Iain Wightwick is a barrister at Unity Stree
a specialist property lawyer, with particu
tenant issues, especially social housing v
nuisance and related anti-social behaviour
hell'), housing conditions/disrepair, homele
private sector housing law.

This is the second edition of the Guide. He also writes *"A Practical Guide to Antisocial Behaviour Injunctions"*, the second edition of that book was published in July 2022.

Iain has thirty-five years' experience of acting for social landlords and tenants and a reputation for creative, cost-controlling approaches to litigation and to alternative dispute resolution.

He is instructed to advise on and appear in many claims concerning housing conditions, mostly for landlords but sometimes for tenants. Until *Churchill v Merthyr Tydfil CBC*, the approach he took to disrepair claims was little known amongst his colleagues. It focuses on his desire to enable social landlords to provide quality homes rather than to pay lawyers' fees.

Shortly after the first Housing Disrepair Protocol was published back in 2003, Iain concluded that tenants should be directed to alternative dispute resolution rather than instructing solicitors to pursue the steps in the Protocol. That approach has saved his clients very substantial sums in legal fees, which he hopes has benefited the tenants of those landlords.

Churchill v Merthyr Tydfil CBC, an appeal brought by Iain from the County Court in Cardiff, has confirmed that *Halsey v Milton Keynes AHA* does not prevent courts from pausing claims for *"non-court-based dispute resolution"*. The CPR have been updated in response to the decision, making ADR much more central to litigation. This is a major step forward and has made it easier for landlords and other public bodies to prevent solicitors from turning customer dissatisfaction into large awards of costs. The claimant's solicitors' firm in *Churchill* went into liquidation, presumably because of the decision. Others have followed, and numerous firms have been intervened.

Iain was also counsel for Swindon Borough Council in an appeal brought against a tenant who was refusing access for a gas safety inspection. The Council had made an application under the Antisocial Behaviour Crime and Policing Act 2014, which the District Judge refused. His Honour Judge Michael Berkley, sitting at Winchester allowed the appeal and confirmed that social landlords can use the 2014 Act to seek an injunction. That procedure is much quicker and less expensive than traditional proceedings under Part 8. Iain can provide a copy of that judgment upon request.

Finally, in the appeal of *Heys v Swindon Borough Council,* another challenge to the decision of a District Judge, this time sitting at Liverpool, His Honour Judge Wood KC overturned a pre-action disclosure ("PAD") order which a District Judge had made against the Council. He agreed with Iain's approach, that a PAD order is unnecessary when a tenant can obtain disclosure through the Data Subject Access Request procedure, free of charge. Again, Iain can provide a copy of the transcript on request.

Iain is always available, whether for a chat about a legal issue or about a mountain bike ride/open water swim/ski.

A Practical Guide to Responding to Housing Disrepair and Unfitness Claims

Second Edition

A Practical Guide to Responding to Housing Disrepair and Unfitness Claims

Policies, Processes and Practice
in Responding to Disrepair
and Unfitness Claims

Second Edition

Iain Wightwick, BSc Hons, Dip. Law
Barrister, Unity Street Chambers, Bristol

Law Brief Publishing

© Iain Wightwick

All rights reserved. No part of this publication may be reproduced, stored in a retrieval system, or transmitted, in any form or by any means, electronic, mechanical, photocopying, recording or otherwise, without the prior permission of the publisher.

Excerpts from judgments and statutes are Crown copyright. Any Crown Copyright material is reproduced with the permission of the Controller of OPSI and the Queen's Printer for Scotland. Some quotations may be licensed under the terms of the Open Government Licence (http://www.nationalarchives.gov.uk/doc/open-government-licence/version/3).

Cover image © iStockphoto.com/CHUNYIP WONG

The information in this book was believed to be correct at the time of writing. All content is for information purposes only and is not intended as legal advice. No liability is accepted by either the publisher or author for any errors or omissions (whether negligent or not) that it may contain. Professional advice should always be obtained before applying any information to particular circumstances.

Published 2025 by Law Brief Publishing, an imprint of Law Brief Publishing Ltd
30 The Parks
Minehead
Somerset
TA24 8BT

www.lawbriefpublishing.com

Paperback: 978-1-916698-83-3

This book is dedicated to:

Michel Kallipetis, KC, who guided us to success in the Churchill v Merthyr Tydfil appeal and to all those who have put up with me during its writing, particularly my wife and my (grown-up) children.

PREFACE

The book is more about the strategies needed to deal with disrepair litigation rather than the substantive law.

Disrepair (or more properly these days, "housing conditions") claims have continued to multiply since the first edition of this book, which is aimed primarily to help those receiving and responding such litigation.

Fortunately, in 2022 after publication of the first edition of this book, I was instructed for the Council in *Churchill v Merthyr Tydfil CBC* [2023] EWCA Civ 1416, a claim which allowed me to take my approach to the Court of Appeal. The Court overturned the existing law and confirmed that litigants can be compelled to attempt alternative dispute resolution.

Before that I had been relying on decisions I had obtained in other claims, including *Hockett v Bristol City Council* (2021) unreported, Ref: B2/2021/1025. In refusing that application for permission to appeal by solicitors instructed on behalf of a council tenant, Lord Justice Bean agreed with my stance. The rationale of his brief judgment was that these claims should not be allowed to continue without an attempt at ADR through the landlord's internal complaints process.

There is good reason for concern about the continuing explosion of claims. This trend is reflected in the escalating costs faced by local authorities.

One contributing factor to this surge is the increased activity of claims management companies. These firms often employ aggressive marketing tactics to attract tenants dissatisfied with their living conditions, particularly during the COVID-19 pandemic. Additionally, the challenges faced by landlords in securing necessary repairs, especially during periods of economic uncertainty, have exacerbated the issue.

Housing conditions claims are not just wasteful in terms of officer time and finances. They can be very stressful for those involved, particularly where landlords face large numbers of claims and their staff are already busy planning and carrying out repairs, maintenance and improvements. I anticipate that all landlords would prefer to direct their resources to repairs rather than legal fees. as would right-thinking people. It would be great if tenant lawyers shared my view that they should hold off sending a Letter of Claim until the landlord's internal complaints process ("ICP") is exhausted, but curiously I have yet to come across one who does recommend the ICP to their clients before taking them on.

With luck, the application of that philosophy to disrepair claims will dramatically reduce the legal bills currently being paid by social landlords. Many of the complaints which tenants are making about housing conditions should never have involved lawyers. You'll need to buy the book to find out more about it though!

The book also addresses how to respond to a disrepair claim in the event that ADR is not appropriate or fails to appease the tenant.

If you are a tenant's representative, I hope that the book will help you to weed out good claims from the many which are at present issued unnecessarily.

Fixed Costs

The Ministry of Justice confirmed some considerable time ago that it is going to implement fixed costs in the fast track and in most money claims up to the value of £25,000, on a date to be fixed. Unfortunately, the implementation for housing conditions claims has been delayed until at least October 2025. While fixed costs have been introduced in the new Intermediate Track, Fast Track costs in housing conditions claims have yet to be controlled.

Fast track claims will fall into four bands of complexity, Bands 1-4 from the simplest case to the most technical and complicated. Fixed sums will be awarded depending on the stage which the proceedings have reached:

pre-issue, post-issue, post-allocation, pre-listing or post-listing, pre-trial. There will be additional trial advocacy fees payable. Tracked possession claims and housing conditions/disrepair are likely to be categorised as Band 3, or Band 4 if more complicated.

This means that, roughly speaking, in cases where damages are less than £10,000, the recoverability of pre-issue costs will be substantially reduced, from the figures we see at present of £5,000-£10,000 to between about £1,000 and £2,250 plus 12.5-17.5% of damages. Total fees going to trial, excluding advocacy will be limited to about another £11,000-£15,000 plus 20-40% of damages. Trial fees will be between £500 and £2,500 for the advocate. Currently those costs are usually claimed at £20,000-£35,000. The total recoverable costs will therefore fall for whoever wins.

While this is welcome news, it does not deal with the major problem of resource allocation caused by housing disrepair claims, because they will all still have to be investigated, and if they are not resolved through the landlord's internal complaints process, will necessitate the instruction of lawyers, either to negotiate a settlement or to defend them. In my experience, settling unmeritorious claims as a commercial decision usually results in the receipt of numerous additional claims, so even if the individual sum of costs recoverable falls, the claimant's solicitor increases their income.

The law described in this book is believed to be correct and up to date at 30th November 2024.

Iain Wightwick
December 2024

CONTENTS

Table of Cases

Table of Legislation

Introduction		1
PART I	**AVOIDING CLAIMS**	9
Chapter One	Estate Management, Tenancy Agreements, Policies and Procedures	11
PART II	**RESPONDING TO THE LETTER OF CLAIM**	19
Chapter Two	The Letter of Claim	21
Chapter Three	The Letter of Claim as a Framework for the Landlord's Response	29
PART III	**THE PRE-ACTION PROTOCOL AND ALTERNATIVE DISPUTE RESOLUTION**	37
Chapter Four	The Centrality of ADR in the Pre-Action Protocol	39
Chapter Five	When Is Notice Not Required?	47
Chapter Six	The Protocol Requirement for Details of Notice	55
Chapter Seven	Counterclaims for Disrepair	63
Chapter Eight	Alternative Dispute Resolution – The Detail	69

Chapter Nine	Making Sure Your Internal Complaints Process Is Fit for Purpose	85
Chapter Ten	The Mechanics of the Complaints Process	103
Chapter Eleven	The Identity of the Claimant	115
Chapter Twelve	The Standard of Repair – Does Liability Arise?	123
Chapter Thirteen	The Specific Defects Alleged	145
Chapter Fourteen	Disclosure in the Pre-Action Protocol	183
PART IV	**AFTER PROCEEDINGS ARE ISSUED**	195
Chapter Fifteen	Expert Evidence	197
Chapter Sixteen	Applications for Summary Judgment / Strike Out / Stay	213
Chapter Seventeen	Drafting the Defence	241
Chapter Eighteen	Transfer and Allocation to Track	245
Chapter Nineteen	Disclosure and Inspection	263
Chapter Twenty	Witness Statements	275
PART V	**PREPARING FOR TRIAL**	281
Chapter Twenty-One	The Trial	283
Epilogue / Conclusion		301
Appendix One	Example Defence	303
Bibliography		321
Index		323

# TABLE OF CASES

Akhtar v Boland [2014] EWCA Civ 872 ... 250

Ball v Plymouth CC [2004] EWHC 134 ... 148

Bavage v Southwark LBC [1998] C LY 3623 ... 50

BCT Software Solutions Ltd v Brewer & Sons Ltd [2003] EWCA Civ 939 ... 110

Binns v Firstplus Financial Group Plc [2013] EWHC 2436 (QB)...108

Birmingham City Council v Avril Lee [2008] EWCA Civ 891 ... 3, 22, 109-112, 246, 247, 248, 293, 294

Birse Construction Ltd v HLC Engenharia SA [2006] EWHC 1258 (TCC) ... 233

Bishop v Consolidated London Properties Ltd (1933) 102 LJ KB 257 ... 48

Bole v Huntsbuild Ltd [2009] EWCA Civ 1146 ... 174

Bradley v Chorley Borough Council [1985] EG 801 ... 140

Bradley v. Heslin [2014] EWHC 3267 ... 232

BT plc v Sun Life [1996] Ch 69 ... 48, 49, 53

Calabar Properties Ltd v Stitcher [1984] 1 WLR 287 ... 107

Chin v Hackney LBC [1996] 1 AER 973, CA ... 116

Churchill v Merthyr Tydfil County Borough Council [2023] EWCA Civ 1416 ... 5, 7, 37, 39, 40, 69, 70, 77, 83, 99, 219, 223-231, 232, 233-234

Dame Margaret Hungerford Charity Trustees v Beazley [1993] 2 EGLR 143 ... 131

David Hamon & others v University College London [2023] EWHC 1812 (KB)] ...232

Doncaster Pharmaceuticals Group Ltd v Bolton Pharmaceutical Co 100 Ltd [2006] EWCA Civ 661 [2007] FSR 63 ... 216

Earle v Charalambous [2007] HLR 8 ... 53

ED & F Man Liquid Products v Patel [2003] EW Civ 472 ... 215

Elmcroft Developments Ltd v Tankersley-Sawyer [1984] 1 EGLR 47, (1984) 270 EG 140 ... 125, 138

English Churches Housing Group v Shine [2004] EWCA Civ 434 ... 107

Field v Leeds City Council [1999] EWCA Civ 3013 ... 218

Gillies v Blackhorse Limited [2011] EW Misc 20 (19 December 2011) ... 257-258, 259

Grand v Gill [2011] EWCA Civ 554 ... 150

Guinle v. Kirreh [2000] CP Rep ... 232

Hall v Manchester Corporation [1915] LJ Ch 732 ... 169

Halsey v Milton Keynes General NHS Trust [2004] EWCA Civ 576 ... 3, 224, 229, 231, 234

Harbutt's "Plasticine" Ltd v Wayne Tank and Pump Co Ltd [1970] 1 QB 447 ... 140

Hockett v Bristol CC (2021) B2/2021/1025 ... 188, 190, 192, 231

HRH The Duchess of Sussex v Associated Newspapers Ltd [2021] EWHC 273 (Ch) ... 216

Hutchison 3G v O2 [2008] EWHC 55 ... 233

Jalili v Bury Council (17 June 2021) (unreported) ... 253

Jillians v Red Kite Housing (24 September 2024) (unreported) ... 167-174

Jet 2 Holidays Ltd v Hughes [2019] EWCA Civ 1858 ... 233

Jones v Geen (1925) 1KB 659 ... 169

Liverpool Mutual Homes v Mensah [2017] WLUK 325 ... 56

Lomax v Lomax [2019] EWCA Civ 1467 (Court of Appeal) ... 232

Loughlin v Blackhorse Limited [2012] EW Misc 8 (CC) (13 January 2012) ... 257, 258, 259

Maclean v Liverpool City Council (1978) 20 HLR 25 ... 131

Mann v. Mann [2014] EWHC 537 (Fam) ... 232

Masterton Licensing Trust v Finco [1957] NZLR 1137 ... 50

McGreal v Wake (1984) 13 HLR 107, 269 EG 1254 ... 139

Midland Heart Ltd v Idawah [2014] EW Misc B48 (11 July 2014) ... 66

Minchburn v Peck (1987) 20 HLR 392 ... 48, 52

Morgan v Liverpool Corporation [1927] 2 KB 131, CA ... 169

Murray v Birmingham City Council [1987] 2 EGLR 53 ... 135, 138

Parker v Camden LBC [1986] Ch 162 ... 255

Passley v Wandsworth LBC (1998) 30 HLR 165 ... 50

PDF II SA v OMF Co-1 Ltd [2013] EWCA Civ 1288 ... 233

Proudfoot v Hart (1890) 25 QBD 42 ... 126, 127, 128, 130, 139

R. (Cowl) v. Plymouth CC [2002] 1 WLR 803 ... 232

R. (Cowl) v Plymouth City Council [2001] EWCA Civ 1935 ... 231

Rahman v Sterling Credit Ltd [2001] 1 WLR 496 ... 66

Ravenseft Properties Ltd V Davstone (Holdings) Ltd [1980] QB 12 ... 131

Rendlesham Estates v Barr [2014] EWHC 3968 (TCC); 1 WLR 3663 ... 174

Ridehalgh v Horsefield and Another & Ors [1994] 3 W.L.R. 462 ... 295

Royal Brompton Hospital NHS Trust V Hammond (No. 5) EWCA Civ 550 ... 216

Shirayama Shokusan v Danovo Ltd (No 2) [2004] 1 WLR 2985 ... 232, 234

Southwark LBC v McIntosh [2002] 1 EGLR 25 and Ball v Plymouth CC [2004] EWHC 134 ... 148

Summers v Salford Corporation [1942] AC 283 (HL) ... 168

Swain v Hillman [2001] 1 All ER 91 ... 215

The Lady Anne Tennant v Associated Newspapers Ltd [1979] FSR 298, 303 ... 216

Tui v Griffiths [2023] UKSC 48 ... 197

Uddin v Islington LBC [2015] EWCA Civ 369 ... 153

Uren v Corporate Leisure (UK) Ltd [2011] EWCA Civ 66 ... 232, 233

Wallace v Manchester City Council (1998) 30 HLR 1111 ... 107, 297

Welsh v Greenwich LBC (2001) 33 HLR 40 ... 158

Williams v Santander UK Plc [2015] EW Misc B37 (CC) (21 August 2015) ... 258, 259

Williams-Henry v Associated British Ports Holdings Ltd & Anor (Re Wasted Costs) [2024] EWHC 2415 (KB) ... 295

Wimpey Homes UK Ltd v Harron Homes [2020] EWHC 1120 (TCC) ... 233

TABLE OF LEGISLATION

Antisocial Behaviour Crime and Policing Act 2014 … 57, 91, 256

Building Safety Act 2022 … 14

Civil Evidence Act 1995 … 209

Consumer Credit Act 1974 … 258

Contracts (Rights of Third Parties) Act 1999 … 115

Defective Premises Act 1972 … 44, 116, 304, 305, 317

Equality Act 2010 … 93

Environmental Protection Act 1990 … 45

Financial Services and Markets Act 2000 … 258

Homes (Fitness for Human Habitation) Act 2018 … 1, 12, 13, 14, 15, 124, 131, 147, 158-159, 160, 166, 170, 173, 206

Housing Act 1988 … 152

Housing Act 2004 … 159, 167

Housing Defects Act 1984 … 134

Landlord and Tenant Act 1985 … 1, 12, 15, 44, 45, 51, 53, 106, 115-116, 124-125, 126, 131, 139, 152, 155, 158, 166, 168, 201, 208-209, 254, 304, 305, 307, 308, 310, 311, 312, 313, 317

Occupiers' Liability Act 1957 … 116

Renting Homes (Wales) Act 2016 … 21, 165

Senior Courts Act 1981 … 295

Social Housing (Regulation) Act 2023 … 14, 86

Welfare Reform and Work Act 2016 … 14

INTRODUCTION

Since 2020, the housing 'disrepair' claims landscape has transformed. The first edition of this book came out soon after the Homes (Fitness For Human Habitation) Act 2018 Act had added sections 9A and 10 to the Landlord and Tenant Act 1985. Although almost everybody continues to use that term it is misleading. It does not take into account the obligations as to fitness imposed by the amendments. Therefore, while I use it in this book for variation, nowadays most such claims include a significant element of alleged unfitness for human habitation. I will refer to them as 'housing disrepair/conditions claims' from now on, but for the sake of variation, I use both the old and the new descriptions interchangeably.

An explanation for my approach to these claims

As a housing lawyer, I have represented both tenants and landlords since starting at the Bar, nearly 40 years ago. I have been instructed in the pursuit and defence of many claims since about 1992 when I was first instructed to advise on defending them for a social landlord. In those days there was no Pre-Action Protocol and often no warning that proceedings were on the way. Usually, the first the landlord knew of a tenant's unhappiness with the repairs process was the receipt of the sealed court papers.

I was invariably asked only how much in damages each tenant should be paid, so that the claims could be settled. But I began to suspect that landlords could not possibly be as uncaring and incompetent as they were portrayed by claimant lawyers in the letters and pleadings. It dawned on me that what appeared to be allegations of serious and persistent breach of repairing duty were often unfounded.

My investigations with social landlord clients uncovered Repairs Teams who were surprised and probably annoyed that their legal teams were settling all claims received when they saw no reason to do so. They provided me with repairs histories, with evidence that they had repaired everything which the tenant had complained of, or sometimes almost everything. Often it transpired that, although the tenant's home might not be in perfect condition, there were myriad reasons for that and the fault did not lie at the landlord's door, or the damage might not be actionable. Eventually I stopped believing what was being alleged and started defending the claims.

Learning how to do so was a long and slow process. Those involved with the repairs system provided witness statements and documents and I drafted Defences and went to court. It was all a bit hit and miss. I did not even use a book on the subject, as we did not have a great library in those days. In 1996 I bought my copy of Stephen Knafler's excellent book, on the subject *"Remedies for Disrepair and Other Building Defects"*. Stephen Knafler sadly died in October 2020. He was only two months older than me, so I was 25 years behind him with the first edition of this book.

The first edition of Dowding & Reynolds ("D & R") did not come out until 1994, and it was too expensive for me. You will need to read the Preface to the current edition to understand that reference. D & R remains the practitioners' equivalent of the bible. My book is about practice rather than the law and I trust that nobody is going to quote from this work in court.

And no practitioner should be without *"Housing Conditions, tenants' rights"* ("Housing Conditions") by HHJ Jan Luba QC, Catherine O'Donnell and Giles Peaker. It is aimed at tenant advisors, so you may need to look at other sources for legal authorities more helpful to landlords.

Those two books will provide you with the substantive law – I can only offer you a practitioner's guide for use in dealing with claims. You will need access to the most recent edition of one or both of those books or use a lawyer who has them, as your opponent should be quoting from them.

But, back in 1992, equipped only with ignorance and hope, we went to trial, and we won, because social landlords do not come from the school of Rachman. As things developed, so did the way of addressing claims. It quickly dawned on me that my clients were not ignoring tenants wholesale, and that some cases were so hopeless that they should not even be allowed to go to trial. So, I started to apply for summary judgment, particularly on the specific performance element of the claim. Additionally, despite the decision in *Halsey v Milton Keynes Area Health Authority*, I applied to stay claims while the tenant exhausted a landlord's internal complaints process. Even if it was right, or had to be taken as binding, the decision of the Court of Appeal was distinguishable on the facts.

As the number of claims increased, so did the urgency of the problem, as claimant firms began to swamp landlords with claims. They were left unable to devote the resources necessary to fight them and legal bills escalated into the millions of pounds for many social landlords. After a series of successes in Wales, and increasing negative publicity for claims farming solicitors, the tide turned, and the industry was almost entirely crushed by the courts. By about 2006, very few claims came my way, much to my satisfaction.

Regrettably that trend has returned, and worsened, fuelled by hostile anti-social landlord press which is in my experience largely undeserved. It was enabled by the 2008 decision of the Court of Appeal in *Birmingham City Council v Lee* [2008] EWCA Civ 891, a case to which I will return in detail below and later in the book (see Chapters Ten, Eighteen and Twenty-One). In my view, it gave the green light to tenant solicitors to charge substantial amounts in costs even though the involvement of lawyers was usually wholly or substantially unnecessary.

Of the many housing conditions claims being pursued, some are entirely justified. This book does not aim to help unscrupulous landlords avoid responsibility for failing to maintain their stock or respond to notice of defects. Some lawyers fight for disadvantaged tenants forced to live in poor conditions by unscrupulous landlords. The lawyers bringing well-founded claims provide an essential service to our society, and I support them fully. Some tenants may be unaware of their remedies or too scared to use them until helped by lawyers. The legislation which protects them, in combination with their tenancy conditions, can be used to impressive effect to improve their lives.

There are other lawyers who also act on behalf of tenants, but who usually find their clients through claims management companies ("CMCs"). CMCs use measures such as cold-calling, advertising on social media and approaching people on the streets. . Even though knocking on doors to sell something is illegal, it's still happening in some places. I have encountered claims in which the tenant invited them in, showed them round and signed a CFA, unaware that they were employees of their landlord. I have frequently listened to tenants at court say they did not want to sue their landlord, or that they have told their solicitors they want to stop doing so, only to be told that they will face a claim for the whole of the costs. The Solicitors' Regulation Authority provided guidance on claims management activity in July 2024[1]. It is essential reading and includes a requirement to advise potential clients as to the availability of cost and lawyer free compensation schemes.

The condition of social housing compared to private rented stock

---

[1] https://www.sra.org.uk/solicitors/guidance/claims-management-activity/

INTRODUCTION

The claims management companies which find these tenants usually work against social housing landlords only. In 2023 during evidence gathering for *Churchill*, we looked at claimant solicitors' websites. Almost all of them made it a condition that the prospective tenant client lived in social housing. Perhaps such lawyers find social landlords easier targets. They seem to attempt to swamp landlords with claims and, whether by accident or design, many of my clients struggle to keep up with the influx of cases.

But social housing providers have received profoundly negative press coverage in the last few years. Numerically, poor housing conditions are far more likely to be found in private rented stock – see the English Housing Survey 2022–23 for the figures:

> "*Private renters were more likely than any other tenure to live in a poor-quality home. **Just over a fifth (21%) lived in non-decent homes,***" (**compared with only** 10-11% in social housing).

> *Private renters were the most likely to live in a home that had* **Category 1 hazards (12%, 572,000),** *followed by* **owner occupiers (9%, 1.3 million),** **local authority renters (5%, 80,000),** *then* **housing association renters (3%, 83,000).** So there are three times (572,000 vs 163,000 as many homes with Cat 1 hazards in private rented stock.

> *Private renters were most likely to be living in a damp home* **(10%, 441,000)**...*local authority renters* **(7%, 109,000)** *and housing association renters* **(4%, 106,000)** ... *owner occupiers* **(2%, 354,000)."* So twice as many damp private homes as social housing.

These figures do not even take into account the relative means of each group of tenants, which makes it more surprising that the number of problems in social housing is so modest compared to the PRS.

The level of costs in these claims

The legal costs mentioned in the Preface provide the context for these figures. Each claim which is settled pre-issue on terms which include paying the claimant's costs is likely to result in a demand for large sums – up to £10,000 is not uncommon in my experience. Currently, the costs claimed by claimant lawyers at trial are usually £25,000–£50,000.

In the Court of Appeal judgment, the level of costs claimed by Anthony Gold, the Claimant's solicitors, was queried by Lord Justice Hughes (at paragraph 37), when he noted they were put at approximately £7,100 in the allocation questionnaire. He said "*We do not know whether there is some special reason for such a level of costs, but Mr Luba did not attempt to suggest that they were justified. We say no more than that, unless there is some special factor, costs at that level look prima facie vastly disproportionate, and that if costs ever fall to be assessed they will need to be scrutinised with some little care*"

Fixed recoverable costs are not going to be brought in for Housing conditions claims until at least October 2025, following lobbying by claimant lawyers. When eventually they are applied to these claims, it could spell a pernicious industry. Regrettably we are some distance away from that and no doubt those lawyers will be continuing their previously successful efforts to persuade the government to exempt them from the restrictions of fixed fees. I discuss fixed fees briefly in Chapter Twenty-One

Tenant lawyers reading it might reflect on the merits of their targeted litigation, and whether they should be earning a living by depriving social landlords of money which could be spent on maintenance and improvement of social housing. Instead, in my view, they should be pursuing claims in the PRS, where there is a significant problem.

It has become fashionable to portray RSLs as cynical profiteers, exploiting tenants and not caring about whether they provide low-cost housing. In responding to these claims landlords should adduce positive evidence about social housing, so that judges learn of the reality, rather than the fiction presented by the Press in the recent past.

This book is more likely to be of use to social landlords, although I hope it will be useful to the private sector as well. I have tried to provide a distillation of the ways in which you can test a claim which comes in, whether you are a lawyer, a housing professional or a landlord. But better still, as a landlord I hope you can refine repairs and maintenance processes so that such claims never see the light of day, because no tenant will want to click on a Facebook advert which says: "Do you want your repairs done?"

I approach claims from the perspective of the Letter of Claim ("LOC") as that is usually the building block of this form of litigation. Such letters should not be sent until a landlord has been told about outstanding repairs and has nevertheless failed to act – see paragraph 1 of the Pre-Action Protocol for Housing Conditions ("the PAP" or "the Protocol") . Further, Social housing tenants are also required to consider alternative dispute resolution, and the landlord's own complaints procedure is placed at the forefront of that suggestion – see paragraph 4 of the Protocol. After *Churchill v Merthyr Tydfil CBC* this should be easier. So when a claimant solicitor sends a LOC and demands the landlord complies with paragraph 5 and onwards, they are wrong in law to do so. In my view landlords need to educate the judiciary to prevent this abuse of the Protocol.

More of that later, but for present purposes, please start to think of the PAP as being more than just a formula that people must robotically follow before inevitably issuing proceedings. It provides the starting point for saying that lawyers should not be involved in a housing conditions claim unless it's unavoidable.

There are bound to be errors, even in this second, updated volume, both of spelling and grammar and, more important, in law and practice. Please do point them out to me, although preferably not in a humiliating fashion.

Best of luck in redirecting some at least of the money which currently goes into the pockets of lawyers (including me) into the repair and improvement of homes!

PART I

AVOIDING CLAIMS

Ideally, no tenant would ever be tempted to engage solicitors, because your estate management is so good that they cannot think of any reason why they would want to do so.

In that perfect world, your housing stock would be maintained so well that it does not have a chance to fall into disrepair, because it is inspected so frequently that all maintenance is carried out proactively. Since the first edition of this book, when i Few property owners will ever even aspire to that level of investment, because it is not cost-effective or environmentally aware. Good estate management in my view is a matter of obtaining a balance between cost, which is ultimately borne by the tenants through their rent, and the standard of comfort they enjoy.

Landlords will make their repairs/improvement policies to comply with the statute and regulation and to fit their budget and rental philosophy. The standard to which properties must be kept is not fixed by any single set of laws, because it depends on the nature of the tenure and the type of accommodation. As a rule, the higher the rent, the better the standard which needs to be set. Of course, the concept of fitness for human habitation now runs through the whole short-term rented property sector, imposing minimum standards.

The size of the estate will, to an extent, dictate the systems employed by the landlord to administer it. The larger the number of properties, the more important it becomes to have a fool-proof and comprehensive planning, works and record keeping policy. But in today's litigation heavy culture, social landlords have been forced to improve their systems, both by the Regulator and by the Ombudsman.

This first section of the book is very short. I merely draw attention to the importance of comprehensive, up-to-date policies and procedures, which you will use to prevent claims and to ensure that those made are unlikely to succeed.

A policy designed to respond to claims is also needed. This book is intended to give some idea of the nature of considerations pertinent to that policy.

CHAPTER ONE

ESTATE MANAGEMENT, TENANCY AGREEMENTS, POLICIES AND PROCEDURES

Given the target audience of this book, I do not anticipate that it will be read by many landlords who do not have up-to-date management policies. Registered Providers must have policies and procedures in place, and they must be fit for purpose. In my experience, up-to-date tenancy agreements are another matter entirely.

Why are they relevant to disrepair claims?

Although 'Estate Management' might include tenancy and environmental management, antisocial behaviour, successions, allocations and so on, this chapter is mainly concerned with maintenance, investment and improvement policies, and the systems needed to support them.

The terms of the tenancy agreement create the basis of the relationship between the landlord and the tenant and govern their respective expectations. Tenancy agreements control much more than the respective duties of each in relation to the repair and condition of the property, so there is no point in this book in trying to address the numerous ways that policies drafted 10 years ago need to be amended.

For the purposes of this book, I assume that landlords will not draft agreements which exceed the requirements of the various statutes governing those duties. In my view, it is poor estate management to go beyond those requirements in the agreement. Policies can always provide that the organisation strives to exceed legal minimums, but the propensity to exploit any such promises cannot be underestimated.

It creates a significant litigation risk to overpromise. See Chapter Thirteen for an example – the experience of Greenwich LBC which generously included the word "*condition*" in its maintenance standards. The 2018 Act has meant that their tenancy now adds nothing to the 1985 Act. Many agreements still refer only to an obligation to remedy to section 11 (structural etc) defects.

Policies help employees to make decisions without management involvement and they ensure that there is a sufficient degree of consistency to avoid a haphazard approach to the control of the estate. When somebody complains that they have not been treated properly, the existence of a realistic and relevant policy benefits both parties.

The landlord can maintain an objective approach and will find it easier to be fair to all tenants. Tenants know the standards they can usually expect, and employees will be able to respond consistently to similar issues. Since the pandemic and Brexit, it has been more difficult to stick to time limits in policies and it is necessary to deal with that matter in evidence

The degree of detail in these policies and procedures is a matter of judgement. In general, the larger the organisation, the more extensive the policies and procedures it needs. Staff members are more numerous and the number of properties in the estate will mean that there are more likely to be untoward or unusual events which need to be approached by all employees in the same way.

It is a question of maintaining a balance between an overly rigid or bureaucratic approach and giving staff the ability to be practical and use their judgement. In terms of the repairs policy, the fundamental guiding principle will be the standards which the landlord is set by the social housing regulator and therefore sets itself as a housing provider.

Policies will need to be reviewed and updated, both at regular intervals and following changes to key legislation, regulations or best practice guidelines. The aims of a landlord may change, and the policy may become outdated, or on a performance review a housing provider may find that it is under-delivering and needs to tighten or improve policies.

In housing conditions law this is particularly pertinent. The coming into force of the Homes (Fitness for Human Habitation) Act 2018 has completely changed the landscape in terms of repairs and improvements. Policies are almost certain to require change, to reflect the fact that merely *repairing* properties is no longer sufficient to avoid legal liability for substandard living conditions.

The Ombudsman has had something to say about this in his *"Spotlight on: Damp and mould-It is not lifestyle"* on damp and mould. He hopes that the word 'lifestyle', when it may be a consequence of limited choices, is banished from the vernacular.

He also argues for an entirely proactive approach to damp and mould, saying even when landlords should go out and look for problems "when all indicators suggest there may be issues." The report is essential reading for every practitioner. It can be found at: https://www.housing-ombudsman.org.uk/wp-content/uploads/2021/10/Spotlight-report-Damp-and-mould-final.pdf.

The requirement to amend policies from reactive to proactive behaviour in respect of damp and mould imposes a substantial financial and administrative burden on landlords. Some claimant lawyers attempt to capitalise on it but in my experience, judges have agreed that it does not impose any new legal duty to pre-empt complaints. Nevertheless, it is clearly good estate management to recognise that property construction type and the nature of the tenant. The question is where such proactive behaviour comes in an already overtaxed repairs policy.

Updating policies

Providers need to take into account properly the changes imposed by the 2018 Act and other related legislation, including the Social Housing (Regulation) Act 2023, the Higher-Risk Buildings (KPI) (England) Regulations 2023, the Building Safety Act 2022, the Code of Conduct for Registered Building Inspectors, the Ombudsman's Complaint Handling Code and the Review of the Decent Homes Standard. That will result in new regulations to action the conclusions in the HHSRS review. The failure to update is evident from the fact that many still use the phrase "disrepair" when they should be referring to "housing conditions".

The greatest danger to landlords is the setting of a quality standard which is too low to satisfy the law, or too high to be affordable. The Welfare Reform and Work Act 2016 forced social landlords to reduce their rents by 1% each year over the following four years. That led to numerous problems and many landlords suffered significant budgetary issues as a result.

In early 2019, the government agreed that social housing rents would be allowed to increase by the consumer price index measure of inflation +1% for the following five years from 2020. Almost every social landlord has raised its rent by the maximum permitted amount. The last financial year (23–24) was an exception to the normal five-year rent settlement, and in November 2022 the Department for Levelling up, Housing in Communities capped rent increases at seven percent. The cap for 2024–2025 was 7.7% and there is a service charge increase.

The National Housing Maintenance Forum is the best source of good practice for maintenance and asset management policies. It helps landlords both with policy and practical guidance to assist housing maintenance professionals.

Rather than discussing policies in detail, the purpose of this section of the book is to concentrate thought on the consequences of the wording of the landlord's repairs and maintenance policies.

Changes caused by the 2018 Act and other new statutes

Most important, such policies can no longer separate repairs and maintenance from improvements. The 2018 Act has required a change to the underlying approach to estate management. A property may not be reasonably fit for human habitation even though not in disrepair as defined by the 1985 Act. This means that works may be necessary even though they result in an improvement to the property rather than merely a repair to those parts of the property which a landlord has agreed to maintain ("the structure and exterior" etc).

The International Standard for Asset Management, ISO 55001, updated in 2024 to include a new "strategic asset management plan", sets a high bar, specifying requirements for the establishment, implementation, maintenance and improvement of an asset management system which can be used by any property owner. It does not mandate any financial, accounting or technical requirements for managing property, but gives guidance on the issues which need to be addressed in a policy.

Repairs and improvements policies

In general, social landlords encounter challenging issues caused by the combination of the nature of the housing stock with some peculiarities of construction, with many tenants who struggle to make ends meet or otherwise to administer their tenancy. Outdated policies give rise to a risk that staff will not properly understand the extent of their duties, particularly as to improvements to address defects under the fitness provisions.

Given the scope of the subject, I cannot go into sufficient detail here to provide a framework for such policies. Realistically, that is the subject of another book.

Complaints Policies

But, for the purposes of responding to claims, the Complaints Policy is of paramount importance. It is therefore essential to operate an efficient and competent policy. In Chapter Nine I look at these policies, in the light of the updated, 2024 Complaints Handling Code.

I will assume that you either have a credible and efficient policy, or that, having read my advice, you are making all efforts to put one in place / update it!

Such policies are important because of the part they should play in the relationship between social landlords and their tenants. Disrepair claims should not be fought out in County Courts all over the country as a matter of course. The legal system should be reserved exclusively for those cases where landlords have been asked, formally, to repair and have failed or refused, and where the Internal Complaints Process has been exhausted yet has not provided a satisfactory resolution for the tenant.

But rather than starting with a detailed examination of the policies or the complaints process, we need to look at things from the point of view of a Letter of Claim. After all, this book is intended for people responding to claims rather than formulating policies. That is nearly always how a landlord is alerted to dissatisfaction on the part of their tenant. It is only in rare cases that a claimant tenant has repeatedly complained or even used the ICP and is still unhappy. Apart perhaps from suggesting that they go to the Ombudsman, in those cases there may be no alternative but to follow the steps in the Pre-Action Protocol and litigate if necessary.

Chapter Summary / Key Takeaways

- Policies set the tone of the organisation

- They need to be updated regularly and in line with developments in the law, statute and society

- Setting the repairs standards in the policy will underpin most decision making in the asset management team

- Social landlords' internal complaints processes are now regulated by statute and controlled by the Ombudsman and the RSH. They must comply with the Complaint Handling Code.

- Creating a customer-friendly Complaints Policy which is efficient and accurate in its determinations can and will save very substantial sums in legal costs and damages. The money that is saved can be spent on the repairs and improvements which you and the tenants both want carried out.

In the remaining chapters you will learn how your asset management policy and your Complaints Policy help to determine how you answer the Letters of Claim which you will inevitably receive, and they also influence how you defend any subsequent claim.

PART II

RESPONDING TO THE LETTER OF CLAIM

Even if repairing policies are excellent, social landlords will receive housing conditions claims. Therefore, however good you are at repairs, you need to know how to respond to claims, because claimant firms view social landlords as easy targets. Most of the remainder of this book will look at claims from a practical point of view, using the Letter of Claim ("LOC") as the springboard.

First, we look at the origins and rationale of a LOC, which provide us with the chapter headings necessary to respond to a claim.

Of course, if the Protocol was used properly by claimant solicitors, unhappiness with repairs and housing conditions would not come to light with a Letter of Claim. Instead, first the tenant would give some form of formal notice to the landlord, whereupon the Complaints Policy can be put into operation. If that process fails, the tenant should in theory go to the Ombudsman. Only if those measures are unsuccessful should a tenant need to engage lawyers.

In fact, there is ambiguity in the Protocol. Paragraph 5.1 does say that *"In order to avoid unnecessary delay and to ensure that notice of the claim is given to the landlord of the earliest possible opportunity, particularly where repairs are urgent, it **may** be appropriate for the tenant to send a letter notifying the landlord of the claim before detailed Letter of Claim is sent"*. The inference is that such a letter should only be sent in an urgent case, whereas ideally the Protocol would specify that the claimant's solicitors must send a one-line letter informing a landlord that they have been approached by a tenant. Much of the time, such a letter would obviate the need for most of the detailed content of a LOC.

But, at the moment, things do not happen like that in England and Wales. Landlords usually receive a LOC out of the blue and feel that they have to respond to them rather than dealing with a service request or a complaint.

My approach to responding to such letters is the same whether or not there is fault on the part of the landlord. If there is a breach of duty, it should be addressed within the landlord's internal complaints process, which is plainly an appropriate form of "non-court-based dispute resolution", not needing lawyers on either side.

CHAPTER TWO

THE LETTER OF CLAIM

While the law of dilapidations is complex, sometimes bewildering and seemingly inconsistent even to lawyers, the Letter of Claim ("LoC") in a housing disrepair case provides a blueprint from which both sides can work toward the resolution of a claim.

Understanding and responding to an LOC is key to dealing with disrepair claims successfully.

The Rationale of the Housing Conditions/Disrepair Protocol

The Protocol first came into force on 8 December 2003, so lawyers have been using – or misusing it for over 20 years. It is therefore surprising that the question of mandatory alternative dispute resolution has remained unresolved until 2024. I am still arguing with claimant solicitors daily, all over the country, as to how the Protocol should be applied. There is insufficient authority at Court of Appeal level and the only frequently cited decision is, in my view, outdated and now wrong in principle. But first, a discussion of the content of the Protocol.

There are now two Protocols, one for England and one for Wales, where the landlord and tenant relationship is now governed by the Renting Homes (Wales) Act 2016 ("RHWA", which came into force on 1 December 2022) and is supplemented by the Renting Homes (Fitness for Human Habitation) (Wales) Regulations 2022. So, when I talk about the Protocol, in Wales practitioners will be referring to the version which contains no reference to unfitness, at least at the moment. As there are extra provisions for enforcement of repair and fitness obligations in the RHWA it is likely that procedure and practice in such claims will divert from claims in England to some extent.

However, the principles I employ remain the same and in most claims the claimant solicitors will make allegations of disrepair as well as unfitness, so that the Protocol will continue to apply in Wales for the short period during which the fitness provisions are not mentioned in the existing version.

The idea of a Protocol was first raised during the Access to Justice enquiry, but social landlords and tenants' lawyers found it impossible to reach a consensus on its content. The Law Society eventually helped to achieve a measure of agreement.

The Protocol does not apply to counterclaims filed in possession proceedings. However, in those claims, tenants and landlords are still expected to act reasonably in exchanging information and trying to settle the case at an early stage (para 3.3). That can be important in terms of avoiding a trial.

The **Guidance to the Protocol** reminds tenants "*to consider other options before using the protocol including the… Ombudsman*".

Although the notes in the White Book say that if the claim is settled, the landlord should pay the tenant's costs and out-of-pocket expenses, the claimant's Solicitors will normally try to insist on payment of costs on a Fast-Track basis, even if the amount of work done and compensation paid is minimal. This is a significant part of the current problem faced by social landlords from disrepair claims.

There is a case on the point – *Birmingham City Council v Lee* [2008] EWCA Civ 891, and it is essential reading for all those involved with such claims. We will come back to it. Essentially, it is only in circumstances where the claim is *justified* that costs can be claimed. If it was only ever a Small Claims Track case, then costs should only be paid on that basis.

Where does the LOC come from?

Many landlords are mystified why their tenants are instructing solicitors who practice hundreds of miles away from the tenants they represent. The claims management industry is responsible for generating the vast majority of these claims. This is 'ambulance chasing', but the victim does not move so is much easier to find. Those companies will generate leads through various well-known methods. Once the tenant is signed up, they offer the lead to firms of solicitors. A few players in the market actually own the entire supply chain – claims management company, solicitors' firm and surveyors' practice.

Letters of Claim arrive, often without any warning from the tenant themselves that they are unhappy. In cases outside London, they are usually sent by solicitors practising in the North of England, who in my experience bring most of the disrepair claims throughout the country. Those firms are often or have been involved in personal injury claims. They are also pursuing Japanese Knotweed and Data Protection claims. However, their ability to bring the former type of claim has been dramatically restricted by the decision of the Supreme Court in *Davies v Bridgend Borough Council*.

Most LOC are vague and unspecific in one or more respects.

At an early stage in the litigation, landlords need to identify the merits of any claim, and the areas in which the LOC is plainly wrong.

Taking the LOC as a structure to identify the areas which need investigation provides as good a springboard as any in looking at how to respond to claims.

The origin of most disrepair claims

Although figures for disrepair claims are not available, Aviva, the insurer, said generally of cold calls and texts in November 2019:

> "Aviva's research found that consumers were targeted with 996 million nuisance calls and texts relating specifically to an injury-related claim (such as whiplash, holiday sickness, etc.), pension, PPI or other financial service-related claims, which translates to 2,728,767 calls and texts per day, or 1,895 made every minute. These calls account for nearly one in four (23.2%) of all cold calls in the UK."

A substantial proportion of tenants who have instructed these solicitors will have answered an advert on Facebook, received a leaflet in a shopping centre or similar, or answered a knock at their front door, a call on their telephone or a text.

The Conduct of Authorised Persons Rules 2014, in rule 4 of the Client Specific Rules, bans cold calling and restricts other marketing in relation to conditional fee claims:

> "Cold calling in person is prohibited. Any marketing by telephone, email, fax or text shall be in accordance with the Direct Marketing Association's Code and any related guidance issued by the Direct Marketing Association."

So, Claims Management Companies should not be recruiting tenants with aggressive marketing, but they seem to do so. On 19 December 2023, the Ombudsman published a warning[2] about "scammers targeting

---

[2] https://www.housing-ombudsman.org.uk/2023/12/19/scam-awareness-and-data-protection-in-the-housing-sector/

social housing residents" who contact people to help them claim money for housing disrepair.

Basics of the Protocol

The Pre-Action Protocol for Housing Conditions sets out the steps which should be taken in the absence of exceptional circumstances when a tenant wishes to sue their landlord for disrepair.

The Protocol gives a roadmap to solicitors, enabling them even as beginners in landlord and tenant law to plan how they should bring a claim. It provides a structure, showing them how to prepare to sue, what evidence to collect and how to rely on it. It therefore repays careful study.

Some solicitors do not seem to know much more than what is in the Protocol and what they have learned along the way. Nor do many surveyors instructed on behalf of claimants seem to know the law behind the physical condition of the building and what satisfies the threshold test of "disrepair" or "unfitness".

So, it is up to a landlord to be questioning and to challenge any assertion by outsiders that their repairs and maintenance policies are deficient.

But doing so is often extremely challenging. Lack of specificity in the LOC often means that it is difficult to know what real merit there is in any claim. Requests for claimant solicitors to provide further details on notice are met with obfuscation and further generalities. This is often because it is not possible to be more specific, as the LOC puts the claim in much stronger terms than the tenant would support in evidence.

These days, the tenant is unlikely to be able to prove any significant number of further instances of notice other than those recorded in the repairs records. Usually if the solicitors cannot provide proper details, it is because only a small part of the allegations are true. We will look at how to discover whether this is so in your case.

The Ombudsman has said (in the Spotlight on damp and mould) that he has asked the Ministry of Justice (see page 2 of the Spotlight on Damp and Mould report) to strengthen the Protocol "*further to promote the use of the complaint procedure*".

Letters of Claim are open to challenge

An LOC can look daunting to the uninitiated. With the various documents mandated by the Protocol attached, it can run to 20 pages and more. Landlords receiving such detailed correspondence might well feel somewhat overwhelmed.

Although on careful analysis, there will usually be some merit in one or more of the allegations in the letter of claim, they are frequently overstated and/or unsupported by the contemporaneous records. Usually, the allegations are so general and wide-ranging that, at first sight, it appears that the landlord has simply handed the keys to the tenant at the start of the tenancy and walked away, allowing their property to crumble while they spend the rent on anything but property maintenance.

Although the onus should be on the tenant to be specific from the outset about the real nature of any genuine complaint they have, it is almost invariably left to the landlord to ascertain the truth. Investigations must discover (1) what had been complained of, and (2) when, if at all. Sometimes it transpires that the tenant is not truly unhappy with the repairs process but had been promised some compensation and has taken advantage of the offer made by their solicitors to obtain it.

What should be challenged?

It follows that claims need to be approached with a sceptical but open mind. Thought needs to be given to every aspect of the allegations. Genuine claims need to be identified at the earliest possible moment within the internal complaints process, and in all cases appropriate offers of works and compensation must be made before costs escalate to even more unacceptable levels. More about the high costs generated in these cases later, but most landlords will be familiar with the surprising figures claimed for costs even in cases settled shortly after inception.

Chapter Summary / Key Takeaways

- The LOC can be used as a template from which to examine and respond to disrepair claims.

- Letters of Claim should not be taken at face value. They may contain allegations which on investigation are not borne out on the facts of the case.

In the next chapter we will consider the various headings of the LOC as a whole and before looking at each of them individually.

CHAPTER THREE

THE LETTER OF CLAIM AS A FOUNDATION FOR THE LANDLORD'S RESPONSE

The LOC can form the basis of an investigation into the claim. It is a checklist of what needs to be researched and determined before a decision is made (1) whether to contest it or to concede, and (2) either way, what works to do and whether to offer in compensation in respect of possible service failures, even if there has been no breach of legal duty.

This assessment should be understood by all involved in these claims, but it should be carried out within the internal complaints process rather than by lawyers. An understanding of the LOC and the new law on ADR is essential to justify that statement and to it should be doing.

The Contents of the Letter of Claim

The content of a LOC is mandated by the Pre-Protocol in Annex A of the Pre-Action Protocol. The Appendix of the Pre-Action Protocol for Housing Conditions contains an example standard LOC. While it is not prescriptive, the form of the LOC in the Annex is almost invariably slavishly copied, although the details are usually woefully lacking in certain respects.

The Protocol requires the following information to be included in the LOC, which I will use in the following chapters to explore how to respond to a claim. It does not mean that you should respond to the LOC by the provision of the information demanded by the claimant's solicitors.

An Explicit Reliance on the Pre-Action Protocol

The letter begins by making a statement which is more often honoured in the breach, in my experience. It states that the tenant's solicitors are using the Protocol, which is intended to avoid litigation except where absolutely necessary.

But usually, tenant solicitors do not adhere to the spirit of it. If followed properly there would be few disputes which merit the involvement of solicitors. This provides the justification for my approach. In its Introduction and the early paragraphs, the PAP contains some requirements to be observed before it is initiated.

First, it says that it should only be used in cases where the tenant has "*ensured*" that their "*landlord is aware*" of the poor housing conditions relied upon in support of the claim. Most people (other than claimant lawyers I suspect) would agree that this cannot mean that a legal claim should be brought after a single notification of the existence of a defect, just because it resulted in no action from the landlord. I take it to mean that (1) after being told about problems the landlord has not responded and (2) the tenant has complained that (1) there has been no response or (2) works have not been done, or (3) not done to a reasonable standard. The Ombudsman describes a complaint as an expression of dissatisfaction, however made. This must be right – a tenant cannot be entitled to claim they are dissatisfied but remain silent and then make a legal claim.

Second, the fundamental stated aim of the Protocol is to "*avoid unnecessary litigation*". The Protocol says this can be achieved by the use of alternative dispute resolution. For social housing tenants this expressly includes the landlord's internal complaints process.

Therefore, the first part of our investigation will involve looking at how the above restrictions should affect the instruction of lawyers by tenants to pursue landlords and on when it is appropriate to follow the majority of the Protocol at all, as ADR should avoid the need for doing so.

Paragraph 5.2 sets out the details of which the LOC should contain. It says that they include the following, and I comment on each because if the ICP is unsuccessful in resolving the dispute, the landlord may still feel it appropriate to respond to the LOC and is entitled to ask to comply properly with paragraph 5.2.

Details of the tenant

Details of the name and address of the tenant and their property.

In my experience, sometimes these details are incorrect, either in naming the wrong tenant, or omitting a joint tenant.

Defects alleged

The letter should provide a full description of the defects and may include a schedule showing each of the defects alleged, room by room.

They rarely do include that schedule, but the landlord is entitled to ask for it, subject to what I say about the ICP.

History of each defect

The letter should describe the history of each defect.

Again, usually they do not set out the history of each individual defect. It is very much more difficult to respond to a claim where the tenant has not provided their version of when each defect was reported, what was done and what work they expect to be carried out.

Notice

Details of notice, or the reason why the landlord should know of the defects.

The letter should specify when notice was given. That should have been done in list or table form in respect of each defect. This detail is central and is rarely provided in sufficient detail to allow the landlord to check their files against the allegations.

Effects of the defects

Details should be provided of the effects on the tenant and their family, individually, listing any personal injury alleged to be suffered. The Solicitors are required to specify whether there will be any additional claimants.

If other potential claims are not mentioned at this point, the landlord can later get a nasty surprise, but even though those claims may succeed the lawyers may get penalised in costs as they should have brought all claims together.

Provision for inspection

The LOC should state that the landlord needs to inspect as soon as possible, provide dates and times for access in list form.

Again, they usually do not do so, but inspections should be arranged through the landlord's complaints team, which needs to contact the tenant direct anyway and cut out the (unnecessary) solicitors. Arrangements made between lawyers almost always cause significant problems and delay. For tenant solicitors they present another opportunity to churn the claim for fees.

Confirmation whether works intended

The landlord should be asked to provide confirmation whether they intend to carry out remedial works immediately or to wait for expert inspection.

The claimant's solicitors should be told that the ICP team will inspect and order and carry out any necessary works without further reference to lawyers. Further, although the Ombudsman says that the ICP should be run at the same time as the Protocol this is totally unnecessary and will obviously lead to duplication of effort, for which the lawyers will expect to be paid. Schedule of intended works

If the landlord is intending to carry out works, the LOC should ask for a full schedule of those works and anticipated start and completion dates, with a timetable.

Again, this is a job for the complaints team. The claimant's solicitors should be told that the ICP team will specify, order and carry out works and their nature and extent is for the landlord as covenanting party to determine.

The LOC will request disclosure of relevant documents and should provide copies of relevant documents from the tenant but rarely does so. A Form of Authority must be included to allow the landlord to disclose such documents.

Again, for reasons I will address, disclosure through and to lawyers is unnecessary and should be resisted. They should be directed towards the Data Subject Access Request process instead (see below, Chapter Fourteen).

Expert Evidence

The letter should say that a Single Joint Expert Surveyor will be instructed on behalf of the claimant if agreement is not reached about the carrying out of works within 20 working days of the letter, upon which the letter should propose a joint instruction. It should enclose a CV and draft letter of instruction. It should invite any objections within 20 working days. If the landlord wants to send their own instructions, they are asked to send them directly to the expert within 20 working days and provide a copy to the landlord.

If agreement is not reached as to the instruction of an SJE, the letter will propose instruction of an expert to inspect in any event. They should invite a joint inspection.

Again, no external, independent expert should be inspecting the property, for reasons I will discuss. Claimant solicitors should be told that it is an unnecessary expense to instruct their own expert and that if they continue, they should not expect the landlord to reimburse the costs of doing so. Claimant solicitors inevitably go ahead anyway, so this is an argument which needs to be raised at trial in respect of costs, if the court finds for the tenant.

Details of the damages and injunction claim

The LOC should conclude with an assertion that there has been a breach of repairing obligations and a request for proposals for compensation, or a suggestion as to general damages, with details of any special damages sought.

I have never seen anything other than a general request for both, save sometimes some optimistic claims for special damages.

General approach of the book

The elements of the LOC provide a good structure for the Chapters Four to Sixteen, following which I consider how to respond in practical terms. An LOC might raise issues which are not limited to the claim itself – it might involve changing building maintenance and improvement policies and procedures.

ADR before going through the Protocol steps

We will start with the question whether it is necessary to follow through all the steps of the Protocol on receipt of the LOC. As I have said, I believe that the parties should attempt ADR before progressing with it. Fortunately, the Court of Appeal and the CPR now support my approach more clearly!

More of this later but start thinking about it now.

Chapter Summary / Key Takeaways

- The LOC is often deficient in one or more respects. However, given that in many cases it should not even have been written at this stage in the life of a complaint about living conditions, that may not be an issue.

- Anyone involved in responding to these claims needs to understand the legal principles behind the claims. In Chapters Four to Sixteen I look at some of those in limited detail.

- From the claimant's point of view, the Letter of Claim should contain the building blocks of the case against a landlord. But it often overlooks the first and fundamental question, whether they should be incurring legal costs at all.

- Complaints procedures should provide a free, quick and efficient way to deal with dissatisfaction with housing conditions

- Tenant solicitors do not approve of the use of the landlord's internal complaints procedure, as it obviates the need for lawyers to be involved.

- Therefore, the first part of this book provides an introduction to the legal requirements of a claim and considers whether the tenant should be using Alternative Dispute Resolution ("ADR") instead.

- If ADR fails, the LOC then should also form the basis of the landlord's investigation whether the claim should be fought or settled, whether works should be done and compensation offered.

- In the following chapters we will look each element of the contents of Protocol and the details required in the LOC.

- But it is important to understand the opening parts of the Protocol, because most claimant solicitors attempt to ignore them, and the landlord needs to know how to prevent them from succeeding in persuading the court to do so.

So first, the Protocol and ADR.

PART III

THE PRE-ACTION PROTOCOL AND ALTERNATIVE DISPUTE RESOLUTION

If the Protocol is observed to the letter, there will be few instances in which solicitors need to get involved. Unsurprisingly, claimant solicitors do not like my way of thinking, as it removes their income stream.

Following *Churchill* and the changes to the CPR, I anticipate that the judiciary will be much more ready to prevent abuses of the Protocol as soon it is amended by the Ministry of Justice. I hope that the involvement of lawyers in social housing disrepair will be minimal.

In this part of the book, I will explain how and why it succeeds in reducing unnecessary disrepair claims and saving costs, which can then be spent on repairs, to the benefit of everyone involved in social housing, except lawyers.

CHAPTER FOUR

THE CENTRALITY OF ADR IN THE PRE-ACTION PROTOCOL

As I have said, the LOC will begin with a statement that the tenant's solicitors are using the Protocol. But they prefer to begin with paragraph 5 and ignore the opening sections, which are all aimed at excluding lawyers until their involvement is necessary.

The Protocol assumes that tenant solicitors will only pursue claims when there has been a significant breach of duty by the landlord. Experience shows that an aggressive approach by claimant solicitors often results in the court allowing claims to run to trial when they should never have been started.

For social landlords the early paragraphs should mean it is possible to avoid the unnecessary use of lawyers. To understand why this should be so, it is necessary to look at the origins of the Protocol and the competing interests of those who drafted it.

In this chapter we will look at paragraphs 1, 2 and 3 of the PAP, because they lead onto a consideration of the fourth, and most important, paragraph. Once you apply those provisions rigorously you can use them to head off claims before they become a legal nightmare.

If the tenant does not comply with the Protocol, the court can impose sanctions and/or order that the other party is relieved of the obligation to comply or further comply with the Protocol – see Chapter Eight. Following *Churchill*, it has proved easier for me to persuade judges that proceedings should be stopped while the ICP is operated.

Paragraph 1 of the Protocol is the Introduction. Paragraph 2 states the aims. Paragraph 3 defines its scope.

Paragraph 1: The Introduction

The Introduction contains four central principles:

- the tenant must **ensure their landlord is aware of the poor housing conditions of which they complain,**

- the Protocol sets out the **conduct which the court will** "*normally expect prospective parties in a claim to engage in*".

- if the claim proceeds to court, **the judge will expect all parties to have complied with the Protocol** "*as far as possible*".

- In the event of a failure by one party to comply, **the court can order a party in breach either to pay costs** "*or to be subject to other sanctions*".

Even after *Churchill*, those four basic principles still give rise to heated argument about how the Protocol should be applied by tenant solicitors. They tend to ignore the earlier provisions in favour of those paragraphs (5 et sew) which require lawyers to spend many chargeable hours on preparation.

This is the lifeblood of the battle between the parties. The landlord, who does not have to earn its living out of litigation and would prefer to spend its income on providing decent housing, wishes to avoid the involvement of lawyers. The tenant's solicitor exists solely to profit from litigation. They cannot earn a living without it. The interests could not be more different, they are polar opposites.

It is easy to understand why the first paragraph of the introduction to the Protocol requires the parties to consider whether the landlord (even) knows of the problems which the tenant is experiencing.

Qualifying requirement in the PAP that the landlord should be on notice

In its first paragraph, it says "*Before using the Protocol, tenants should ensure that their landlord is aware of (their poor housing) conditions. **The Protocol is intended for those cases where, despite the landlord's knowledge of the poor conditions, matters remain unresolved**.*"

This is often the first issue in housing disrepair claims. Landlords are surprised to receive a LOC from a claimant tenant's solicitors. They check their records and find that there are no outstanding complaints that repairs have not been carried out.

Alternatively, although a landlord might be aware of one or two of the defects in the LOC, most of them will not have been brought to their attention. They often express surprise to the solicitors that the claim has been threatened, but, in my experience, rarely do anything about the lack of notice.

This is also often interpreted by tenant lawyers to say that, if the tenant just tells their landlord of a problem and it is not rectified, they are entitled to consult solicitors, institute the Protocol and bring legal proceedings in the expectation that their costs will be paid under paragraph 11 of the Protocol and *Birmingham CC v Lee*. Generally, the court does not agree with this line and after the changes to the CPR it is less likely to do so.

So as a preliminary argument, if you check the records and there is proof that the tenant had reported certain defects, but not those complained of in the LOC, it is reasonable to say that initiation of the Protocol is premature, because the landlord was not even aware of the issues, let alone that a tenant was dissatisfied with the repairs process.

This should be enough to excuse further compliance with the PAP and follow the repairs process without even treating the LOC as a complaint.

But the wording of the CHC calls that practice into question, as it says that any expression of dissatisfaction however framed amounts to a complaint. However, the Ombudsman also firmly says that complaints should be distinguished from service requests, so it is possible to respond to a LOC by saying that no *service request* has previously been received and therefore the landlord is pursuing its standard repairs procedure, without initiating the ICP.

In theory it is possible to hold out at this stage and defend any proceedings on the basis that the works were carried out within a reasonable time so no complaint, let alone a claim was justified.

In practice I have not seen this done, as landlords prefer to take the LOC as a complaint and instruct the ICP team to deal with it, so it can be addressed outside the normal repairs process, in a manner which generates more extensive record-keeping, useful to narrow the issues and, if necessary, defend the claim.

A complaint can be, and often is, resolved by a finding that works are necessary, but no compensation should be paid because the records show that notice had not been given.

We will look at notice in more detail in Chapter Five.

Paragraph 2: The Stated Aims of the Protocol: ADR is central to its operation

In its second paragraph of the Protocol specifically states that its first aim is to "avoid unnecessary litigation". It then lists others, which we will address in other chapters. The sixth aim is to *"keep the costs of resolving disputes down"*.

As you are likely to know, tenant solicitors using the Protocol who succeed in extracting a promise to do works and a small payment of compensation often then produce a costs schedule for the landlord, relying on *Birmingham v Lee*. Usually, they claim between £5,000 and £10,000, a totally disproportionate amount measured against the value of the works and the agreed compensation. Thus, in many cases, when it is not applied properly, the Protocol fails in its central aim if the landlord concedes and pays.

Methods of ADR are addressed in paragraph 4. If the landlord and the tenant themselves both engage in ADR properly, in most cases there should be no need for lawyers to be instructed and they will not be entitled to any, or any significant costs. We will return to this aspect in Chapter Eight after we have looked at when the Protocol will apply and when parties can ignore it.

Paragraph 3: The Scope of the Protocol

Paragraph 3 of the Protocol describes when the Protocol should and should not be used. First, although the Protocol must be used in most disrepair claims, there are some circumstances in which it is not relevant, e.g. when a counterclaim is made in possession or other proceedings against the tenant. That deserves separate consideration, in the next chapter.

Paragraph 3 also sets out the circumstances in which parties *must* use the Protocol. If someone is making a personal injury claim which arises because of a failure to repair, or the defective state of premises, the Protocol will be relevant. However, just to complicate matters, if an injury claim needs medical evidence other than a GP's letter, the claimant solicitors must follow the Personal Injury Protocol, but only in respect of that element of the claim. This reduces the limitation period to 3 years.

Also, if a disrepair claim is urgent, solicitors are allowed to bring separate disrepair and personal-injury claims, which might then be case-managed together or consolidated. But provided the disrepair claim is truly urgent, a landlord would be liable for the costs of both and could not argue that the latter was unnecessary. Such situations should be very rare for social landlords.

The Protocol should also be used when people other than tenants make such claims, for instance sub- tenants and members of the tenant's family.

Unwary landlords can be caught out by dealing with claims in respect of a tenant, only to receive separate and additional claims from others living in the property. If settling a claim, care should be taken to ensure that any other possible claimants are included in the terms of the settlement agreement.

Previously most claims were pursued primarily under section 11 of the Landlord and Tenant Act 1985 and under the covenants in the tenancy. Claims now rely on sections 9A and 10 of the Act too. The Protocol also covers claims brought under the various other forms of legal remedy available to occupants – the Defective Premises Act 1972, claims in common law nuisance and negligence, etc.

The LTA 1985 only applies to terms of less than seven years, all existing periodic tenancies and new and assured tenancies with a fixed term of seven years or more. Also, if the landlord of a longer letting can terminate the tenancy within seven years of its start date, the 1985 Act will apply.

If you are dealing with anything other than a standard periodic assured or secure tenancy, it pays to consider whether it will be excluded from the provisions of the Act. It is rare to come across a residential lease for a term of more than a few years, or under about 40 years in London and

100 years elsewhere, so most people making these claims will be able to rely on the implied terms of the 1985 Act.

The Protocol is not relevant where a claim is brought under section 82 of the Environmental Protection Act 1990. They are dealt with in the Magistrates' Court.

The Protocol should be used whatever the value of the claim – thus even if it is only a small claim, the parties are obliged to follow it. In my view that makes ADR even more important.

Chapter Summary / Key Takeaways

- The terms of the Protocol should dictate the way a landlord should be alerted to disrepair problems, and how they respond to that notification.

- The stated aim of the Protocol is to keep costs of litigation down, by avoiding unnecessary litigation.

- The first two paragraphs of the Protocol alone provide ample material to challenge claimant solicitors on their invitation to engage in paragraph 5 and onwards.

- Taken in conjunction with paragraph 4, if applied properly, few claims should ever progress to a point at which lawyers are required.

- The scope of the Protocol is unlikely to be an issue in most cases received by landlords, but it is worth thinking about how its principles might be applied, e.g. in counterclaims.

Because the issue of notice is so fundamental to disrepair claims, the following chapter looks in detail at the questions of when notice is not required and the exceptions to that rule, before we look at the question of notice as set out in the Protocol.

CHAPTER FIVE

WHEN IS NOTICE NOT REQUIRED?

Notice is almost invariably a battleground in disrepair claims. You will need a thorough understanding of the legal principles behind the question. We are looking at it now because a landlord will not be liable for any significant damages for loss of amenity unless the tenant can prove that they were aware of a defect, and it was not addressed within a reasonable time.

It is important to recognise situations in which the tenant may argue that the landlord is liable even though they have not had notice of the defect. The reason that this surprising principle exists lies in the ability of the tenant to know of the defect. Most tenancies will provide that the tenant must give notice of defects so that their landlord can repair, and that a failure to comply is a breach of contract. This should prevent tenants from recovering damages, because they have entirely failed to mitigate their loss. But the principles discussed in this chapter may still be relied upon by the tenant's lawyers.

Notice is important whether the defect does amount to disrepair, renders the property unfit for human habitation or is merely something which the landlord will usually address within its service criteria despite the fact it has no legal duty to do so. This is because, in the landlord's formal Complaints Procedure, works might be necessary or compensation payable for a service failure as well as a breach of legal duty. We will look at that principle later.

The law in respect of notice is tricky and sometimes counterintuitive so you need to understand the subtleties. You might refer to two books, as mentioned in the Introduction. First, for a more concise consideration,

"*Housing Conditions, tenants' rights*", by HHJ Jan Luba QC, Catherine O'Donnell and Giles Peaker, and for a more in-depth study, "*Dilapidations, The Modern Law and Practice*" by Nicholas Dowding KC, Kirk Reynolds and Alison Oakes.

You should be able to cite both in correspondence and in court in argument to support your stance.

When a tenant is not expected to notify the landlord of a defect

In some circumstances a tenant cannot be expected to know of a defect because it has occurred outside their demise. Therefore, they cannot be expected to report it unless it has caused damage within their home and causing them loss of amenity. So, in those situations, the landlord is said to be liable to repair the defect from the date on which it arises. That is not a problem, but if a tenant then claims damages for a period during which the landlord was not in fact aware of a defect, the rule might seem unfair. But it is limited in its application.

When the defect is not in the demised property

Defects to the common parts are included in this principle. For instance, if a dead pigeon blocks a downfall overflow pipe above a flat and causes a flood which damages the tenant's furniture, that defect gives rise to liability from the outset and the landlord is required to repair and to compensate the tenant for their losses.[3]

The rationale of the principle is that the requirement of notice in cases where a defect is in the demised property itself is really an exception to

---

[3] *Bishop v Consolidated London Properties Ltd* (1933) 102 LJ KB 257; *Minchburn v Peck* (1987) 20 HLR 392, *BT plc v Sun Life* [1996] Ch 69 and other cases – see Dowding & Reynolds at 22–16

the general principle that a landlord who covenants to keep a property in repair agrees to do so at all times, so effectively it is the landlord's problem when there is any defect.

Of course, a landlord who has entered into a repairing covenant should be liable to repair, for example, both a defect in the roof of a block of flats and the immediate damage caused to the property when it manifests itself in a flat below.

But in housing disrepair, the claimant's solicitors may seek to apply the principle to damages for loss of amenity over a period of years, despite the fact their client has not reported the water ingress. Alternatively, the claimant might have reported it some years previously but was out when the repairs team attended to inspect and did not rearrange the appointment.

Although the general rule is clear, fortunately there are several exceptions and the rule that a claimant must mitigate their loss can also help the landlord.

Where the defect is caused by an occurrence wholly outside the landlord's control

In the *BT v Sun Life* case, the court did not express any concluded view about cases where damage occurs which is entirely outside the landlord's control. The example given was roof damage caused by a branch falling from a tree standing on a neighbouring property outside the landlord's control. Provisionally the judge said that he could not see any reason why that case should not be a further exception to the general rule. In theory tenants should be insured against that sort of occurrence.

That exception is limited to events which originate on land in the possession and control of a third-party. Where an unforeseeable defect arises on the landlord's property[4] the exception will not be applied. In another case[5] Hobhouse LJ doubted that it is relevant that the defect was outside the landlord's control, saying that it is only when the landlord or the tenant is responsible for the defect that causation becomes relevant. In that case, a frozen pipe burst and caused damage. The court held that this was not an event which was wholly outside the landlord's control, because frozen pipes are not uncommon in this country. Landlords should take preventative measures such as insulating them. This might be contrasted with the gradual deterioration of pipework within the structure, or in a loft which the landlord might not be expected to inspect.

The lease may require notice before liability to repair arises

But short-term tenancies usually provide that the landlord's duty to repair only arises upon the giving of notice. Generally, provided a covenant to that effect is clear enough, the courts will uphold it, and the landlord is not under any obligation to repair until the tenant informs them of the damage to their flat and, therefore, by inference, of a defect in the structure.

In such a case[6] the landlord will not be liable for the initial damage, unless they fail to repair within the time stipulated in the tenancy, but even then, should only be liable for damages for loss of amenity rather than the original effect of (say) a flood caused by a roof defect. This might seem unfair on the tenant, but household insurance is designed for such eventualities.

---

[4] as in *Bavage v Southwark LBC* [1998] C LY 3623

[5] *Passley v Wandsworth LBC* (1998) 30 HLR 165

[6] e.g. as in a New Zealand case, *Masterton Licensing Trust v Finco* [1957] NZLR 1137

But in housing disrepair claims, it has been argued successfully at first instance that section 12 of the 1985 Act prevents a landlord from requiring a tenant to give notice of disrepair before liability to repair arises, as the section prevents a landlord from contracting out of their duties. That principle has yet to be tested on appeal. In this context, there is a difference between the liability to repair and liability to pay general damages for loss of amenity during the period prior to the tenant giving notice of damage to their flat.

The covenant has the potential to operate unfairly to a landlord

The rule has the potential to operate unfairly against the landlord if misapplied. Take an example where there is a roof leak in a building where there is no access to the roof (except e.g., by scaffolding), or there are pinprick defects in a flat roof surface invisible to the naked eye. Water ingress through the ceiling occurs in a flat but the tenant fails to report it for a period of years.

That would cause the tenant knowingly and voluntarily to suffer any loss of amenity caused by the water penetration. If this principle is applied without any further analysis, the landlord might appear to be liable for that loss of amenity even though they had no idea that the roof was in disrepair. If, for instance, the tenant is not using a room or they are absent from the flat for long periods, they could deliberately accrue a claim for damages against an unsuspecting landlord.

The tenant has failed to mitigate the damage they suffer

In such a case, the tenant who fails to notify their landlord of water penetration and therefore suffers continuing loss of amenity fails to mitigate the damage which they are suffering.[7]

Although they will be able to insist on the landlord repairing the roof leak and any damage to plaster, furniture and decorations caused by the initial flood, there is no good reason that they should recover damages for any loss suffered because of their deliberate silence after they first noticed the damp penetration.

Damages are likely to be significantly lower where there has been a failure to mitigate. The difference between liability for the initial damage and for the damage suffered after a failure to report could be very substantial. If a tenant notices a few drips coming through his ceiling and reports it immediately, the leak might be fixed before they suffer any significant loss of amenity and before any decorations, floor coverings and furniture are damaged. It depends on the speed at which the initial leak causes damage. If it is sudden and catastrophic, all the decorations will have been damaged from the outset. If gradual, any failure to report would cause the damage to be more serious.

If the tenant says nothing about it until years later, they might claim substantial damages for loss of amenity. They should not be awarded them for the period during which they did not complain, because they have entirely failed to mitigate their loss. They are entitled to insist the landlord repairs the defect, but only to damages perhaps reflecting minor staining to the decorations which would have remedied much sooner had they reported the defect. Further, it is arguable that the landlord should counterclaim against the tenant for the additional damage caused by their act of waste.

---

[7] see *Minchburn v Peck*, above, and para 22–22 and 33–37 in Dowding & Reynolds (although the Court only reduced damages by 10%, for reasons unknown)

Thus, the principle that notice is not always unfair.

Blocks of flats subject to the statutory consultation procedure

The rule might also be prejudicial to a landlord who must consult tenants before incurring maintenance costs underwritten by service charges. If the landlord's repairs cannot be started before carrying out the consultation procedure under section 20 and 20 ZA of the 1985 Act, and the landlord cannot afford to repair without receiving interim service charges, they may be liable in damages for loss of amenity even though they could not possibly have started the repairs.

But the consultation procedure is subject to an exception for emergency or urgent works. Also, the lease might be expressly subject to contribution and payment by the lessee of the service charges necessary to fund the works. In another case,[8] Carnwath LJ suggested that the court might have to consider whether the rule in *BT v Sun Life* "*requires some modification to take into account the practicalities of the modern relationship of residential lessors and lessees*". In my view it should be revisited, so that a landlord is obliged to carry out repairs but not liable to a tenant who fails to report the existence of a defect.

Where the defect arises in an area of the building in the possession of another tenant

In such a case, it seems that there are two possible scenarios.

First, where the tenant in a flat above a claimant commits some deliberate or negligent act which causes damage below, e.g. allows their bath to

---

[8] *Earle v Charalambous* [2007] HLR 8

overflow, or goes on holiday during the winter and leaves the windows open, and the resulting flood into the flat below causes damage.

Provided there is nothing wrong with the installation for the supply of water or the intervening structure which allows the flood to descend, then that cause appears to be wholly outside the landlord's control. Again, it is the sort of event against which an insurance policy should be obtained. Of course, the landlord would still have to repair the damage to the structure but may be able to recover from the other tenant.

But if a pipe bursts, the landlord may be liable if their breach of duty caused it. That might occur because of faulty plumbing, even years before, which left a weakness in the pipe system. A landlord should be responsible for the damage which that causes.

Again, that exception must be subject to the principle that the landlord would become liable for any loss of amenity suffered after they receive notice if they do not then remedy the defect in the neighbouring property within a reasonable period of time.

Chapter Summary / Key Takeaways

- The issue of when notice is not required will confound many. The principles do not seem to be entirely fair, but there is a logic to them.

- The guidance above has scratched the surface of the issue and should provide some useful points of argument.

In the next chapter we look at what the Protocol says about the tenant's duty to give notice and the implications for a claim.

CHAPTER SIX

THE PROTOCOL REQUIREMENT FOR A CLAIMANT TO GIVE DETAILS OF NOTICE

The Protocol assumes that notice of a defect is necessary before liability to repair arises. Perhaps not unreasonably, it expects a tenant who wishes to have works carried out to tell their landlord of the defect.

As discussed in the last chapter, when the defect is outside the tenant's home, a landlord might be liable to repair despite not actually having been given notice. Whenever there is penetrating damp, there is never any dispute that a landlord is required to carry out repairs, e.g. to a roof of the block of flats in which a leak is occurring into a home below.

The Protocol says that a defect which is affecting a tenant should not give rise to liability until the landlord is aware of it. Further in any event, as discussed, most tenancies will contain a clause requiring the tenant to report disrepair whether it is because of a breach of contract by the tenant preventing liability for consequential damages from being payable, or a total failure to mitigate. But it must be pleaded and proved as a defence by the landlord.

Insisting on compliance with the Protocol in respect of notice

Before going through the steps in the Protocol, the tenant must prove notice and further give the landlord a reasonable period of time in which to carry out works.

The first response to the LOC – when notice not given

It follows that, in the reply to the LOC, if the tenant has not previously complained that repairs are not being carried out, landlords should refer to this paragraph of the Protocol first. They should say that the tenant should not be using the Protocol yet because the landlord was not aware of the defects. For this reason, the landlord should not respond to the LOC with a reply within the Protocol (i.e. complying with paragraph 6 and providing disclosure etc) but treat it as notification from a tenant of the existence of a defect which the landlord must remedy.

The landlord is entitled to take the LOC as 'notice' and respond to it outside the Protocol. If the tenant then goes ahead and issues proceedings, the landlord is entitled to say that this is a breach of the Protocol and should be the subject of sanctions. Most important, the landlord is excused from further compliance with the PAP. We will address those sanctions below.

Further, by the date of issue, if a landlord has an efficient repairs service, works will have been carried out and the claim can be met with an application for summary judgment – see Chapter Sixteen.

Access injunctions

If the tenant refuses to allow contractors in to carry out work, an application for an access injunction can be made. It will follow that a tenant cannot then claim specific performance of the repairing covenant on the grounds that a landlord is refusing to repair. See *Liverpool Mutual Homes v Mensah* [2017] WLUK 325 for an example of the factors the court will consider in the exercise of its discretion. As was frequently the case pre-Awaab's case, when the landlord called tenant to arrange access it "*was met with a telephone response from the tenant ... to the effect that she had been told by her solicitor not to allow access*". The illness of the tenant's daughter was not accepted as a significant factor in her refusal of access.

The judge did not accept the various reasons she advanced for not letting the contractors in.

An application for an injunction can now be made under the Antisocial Behaviour Crime and Policing Act 2014, using a Form N 16A, following the appeal in *Swindon Borough Council v Wood* (21 August 2021, County Court at Winchester). HHJ Michael Berkley agreed that any behaviour which is capable of causing a nuisance and annoyance in relation to a person's occupation of residential premises or to the exercise of housing management functions may justify the making of an injunction, possibly including a power of arrest. Of course, the grant of such an injunction is always a matter of discretion and in my view, it is best to confine such applications to instances where there is some risk to others from the tenant's refusal of access, or at least the interference with housing management functions has been significant and unusual. Please ask me for a transcript and note that it is only a County Court decision.

Unjustified claims for injunctions for specific performance

If the claimant does then include a claim for an injunction in any claim, the landlord should apply for summary judgement against the claimant on that part of the claim – see Chapter Sixteen.

Treating the receipt of the LOC as the receipt of a complaint

As an alternative to this stance, rather than treating the receipt of the LOC as notice of a defect, in most cases the LOC should be treated as a complaint. We turn to an investigation of how that is done in the context of cases where at least one defect was known of by the landlord.

Either way, the claimant solicitors are obliged to comply with (and should be referred to) the 2024 SRA guidance[9] on claims management as follows:

> *"Explaining claim options*
>
> *To act in the best interests of a client during a claim you should explain to each client during your pre-contract stage about any other potential routes that may be available to them to progress their claim. This includes making certain your client has been informed about, and has understood, that an established industry ombudsman or public compensation scheme exists (as relevant to that specific area of claim) and that they can approach those schemes directly themselves and without professional assistance or incurring charges for the cost of that assistance."*

Response to the LOC when notice has been given on one or more defects

In a case where a tenant has previously given notice of at least one of the defects on which the LOC relies, it is not as easy to respond by saying that the LOC is being taken as the first notice of the defects.

A landlord could approach the reply to the LOC on a hybrid basis, separating the defects relied on into those of which notice has been provided, or of which the landlord is or should be aware, and those which are entirely new. However, that would lead to such complexity that it is usually best to deal with the issues together.

In practice this means instituting the internal Complaints Process, but keeping a clear distinction between defects of which there was previously

---

[9] https://www.sra.org.uk/solicitors/guidance/claims-management-activity/

notice, and those which were drawn to the attention of the landlord for the first time in the LOC.

In the case of defects where notice had been given, compensation might be payable for failure to carry out the works within a reasonable period and to a reasonable standard. This depends on why works have not been completed, or completed to a less than satisfactory standard

Otherwise, if notice had not been given of a defect but the Complaints Process finds that works are necessary, provided they are completed within a reasonable time, no compensation should be offered in respect of those defects as there will have been no breach of duty.

Notice is often central to the defence of claims

If the Complaints Process is unsuccessful in resolving the tenant's concerns and the tenant's solicitors pursue the claim, the arguments on notice will have to be raised as a defence to the claim in court and evidence will be needed on the issue.

Notice needs to be pleaded and proved, and can be challenged

Usually, the LOC will be deficient in the manner it makes allegations about notice. They are vague and there are no particulars. While the landlord will not be responding within the Protocol, the complaints officer needs to address what evidence of notice exists and conclude whether the allegations made by the tenant's solicitors are justified in any way.

At the pre-action stage it is only necessary that any lack of particulars is raised, either in the complaint finding or in subsequent correspondence. It will then be pleaded in the Defence and an application can be made to the court asking for an order that the claimant provide further and better particulars, under CPR 18.

Chapter Summary / Key Takeaways

- Often landlords do not appreciate the significance of the Introduction to the Protocol.

- Except in a few cases in which a tenant has complained of disrepair and nothing has been done, tenant solicitors always ignore the importance of the need to prove notice and a failure to repair as a precursor to writing the LOC.

- Upon receipt of the LOC, landlords often fail to use the content of the Protocol to respond appropriately to it. Many thousands of disrepair claims are started unnecessarily because both parties fail to follow the Protocol properly.

- Therefore, if a landlord is confident that they can prove that they have not received notice of any of the defects relied upon and liability does not arise without notice, they should carry out works pursuant to the notice they have received in the LOC and refuse to proceed with the remainder of the steps in the Protocol.

- If there was no constructive or actual knowledge on the part of the landlord, compensation for loss of amenity will not be payable. But if the tenant subsequently alleges that they are still unhappy with the standard or extent of repairs done, the Complaints Process should be instituted.

- Notice is likely to be a significant issue in the proceedings, and landlords need to ensure their recording systems are accurate and contain sufficient detail to disprove a tenant's vague assertion that they have previously complained of a defect but have been ignored.

In the next chapter we will look at counterclaims, when the Protocol need not be followed, and what can be done about the problem which that creates.

CHAPTER SEVEN

COUNTERCLAIMS FOR DISREPAIR

Protocol need not be followed in some disrepair disputes

Landlords are accustomed to receiving counterclaims for disrepair in possession claims. The parties do not have to follow the Protocol in a counterclaim for disrepair. However, this does not mean that a tenant will necessarily be allowed to adjourn possession proceedings just because they bring a claim for disrepair.

For instance, a tenant may be accused of serious antisocial behaviour or may have substantial rent arrears. But when the parties attend for the first hearing (the CPR 55.8 Return Date), the landlord is wrong-footed when the tenant's solicitor says that there is outstanding disrepair.

Occasionally there may be some merit in the allegation, or at least the defects might exist. There may be repairs which have not been carried out for a variety of reasons. Sometimes because the landlord has genuinely failed to comply with its obligations.

Surprise counterclaims

More often, a landlord consults its repairs records and finds that there is no mention of the defects relied upon in its systems. Alternatively, the tenant may have had some repairs done and the remedial works were not quite finished off or they were not done to a perfect standard. Again, often, on inspecting their records, they find there were no outstanding concerns concerning repairs.

A party who wishes to bring a counterclaim must comply with CPR 20.

Before the Defence is filed

The defendant does not need permission to file a counterclaim as long as it is done as part of their Defence. In counterclaims, it is worth considering whether you can proceed with the possession claim with an order for a split trial even though the counterclaim has been raised. If the claim is of any significant urgency or seriousness, there is nothing to prevent the court from considering the grant of a possession order on a summary basis, while adjourning the counterclaim for disrepair.

Such an order might be appropriate where there has been serious antisocial behaviour, and the counterclaim could be pursued whether or not the tenant remains in possession. It may be wise to apply for an ASBI (see my other book on them!). Equally, if rent arrears are very substantial and the disrepair is objectively modest, you may be able to argue that there is clearly no defence to most of the rent claim and therefore a possession order should be made, although possibly suspended, depending on quantum.

However, if a counterclaim is drafted after the close of pleadings, the defendant must apply for permission (CPR 20.4 (2) (b)). If pursued late in the day, you should consider whether to object and to ask that the possession claim be tried immediately, without an adjournment to provide for the disrepair claim to be heard at the same hearing, or applying for summary judgment on the whole of or part of the counterclaim (see below and Chapter Sixteen).

Imposing terms on the grant of permission to pursue a counterclaim

In both cases, the landlord should argue that, although the counterclaim should proceed, or the court might give permission to pursue a disrepair counterclaim, permission to pursue the counterclaim should be conditional upon the tenant making interim payments of rent and arrears, with a provision that a possession order should be made if the tenant fails to keep up their payments. Additionally, if there have been problems with access, they can be addressed by way of undertaking or injunction.

Systems to prevent surprise counterclaims

Given the number of claims in which an ambush disrepair defence is raised, it is worth thinking about how to pre-empt such delaying tactics. I recommend the introduction of a protective policy when considering whether to bring a possession claim. If the landlord already makes personal visits or requires an interview when contemplating eviction (as they should), there should be a mandatory requirement for the officer or employee concerned to ask in detail about the condition of the property.

The tenant should be asked specifically whether they have any concerns about the condition of their home, and the answer must be recorded in sufficient detail to render it credible. Then if the tenant later raises it in the possession claim, the landlord will already have documentary proof that the issues were not previously mentioned and the Counterclaim has been raised as a spoiling tactic rather than a genuine area of dispute.

Application for summary judgement on the counterclaim / a split trial

Although the court will be reluctant to separate the question of possession from a counterclaim for disrepair, in certain circumstances, if a landlord's evidence is good enough, the court might be prepared to make a possession order and adjourn the counterclaim for disrepair to be dealt with separately.

This is particularly pertinent if arrears are very high compared to the possible value of any counterclaim, or if there are allegations of antisocial behaviour. In the latter case it may be better to apply for a split trial of the ASB allegations before dealing with the disrepair claim.

In many cases an application for summary judgement against the counterclaiming defendant can be made. Often the records show that prior to the issue of proceedings there was no substantial dissatisfaction on the part of the tenant and therefore, even if there are defects in the property, the landlord did not have notice of them. Obviously in such a case it would be necessary to show that the landlord has completed any necessary works within a reasonable time after notification.

Applications for summary judgement against disrepair claimants form part of the process of defending claims anyway, so I will look at this area in more detail later in the book.

There are statutory restrictions against bringing possession proceedings where there is outstanding disrepair, but in my experience, those circumstances never arise in social housing, so it is not worth addressing them here.

Damages claims after a possession order

A defendant tenant might even ask for the permission of the court to make a counterclaim after a possession order has been made,[10] although a landlord will be alive to a possible abuse of process in respect of any claim which is not raised at the earliest possible stage in the proceedings, particularly where a tenant has been legally represented.

---

[10] *Rahman v Sterling Credit Ltd* [2001] 1 WLR 496 and *Midland Heart Ltd v Idawah* [2014] EW Misc B48 (11 July 2014)

The case law is not very helpful to landlords on the point though and it is usually better to press for an early trial/summary dismissal of the counterclaim.

Chapter Summary / Key Takeaways

- The scope of the Protocol is wide, but usually a landlord is not able to deflect a counterclaim for disrepair by requiring a tenant to go through it before pursuing a counterclaim.

- Instead, there are other ways of addressing a counterclaim brought as a tactical defence. The most fruitful approach is likely to be an application for a split trial or an application for summary judgement on the counterclaim. For those applications, the landlord needs excellent records and a clear approach to the issues raised by the tenant.

But this chapter has been a divergence from the more usual circumstances of a disrepair claim. In the next chapter we look at how to get the court to apply the Protocol properly, through the use of ADR.

CHAPTER EIGHT

ALTERNATIVE DISPUTE RESOLUTION – THE DETAIL

In most cases, when an LOC is received, even if the landlord was on notice, they were not aware that the tenant was allegedly unhappy with the repairs process, or at least unhappy enough to contemplate a legal claim. The Protocol allows for this eventuality in its opening paragraphs. It provides that the parties must consider ADR. This reflects the whole tone of the Civil Procedure Rules. It is one of the fundamental tenets of the 'overriding objective'. Since *Churchill* it has been given greater prominence in the Rules, and now there is ample justification available to a judge faced with a premature claim.

In this chapter we will consider how the CPR, the Pre-Action Protocol for Housing Conditions and the Practice Direction relating to the Protocols fit together to make a compelling case for pre-litigation ADR through use of the landlord's complaints process. The notes in the White Book Volume 1 (at C1A-004) are very helpful if you are preparing a submission to the court about ADR, as is section 14 in Volume 2 on ADR. They contain references to the principles and cases I discuss below.

We will look further at the law behind mandatory ADR in the chapter on summary judgement/strike out/stay applications.

The CPR are very clear in their aim of discouraging unnecessary litigation.

The Overriding Objective

The central principle ("the overriding objective") of the Rules includes the principle they enable the court to deal with cases justly and at proportionate cost (CPR 1.1 (1). Following *Churchill*, the Rules have been substantially amended. As from 1 October 2024 the overriding objective **expressly includes** "*promoting or using alternative dispute resolution*"- in other words not just actively encouraging but mandating it if necessary.

The case law on this issue is discussed in Chapter Sixteen, when I talk about applications to stay the proceedings. The application needs to be accompanied by a skeleton argument which sets out the CPR, PDs and PAPs and the case law and other materials.

Asking the court to order ADR

By CPR 1.2 the court is obliged to give effect to the overriding objective in exercising powers given to it under the rules, or in interpreting them.

- The parties are required by CPR 1.3 to help the court to further the overriding objective. This specifically means that the court should weigh up the proportionality of allowing a case to go to trial rather than staying it for ADR.

- The court's duty to further the overriding objective is carried out by active case management, including, in CPR 1.4 (2) (a), encouraging the parties to cooperate with each other in the conduct proceedings (or indeed in avoiding unnecessary litigation).

- Most importantly, CPR 1.4 has been amended to include as part of the Court's duty to manage cases "(e) ordering or encouraging the parties to use, and facilitating the use of, alternative dispute resolution".

- Further, subparagraph (f), requires the court to help the parties to settle the whole or part of the case.

This new regime is supported by the provisions of CPR 3.1, which gives the court the power to impose sanctions failing to engage in ADR when read with the Practice Direction to the Protocols:

- CPR 3.1 (2) (g) provides similarly that the court may: *"stay the whole or part of any proceedings... either generally or until a specified date or event"*;

- CPR 3.1 (2) (o) says that the court can "**order** *the parties to engage in alternative dispute resolution*";

- CPR 3.1 (4) provides "*Where the court gives directions it will take into account whether or not a party has complied with the Practice Direction (Pre-Action Conduct) and any relevant pre-action protocol*".

Although the Court is specifically reminded by the CPR and PD of the ability to impose a sanction in costs, such a post-trial penalty is of limited benefit to a party which has had to spend substantial periods of time in the preparation of responses to disrepair claims. Further, most of the time the costs ordered against the unsuccessful tenant are much lower than those incurred. So, the inclusion of these new powers reflects a complete change to the attitude of the Court toward alternative dispute resolution.

The various Pre-Action Protocols provide for differing methods of alternative dispute resolution depending on the nature of the parties. In housing disrepair litigation, many cases involve social housing landlords and their tenants.

In Chapter Four we considered paragraphs 1, 2 and 3 of the Housing Conditions Protocol, which presuppose that solicitors will only be instructed when necessary.

Most people would take this to mean where a relationship has broken down fundamentally and the parties are not in fact capable of problem-solving communication with each other. This is not how claimant lawyers interpret it. They proceed on the basis that a tenant is entitled to instruct solicitors provided there are works, whether or not the parties have fallen out.

The Housing Conditions Protocol is unusual in specifying an internal complaints procedure as a recommended form of ADR. It does so in paragraph 4.

Paragraph 4.1 of the Pre-Action Protocol – the Requirement to Consider ADR

Paragraph 4 of the Protocol for Housing Conditions concerns ADR.

By paragraph 4.1, the parties are required to *"consider whether some form of ADR procedure would be more suitable than litigation and if so, try to agree which form of ADR to use."*

Either party might *"be required by the court to provide evidence that alternative means of resolving their dispute were considered."* See the discussion of how to use this provision in Chapter Sixteen on preparing applications to stay.

I believe that it is not by chance that this paragraph precedes the provisions relating to the LOC and the landlord's reply. It would make no sense to initiate a cost and lawyer free process only after significant legal fees have been incurred, which the tenant's advisers expect the landlord to pay.

The Ombudsman is talking to the Ministry of Justice about strengthening this obligation. I anticipate that it will say that, in normal circumstances, the court will expect the tenant to have exhausted the ICP.

It is legitimate for a landlord to request the tenant's solicitors' cooperation in avoiding litigation, including even the use of the Protocol. Read in conjunction with the Introduction, paragraph 1.1, this means that the lawyers' steps in the Protocol should not be pursued unless it is *necessary* because the landlord has failed, despite knowing about "poor conditions" to remedy them *and* attempts at ADR have failed.

Thought must be given as to whether ADR in general would be "*more suitable than litigation*". What does that mean? Factors such as the landlord's approach to notice of defects, the urgency of the situation in terms of the amenity of the property and the financial position of the parties might be relevant. Clearly it is easy to make out a case that cost-free and speedy ADR would be more suitable than litigation.

Thus, a landlord needs to alert the tenant's solicitors immediately to the requirement to "*consider*" ADR. While, as presently worded, the Protocol does not *mandate* the parties to attempt ADR, that may not always be the case in the future.

In the meantime, the "consideration" of ADR is policed only once proceedings have been issued and then only if a party raises an objection to the continuation of the claim based on a breach of the PAP.

Paragraph 4.2 of the Protocol – ADR options

The first line of defence is that a landlord was unaware of the tenant's dissatisfaction at all so the normal repairs process has been put into action.

If that does not apply, because there is evidence that the landlord was on notice of any issue, or the defect has been investigated and dealt with, but the tenant remains unhappy, we move on to how ADR can then be used despite the tenant instructing solicitors.

The Protocol provides specific options for resolving a dispute. In particular, for all tenants, mediation can be considered (paragraph 4.2 (a).

Private landlords may find this particularly useful and there are some free court mediation schemes. Also, for private tenants, the Protocol provides in paragraph 4.2 (d) that *"the landlord, letting agent or property manager may be a member of a redress scheme enabling unresolved complaints about housing conditions to be independently resolved"*.

However, a social landlord has a wider variety of ADR options open to it. Paragraph 4.2 (b) and (c) suggest that any remaining unhappiness can be addressed within a landlord's own *"complaints and/or arbitration procedures."* This protocol 1 of three which encourage the use of an ICP- the Judicial Review and package travel claim protocols also point towards this form of non-court-based dispute resolution.

There are further suggestions for both council and housing association tenants in paragraph 4.2 (b) and (c), by use of the Right to Repair Scheme or using the Housing Ombudsman's Service.

But I am going to put this in bold, so that it becomes fundamental to your thinking:

A social landlord is entitled to suggest that the tenant uses its own complaints procedure

So, in cases involving both social housing and private tenants, landlords can suggest to the tenant's solicitors that ADR through a cost free and speedy process is attempted before the remainder of the Protocol is followed.

For obvious reasons, a local authority or housing association complaints procedure is likely to be the best means of ADR. It is free to both parties at the point of use, very speedy and potentially flexible.

As i have said, the response to the LOC should also refer to the July 2024 SRA Guidance on claims management activity.[11]

How does a landlord insist on ADR after receiving an LOC?

What does this mean in practice? A landlord should reply to the tenant's solicitors, saying that it is premature to go through the Protocol, because the parties have not attempted ADR through the landlord's own internal complaints procedure.

Usually, if a landlord replies to the tenant's solicitors' LOC saying that they wish the tenant to be advised to pursue their internal complaints process, the solicitors will object. Often it is said that the tenant has already complained, and it has got nowhere. Otherwise, claimant solicitors will allege that the complaints procedure is not independent and therefore can be dismissed as an option.

In my experience, in most cases, tenants have not raised any complaint at all. Even if they have, no formal complaint will have been made through the complaints process. Alternatively, such a complaint will have been made in respect of one, often small, aspect of the claim which is now being pursued. Most of the allegations made in the LOC were not included in the complaint made by the tenant.

---

[11] https://www.sra.org.uk/solicitors/guidance/claims-management-activity/

Replying to the LOC

This therefore is the first issue to raise in a claim. The facts of every case are different and the response to the LOC must fit those facts exactly. If the tenant has taken the landlord completely by surprise, a complaint investigation should be launched into the entire claim.

If the tenant has been unhappy with dampness in the kitchen and has been asking the landlord to come back to remedy it, that should be dealt with separately to those allegations which are brought to the landlord's attention for the first time in the LOC.

Of course, the likelihood is that a continuing complaint of damp in the kitchen or bathroom is the result of condensation, which might not be disrepair. But more of that later.

So, the response to the LOC should be a clear statement of whether notice was given of any of the defects, and if so when, together with a reassurance in respect of all defects that they would now be thoroughly investigated under the formal complaints procedure.

Immediately upon receipt of an LOC, a check needs to be made to ascertain whether the tenant has notified you of any defects, and if so which defects and when you got notice. If there has been notice, how did you respond, when were works carried out and what was the result?

If the tenant has given you notice of defects and you have done works, has the tenant complained to you that the works were not done to their satisfaction, either within a reasonable time or to a reasonable standard?

If they have complained, was it an informal or formal complaint? You need to check your records and make sure of your ground before you reply to the LOC.

If you are going to invite a complaint by the tenant, you will need to provide a link to or copy of your (updated) complaints procedure, or if you are a private landlord, the details of the redress scheme which enables complaints about housing conditions to be independently resolved.

In the meantime, pending the completion of that process, a landlord is entitled to argue that pursuing the remainder of the Protocol is premature. See Chapter Sixteen for the case law you will want to mention briefly, although most claimant solicitors will by now have heard of *Churchill* and will probably try to rely on it themselves.

The tenant solicitors' reaction to the reply

Such a response will invariably be extremely unpopular with tenant solicitors. There is no need for lawyers to be involved in an internal complaints procedure on either side. If the tenant can voice their concerns, either on the phone, by email or through a website complaints form, they can ask for repairs to be done and for compensation to be paid. In most cases this should put an end to the intimated legal claim.

But the tenant's solicitors will then make a claim for their costs. A landlord will be able to say that the tenant should not be entitled to the refund of any legal costs they have incurred.

Why should a tenant be able to pursue a complaint without lawyers?

Tenant solicitors say that their clients are disadvantaged, or unable to articulate their complaints and therefore the form of ADR is unsuitable because they are disadvantaged against a landlord. Social landlords will appreciate that this is unlikely to have any foundation. Employees are well used to dealing with people who struggle to articulate themselves. They are acutely aware of the difficulties which their tenants can face and are sympathetic, mostly contrary to private landlords driven by profit.

It is insulting to most social landlords to be told that they will take advantage of their tenants in a complaints process. This is a point which needs to be made to tenant solicitors, backed up by evidence, if necessary, in the event the claim goes to court.

The Protocol also refers tenants to several sources of advice and assistance about repairs rights and tenants should be referred to them by the landlord:

- Shelter's website

- the Citizens Advice website

- the Government's publication "*Landlord and tenant rights and responsibilities in the private rented sector (April 2019)*"

- the Government's guidance in social housing "*Good Practice Guidance on housing disrepair legal obligations (January 2002)*

Tenants may additionally consult, free of charge, various housing advice services depending on where they live. The result is that they need not approach the dispute without help if needed. In most cases it is not necessary to seek the assistance of someone to complain that there is a defect in a property. But if there is, there are few tenants who are ignored by social landlords and permitted to live in substandard accommodation.

All those involved in claims against social or private landlords on disrepair/housing conditions claims will need to be familiar with the content of these advice sources because: (1) they provide the guidance you will need to understand the nature of disrepair/housing conditions and to ensure your Complaints Process is up to the job of heading off claims at the pass; (2) you will need to refer tenants who are unsure about the formal complaints process to them.

Halting the use of the Protocol in the response to the LOC

As the first step in any tenant's journey through the Protocol is mandated to be ADR, landlords should stand up to threats to sue them by saying that the involvement of lawyers is premature. They should ask the tenant's solicitors to advise their client to try the complaints process.

That needs to be done by a letter which sets out the basis for the request to consider the use of ADR, and the basis for choosing the social landlord's own complaints process. The letter can be drafted using the material set out in this and the next chapter.

We will now consider how this is done through reliance on provisions of the CPR and PDs.

The Practice Direction ("PD") to the Pre-Action Protocols

The Introduction to the PD for Pre-Action Conduct and Protocols and its early paragraphs are also relevant in disrepair litigation. The Introduction is helpful as it sets the tone of the approach which the court is expected to take to discouraging unnecessary litigation. It also sets out the manner in which the court can control the behaviour of the parties in respect of breaches of the Protocol. I anticipate that it will be amended at some point to strengthen the implementation of the stronger ADR push.

The Practice Direction – requirement to consider ADR

In brief, the PD to the Protocols provides at:

- paragraph 8, that *"litigation should be a last resort."*

- paragraph 11 that: *"If proceedings are issued, the parties may be required by the court to provide evidence that ADR has been considered. A party's silence in response to an invitation to participate or a refusal to participate in ADR might be considered unreasonable by the court and could lead to the court ordering that party to pay additional court costs."*

Sanctions for refusing to consider ADR

The Introduction is supplemented by paragraphs 13, 14, 15 and 16.

Paragraph 13

- *"If a dispute proceeds to litigation, the court will expect the parties to have complied with a relevant pre-action protocol or this Practice Direction. The court will take into account non-compliance when giving directions for the management of proceedings (see CPR 3.1 (4) to (6) **and** when making orders for costs (see CPR 44.3 (5) (a))…..*

- *The court will consider whether all parties have complied in substance with the terms of the relevant pre-action protocol or this Practice Direction and is not likely to be concerned with minor or technical infringements, especially when the matter is urgent (for example an application for an injunction)."*

The landlord does not have any protection from the tenant solicitors' approach to these claims in pursuing relentlessly the Protocol in the face of requests not to do so. But if they then issue proceedings, their breaches can be brought to the attention of the court and addressed by the imposition of sanctions.

When raised at an early stage in the proceedings, this paragraph allows the court to make case management decisions which result from a failure to engage in ADR. Sanctions are not limited to costs at the end of the proceedings.

Claimants rely on historic case law to assert that the court should not order a stay for ADR. But the new regulatory, statutory and judicial approach has removed all support for the argument made by the tenants.

Paragraph 14

That is expressly provided for by paragraph 14 (c), which says that *"the court may decide that there has been a failure of compliance when a party has ... unreasonably refused to use a form of ADR or failed to respond at all to an invitation to do so."*

So, there is a specific provision allowing the court to change the course of a case by making a case management decision based on a refusal to respond to an invitation to ADR or the unreasonable refusal of ADR.

Paragraph 15

Addresses sanctions which the court can impose when it finds a breach of the Protocol: *"where there has been non-compliance with a pre-action protocol or this Practice Direction, the court may order that:*

- *the parties are relieved of the obligation to comply or further comply with the pre-action protocol or this Practice Direction;*

- *the proceedings are stayed while particular steps are taken to comply with the pre-action protocol or this Practice Direction;*

- *sanctions are to be applied."*

Crucially, subparagraph (a) means that a landlord **should not be criticised** for failing to respond in detail to the LOC under the PAP-they are excused from continuing with paragraphs 5 and onwards.

Many judges may not be wholly familiar with the powers they have been given for dealing with breaches of the Protocol. But once they know that a claimant who refuses properly to consider ADR cannot then push ahead with the Protocol, it removes the possibility that they will say both parties are guilty of a breach.

The court can also order that the proceedings are stayed while the parties comply with the PAP, which in practice now means paragraph 4.2. Further, while the obligation in that paragraph is to "consider" the ICP, the tenant can be asked to provide evidence of that consideration. Turns out not to be sufficient to persuade the court that opposition to an ICP is based on reasonable grounds.

Finally, paragraph 15 (c) allows the court to impose sanctions on a party who has unreasonably refused to use a form of ADR. Such sanctions might include costs, but the claim can be stayed or even struck out for such refusal. The CPR now support a stay at least and, upon default by refusal to engage, could support a strike out.

Paragraph 16

Paragraph 16 provides: *"the court will consider **the effect** of any non-compliance when deciding whether to impose any sanctions ..."*

Thus, if a tenant refuses to engage in the Complaints Process under paragraph 4 of the Protocol, a landlord can argue that the **effect** of the non-compliance is to have caused unnecessary legal costs and, if it is not remedied, inevitably to lead to far greater waste. Thus, the court has powerful material on which to justify a stay.

Since *Churchill* this is an argument which has found favour with the court and prevents a tenant from succeeding in their standard response that the landlord has been in breach of paragraph 6 and beyond so there should be no stay for the ICP.

Therefore, if the argument is made immediately upon receipt of the LOC, the tenant's solicitors will then be at risk as to sanctions should they issue proceedings prematurely.

But they are not prevented from litigating forever. Their access to justice is not impeded, merely delayed for a short period while more proportionate means of resolving the dispute are attempted.

I discuss these provisions in more detail below, although normally *Churchill* and the amended CPR *should* now be enough to persuade an unwilling claimant solicitor to advise their client to exhaust the internal complaints process before going back to them and continuing with the claim.

Arguing for a more effective sanction than costs for failure to use ADR

So, although there is no specific sanction such as strike out mentioned in the Introduction, the court is not prevented from imposing such a serious penalty. Paragraph 16 gives examples of specific costs penalties only, rather than including every form of sanction.

Other sanctions which may be appropriate *include* an order for costs of the whole or part of the proceedings on an indemnity basis, depriving a successful party of interest, or giving penalty interest to a successful party. However, those latter sanctions are more likely to be ordered at the end of the proceedings.

It is necessary for the rules specifically to provide for those costs sanctions, because pursuant to CPR 44.2, the normal order for costs after a successful claim is that the loser pays them. These provisions allow the court to depart from that rule. But remember that while paragraph 16 expressly mentions costs, it does not exclude other forms of sanction, and they are relevant in appropriate circumstances.

Chapter Summary / Key Takeaways

- There is an obvious and pressing need for public authorities to avoid litigation if they can do so.

- The Housing Conditions Protocol is one of only three which expressly provide that the parties should consider the use of an internal complaints process.

- Properly applied, the Protocol, its Practice Direction and Introduction together can provide the materials to steer tenants away from unnecessary claims.

- The court can impose sanctions for a party's failure to follow the Protocol, which can include a stay of the proceedings, orders for costs and even a strike out.

In the next chapter we will look at complaints processes and the reason that they need to be overhauled by most landlords.

CHAPTER NINE

MAKING SURE YOUR INTERNAL COMPLAINTS PROCESS IS FIT FOR PURPOSE

There is no point in telling the court that you wish the claim to be stayed or even struck out pending compliance with your internal complaints process unless that procedure is up to the job.

Developments since the 2020 White Paper

The Social Housing White Paper published on 17 November 2020 and updated on 22 January 2021 as the "Charter for Social Housing Residents". It has addressed numerous relevant issues, including complaints and redress procedures.

The Grenfell Tower enquiry found that tenants had raised concerns about the safety of the building, but they had been repeatedly ignored by the landlord.

Much has changed since the White Paper was published. It has led to:

- Increased scrutiny of operational activities and performance measures;

- New requirements for resident engagement and complaints, including the Ombudsman's Guidance on the Pre-Action Protocol and the Complaint Handling Code;

- A greater emphasis on safety, 'resident voice', performance monitoring, and home ownership;

- Stronger enforcement powers for the Regulator of Social Housing (RSH);

- The RSH being required to set up an advisory committee;

- The RSH being expected to develop a publicity strategy to inform tenants of its role and purpose;

- The RSH being expected to be more transparent in how it works;

- The RSH being expected to have greater engagement with tenants.

The government introduced the "Social Housing Quality Resident Panel" for resident engagement. The 2023 Act also allows the Regulator and the Housing Ombudsman the power to issue guidance to social landlords.

Social housing landlords are also required to install smoke and carbon monoxide alarms in properties. This should lead to a substantial increase in remote monitoring systems, to the benefit of all.

In March 2024 the Housing Ombudsman issued a consultation paper about his proposed approach to issuing good practice guidance and its approach on self-assessments.

One of the effects of the reforms has been to provide impetus to the claims farming industry, which portrays itself as championing the needs of social housing tenants. This has been further fuelled by practices like the "naming and shaming of failing landlords". At present, social landlords must work in this environment to defend claims which capitalise on the negative atmosphere created by these influences. This means that complaint handling needs to be able to withstand the scrutiny of the Regulator and the Ombudsman. We need now to look at the latest Ombudsman's Complaint Handling Code, which will shape your Complaints Policy.

Lessons from the Awaab Ishak case

During the period the case of Awaab Ishak came to light. He died on 21 December 2020 of breathing difficulties caused by mould in the family home.

Anthony Hodari solicitors, a firm of which many landlords will be aware, engaged Awaab's father (Mr Abdullah) as a client seemingly without him realising he had instructed solicitors to sue his landlord. He told the coroner that he "*was sent paperwork to sign, but he believed it was to give consent for RBH to carry out work.*" Over the years I have heard many tenants say similar things.

This was a misconception which turned out to be a fatal for Awaab.

Anthony Hodari solicitors sent the landlord, Rochdale Boroughwide Housing ("RBH") a letter of claim 12 June 2020. RBH is not a local authority landlord, but the "*UK's first tenant and employee co-owned mutual housing society*". At the time it faced 450 other outstanding claims and there were 600 damp and mould cases in its backlog. It was also six months into the pandemic and the lockdowns, when all landlords were facing almost insurmountable difficulties in carrying out works other than those which were urgent.

That letter does not appear to have been in the brief form suggested for urgent cases in paragraph 5.1 of the Protocol. That provides: "*it may be appropriate for the tenant to send a letter notifying the landlord of the claim before detailed Letter of Claim is sent.*"

Thus, it may not have indicated any urgency in this situation, a conclusion strengthened in my view by the solicitors' subsequent conduct. Additionally, RBH's Disrepair Manager later said that they were not aware that Awaab was living at the one-bedroom flat, perhaps because the solicitors did not mention him in the LOC. The available material does not say either way.

On 13 July the Disrepair Manager was made aware of the situation and the following day he carried out an inspection in which he does not appear to have discovered that Awaab and his mother lived there, presumably because he was not told.

Following the inspection, Rochdale wrote to the solicitors with details of the intended works. At that time, social landlords generally thought they were not allowed to start works without getting them approved by tenant solicitors. The Disrepair Manager said that they had "*received instruction numerous times that we were not allowed to carry out any repairs until they had been agreed by both parties*".

Back in 2020, landlords were usually warned in the LOC that if they tried to contact the tenant direct and arrange works or went ahead and carried out or tried to carry out works, they would face injunction proceedings. Such warnings were sobering to read and caused most landlords not to risk ignoring the tenant solicitors.

This mistaken belief is understandable as it arose from the wording of the Protocol, which provides for a process which must be followed by those required to participate in the Protocol. Paragraph 6.3 (d) requires the landlord to send "*a full schedule of intended works, including anticipated start and completion dates and a timetable for the works.*" That *appears* to require a landlord to hold off starting them until the tenant solicitors have approved them.

That view of the Protocol is wrong and should have been ignored. In Chapter Fifteen I discuss this point of law – the method of repair is a choice for the landlord to make and the opinions of the tenant's surveyor are usually unnecessary and irrelevant. It is only if a landlord's choice of remedy is so deficient as to be properly described as professionally negligent or incompetent that a tenant's surveyor should be mandating the method of rectification.

Unfortunately, the Protocol did not make this clear. It should have said (and in the future no doubt will say that landlords should not delay works while waiting for approval of any specification

Returning to the historic practice of tenant solicitors preventing works until they had their say, the approval process can take quite a time if it is done properly and accurately. Weeks rather than days was quite usual historically. In my experience, tenant solicitors usually delayed that process significantly, e.g. in seeking their own surveyor's views on the schedule, disputing the nature and extent of the proposed works etc. All the while increasing the chargeable hours with tasks required under their interpretation of the Protocol…

In the event, after the visit, RBH was able to send a schedule to Anthony Hodari. But they did not receive a reply from the solicitors. Subsequently the Disrepair Manager said that if he had known that Awaab was living there, he would have gone ahead without waiting for approval.

RBH continued to get no reply from the solicitors. It subsequently transpired that by September 2020, less than two months after they had sent their LOC and three months before Awaab died, they had decided to drop the claim, presumably because they thought it had no merit.

Stephen Lund, a director of the solicitors' firm, told the coroner that the firm had not told RBH that they were dropping it. If they had done so, the landlord would have contacted the tenant directly and carried out remedial works. Perhaps things would have turned out differently.

RBH did not go behind their policy of waiting for approval from claimant solicitors and Awaab died on 21 December 2020 while RBH were still waiting for permission to attend. With the benefit of hindsight, they told the coroner that they were mistaken.

I believe that they behaved just as most social landlords would have done at the time. They had the threat of injunction looming over them if they disobeyed the claimant lawyers' prohibition on works without consent.

The Ombudsman's Complaint Handling Code published in July 2020 said that a landlord's complaints policy might exclude complaints when:

> "*Legal proceedings have been started. Landlords should take steps to ensure that residents are not left without a response for lengthy periods of time, for example, where a letter before action has been received or issued but no court proceedings are started or settlement agreement reached.*"

The Code published in 2022 was updated to confirm explicitly that "legal proceedings" meant their issue (not the sending of the LOC). So, after Awaab's case the Ombudsman recognised that his Code should make it plain that landlords could continue the complaints process even though an LOC was received.

Additionally, there was nothing in terms of case law to clarify the apparent requirement in the Protocol to seek consent before carrying out works.

Cases where the tenant's solicitors advise them to refuse access

I am still seeing some claims in which solicitors, seemingly ignorant of the change in the legal landscape, warn landlords not to start works without their approval.

Fortunately, nowadays since the wide-ranging publicity surrounding the case and the Ombudsman's Guidance (below), landlords just get on with the works and ignore claimant solicitors if they tell them not to do so.

Additionally, in cases where access is refused, the law has moved on, at least at County Court level. When the tenant's solicitors tell their client not to allow access, the landlord must ignore them and push ahead with an inspection and all appropriate works and apply for an injunction if they do not back down.

Every landlord should have a standard process for obtaining an order against a tenant, which can now be pursued in a much quicker and cheaper process using a form N16A under the Antisocial Behaviour Crime and Policing Act 2014 – see Chapter Six on access injunctions.

Part of your response to any suggestion from the tenant that their landlord has told them to refuse access for inspections and works should be to tell the tenant that such advice can put their safety at risk.

Additionally, you might write to the solicitors warning them that you intend to apply for an injunction and will repeat to the court that the tenant has told the repairs team to refuse access on their solicitors' advice, so you will (not unreasonably) be seeking an order for costs against them.

Photos and videos should be taken to safeguard evidence of the condition of the property and the interior environment at the time.

The Ombudsman's Guidance October 2021

The Ombudsman published his "*Guidance on pre-action protocol for Housing conditions claims and service complaints*" to help landlords divert legal claims toward the ICP. It also helps with the argument that access should be provided and works carried out immediately, without waiting for tenant solicitors to approve them.

At the time the Guidance was published, the Ministry of Justice and the courts had not given such a strong steer toward ADR, and it was not compulsory within the CPR. The Ombudsman therefore said that it was a tenant's "prerogative to follow the protocol and make a claim".

He said:

"Even when a landlord receives correspondence initiating the protocol, it is important that they do not disengage from either the ICP or the repair issue itself. Commencing the protocol does not constitute legal proceedings and ADR can be pursued at any stage of the protocol... The Ombudsman's view is that a matter does not become 'legal' until proceedings have been 'issued'.

The Ombudsman also stresses the importance of landlords remaining committed to inspecting properties as soon as a claim is raised and to completing the repairs needed as soon as is practicable. Where a resident has been advised by a solicitor to deny access to complete the repairs, the landlord should consider alternative methods of gaining access, such as seeking an injunction."

The Ombudsman also required landlords to do all they can to mitigate the impact and provide appropriate support to residents suffering from damp and mould because of "non-structural" issues. This is a reference to what used to be called "lifestyle". Of course, the Spotlight report deprecates the use of that word, pointing out that many tenants are unable to heat their homes due to fuel poverty, which also frequently causes them to reduce ventilation.

We need now to look at the Ombudsman's Complaint Handling Code.

The Housing Ombudsman's Complaint Handling Code 2024

The Ombudsman has published his updated Complaint Handling Code, and on 1 April 2024 it became statutory, meaning that any landlord within the Ombudsman's Scheme must follow its requirements. It can be found at https://www.housing-ombudsman.org.uk/landlords-info/complaint-handling-code/.

This has an important consequence in the context of the arguments raised by tenant solicitors, who were previously able to say that the process had no statutory backing.

The Ombudsman believes that the CHC represents best practice in complaint handling. If your policy does not comply with the Code, you must provide a detailed explanation for non-compliance in your self-assessment and confirm the date by which you intend to comply.

Therefore, your complaints policy needs to align with the nine sections of the Code, and you should be able to explain and justify its provisions to the Ombudsman. The areas concern:

- Definition – what is a complaint?

- Exclusions – what will not be treated as a complaint

- Accessibility – making it easy to make a complaint- meeting the requirements of the Equality Act 2010 and offering reasonable adjustments where appropriate

- Staff – landlords should have a designated person or team to respond to complaints

- Process – sets out a clear 2 stage complaints process

- Stages – sets out the timescales to provide a response at both stages including the use of extensions. If a landlord is going to take longer to provide a response, they need to tell the tenant and keep them informed.

- Putting things right – considering the impact on the resident and setting out what will be done to put things right

- Self-assessment – landlords must complete an annual self-assessment of their compliance against the Code

- Scrutiny – appointing a Member Responsible for Complaints to have responsibility and accountability for complaints

Amendments to a complaints policy following the Complaint Handling Code

I assume that by now every social landlord has an updated ICP policy or is drafting a revised policy. This book cannot go into great detail on the wording is there are too many variables. In the past few years, I have re-written a number of policies for clients, and ***it is surprising how a generic, organisation-wide policy can fail to address properly housing conditions complaint.

Further you should note that there are numerous potential pitfalls in this Code and care must be taken not to slip up at the first hurdle. When re-formulating the Policy, you will need to go through each provision and consider how it can be adapted to your particular circumstances.

Some observations and examples:

1. **Definition**:

    a. The definition of a complaint includes a Letter of Claim ("LOC").

    b. Therefore, as the Ombudsman has said, Stage 1 **must** be put into operation immediately upon receipt of an LOC.

    c. Claimant solicitors will object, but there is nothing wrong with insisting that it should be exhausted before they incur any substantial costs. In this regard the Introduction to the Pre-Action Protocols and the new CPR will support the landlord in refusing to proceed with the remainder of the Pre-Action Protocol.

2. **Exclusions:**

   a. The list does not have to be followed slavishly; it is intended to protect landlords rather than provide a straitjacket.

   b. For instance, in housing conditions claims, it is not possible to shut out e.g. matters which arose more than six months ago, because of the nature of the claim. But claimant solicitors will argue that the ICP cannot be employed as the complaints go back six years.

   c. This is illogical-as exclusions are intended to protect the landlord, rather than give reasons to claims farmers why the ICP should not be operated. A landlord can waive reliance on the exclusions.

   d. If your ICP currently excludes these claims, you are still free to take a decision that you will not rely on the exclusion and will run the policy in any event. But that is a good sign that your policy needs updating.

3. **Accessibility:**

   a. Policies must provide assistance for vulnerable tenants to engage in the ICP. Many claimant tenants suffer reading difficulties and other disadvantages, and it is highly unlikely that many or any of them have read or understand the CFA they have signed.

   b. Most landlords can support tenants who are clearly unable to fend for themselves within an ICP, and in my experience they do so as a matter of course. But claimant solicitors will argue that they are needed to put their client's case in the ICP.

    c. In fact, their interference is usually counter-productive, for instance because in the LOC they rely on every defect found by the individuals who have visited the property (employees of claims management companies perhaps, or sometimes surveyors). They usually say that there have been multiple instances of notice of every defect. The truth is almost always very different and needs to be obtained direct from the tenant within the ICP, thus greatly narrowing the ambit of the dispute.

4. **Staff:**

    a. It is not realistic to expect staff handling general complaints to be able to address housing conditions claims without proper training.

    b. Staff need to be educated to recognise what is disrepair or unfitness, when it is actionable and what should be done about it.

    c. Further, they must know how much the court is likely to award in compensation to offer a similar amount if they find the maintenance team have breached their duty.

    d. They are also considering service failures, so can recommend that works are ordered which might be offered by the landlord within one of their policies while not being required by statute or contract.

    e. In normal circumstances the Stage 1 complaints Officer will be a surveyor, who has full access to the repairs, communications and works records.

    f. It is also important to ensure that officers considering Stage 2 complaints are familiar with the law so they can carry out a proper review as opposed to rubber stamping the Stage 1 decision.

5. **Process:**

    a. The Ombudsman requires that an ICP should have only two stages so that complaints can be dealt with swiftly. In my view this a potentially significant benefit of an ICP, because it is unlikely that Stage 2 will involve any form of board or hearing. The result is that complainants do not have a forum in which to air their views before more independent people such as councillors or even paid complaints adjudicators. This provides an opportunity for claimant lawyers to argue that the ICP is not independent and that they can get involved at an earlier stage if the redress offered at Stage 2 is considered insufficient.

    b. The Code requires complaint handlers to "give the resident a fair chance to set out their position". It is important that your policy allows and requires this to happen at both stages. The court needs to know whether a tenant was satisfied with Stage 1 works and compensation, and if not why not.

6. **Stages:**

    a. While timescales are included as steps which **must** be taken within short timescales, landlords can inform tenants if an extension is needed.

    b. As all social landlords will know, much of the time it is usually difficult or impossible to comply with these timescales, partly because of overwork and partly because they can be complex, particularly if the complaints officer works from the Letter of Claim rather than asking the tenant what really concerns them.

    c. Every landlord will be aware of the irony that, if a tenant goes to the Ombudsman, it is likely to be between a year and 18 months before their complaint is addressed. It is rare indeed that, by the time a decision is received, works remain outstanding. But if defects do remain by then, that is a sign that the repairs process may need overall.

d. Extensions of time can be for up to 10 days, or if there is good reason, longer. Reasons for the extension must be explained clearly to the resident. It may be wise to contact the Ombudsman and inform him that demand on resources is such that the timescales are unrealistic, so that you will need an extension in almost every complaint about housing conditions.

e. Decisions must be provided immediately, and landlords should not wait until works are ordered, or carried out. This is very important-the complaint finding will include full details of the works ordered and when they will be carried out, although I would recommend that the decision is not delayed if the information is not immediately available.

7. **Putting things right:**

a. This means that complaints officers must know what they are obliged to order in law, and what they can offer additionally within their discretion, and without legal liability.

b. Separate those remedies, being clear to the tenant whether they are offered as part of redress for breach of duty, for a service failure, or as a 'gesture of goodwill'. It is essential to specify any works which are being carried out as a result of a tenant's failure to comply with tenancy conditions, e.g. by deliberate damage or failing to clean/decorate/ventilate – see Chapter Thirteen on dealing with causation of damp and mould though. Failing to heat may be the result of fuel poverty rather than choice.

8. **Self-assessment etc:**

   a. This imposes yet another duty on social landlords, and the officer time spent preparing the annual report will have to be paid for by tenants out of their rent.

   b. The process may be helpful, so paying for itself by reflecting improved complaint handling and reduced litigation.

9. **Scrutiny and oversight:** more duties for which the tenants must pay, but again, if landlords learn from their complaint handling, it might lead to the provision of a better service and a reduction of litigation.

Landlords also need a policy which addresses unreasonable, persistent or vexatious complainants. In recent years numbers of such people seem to have risen, as society seems to have encouraged people to be dissatisfied, and to complain.

So, use of the exclusion of vexatious complaints can protect a landlord from serial complainants, as the court has the power to dismiss legal claims, declare that proceedings are "totally without merit" and subsequently impose restrictions on tenants who bring unmeritorious claims.

Even prior the decision in *Churchill*, the CPR, their PDs and the PAPs provided sufficient justification for forcing tenants to exhaust the ICP. Now the combined effect of legislation and legal authority means that (1) a claim should not proceed to litigation until the internal complaints procedure has been exhausted and (2) if a claim is started unnecessarily, it can be stayed or even dismissed if a tenant refuses to engage in the ICP. Until *Churchill* and the updates to the CPR, some judges were reluctant to put those principles into practice.

In the near future I hope that this principle will be strengthened by the amendment of the Protocol and further Court of Appeal decisions, so preventing many unnecessary disrepair claims.

The best way to ensure that the ICP is used is through the tenancy agreement. It should be a condition of the tenancy that (perhaps except in urgent cases) the ICP must be exhausted before lawyers who expect their fees to be paid by the landlord become involved. Provided the term is phrased so that it is not unfair to a tenant, it will be enforceable.

Local authority providers -generic vs specific complaints policies

There is likely to be a difference between local authorities and other social landlords' complaints policies. The areas that they must address can be very different. Local authorities have wide ranging responsibilities and a policy which deals with, e.g., social services complaints might need to be phrased differently to one dealing with complaints about disrepair. My observations below apply to policies dealing with that specific issue.

Chapter Summary / Key Takeaways

- Grenfell and Awaab Ishak's case provided an important impetus for change in relation to housing conditions law and particularly claims involving damp and mould problems

- Responsibility for Awaab's death was multifactorial

- The subsequent publication of the Ombudsman's Guidance and the Complaints Handling Code, together with changes in the law have provided landlords with the justification for acting swiftly in response to Letters of Claim

- Of particular relevance to this book, they have enabled and mandated the use or continuation of an internal complaints process even after receipt of a Letter of Claim.

- Complaints policies may need to be updated to take into account the content of the various requirements/guidance given

- The CHC is designed to be helpful as a template but adaptable to the particular circumstances of a landlord, save in respect of the time limits. Those time limits are capable of extension.

- It is possible to make an application to stay or even strike out claims which have been pursued in defiance of the necessity to consider properly the availability of a cost-free alternative to litigation.

- When updating your tenancy agreement, ensure that there is a contractual requirement to exhaust the ICP before initiating the Pre-Action Protocol.

In the next chapter we will consider the machinery of a landlord's formal Complaints Process and how it should work in practice.

CHAPTER TEN

THE MECHANICS OF THE COMPLAINTS PROCESS

Assuming that the complaints process is up and running, those dealing with disrepair claims have to look for specific features. After complaints are resolved the question of costs may be raised by the claimant's solicitors.

Completing the complaints process

If your process is staffed by competent people who can dispassionately and effectively investigate the history of the property, work out why any defects exist and whose fault that might be, you will be able to respond to a claim with the sort of detail and accuracy which enables a landlord to dispose of the claim. The complaints team must know what works to order and whether compensation is payable and, if so, how much.

A properly investigated complaint will provide a full analysis of the nature and history of every defect, whether the landlord knew or should have known about it and whether the landlord's response was reasonable.

Often Letters of Claim include numerous defects which do exist but have never worried the tenant and therefore have not been reported. That much is usually obvious from the repairs history, but it is important to hear it directly from the tenant themselves, because it determines the true ambit of the claim and will dramatically reduce the amount of work a landlord needs to do if the claim continues in court.

Visiting the tenant

Provided the tenant is cooperating in the process, care should be taken to obtain the history of their dissatisfaction directly from them, by talking to them in person if possible. That process will invariably elicit information that can have a determinative effect on the decision.

So, the Surveyor who makes the inspection should be tasked with running through the list of defects with the tenant, checking when they believe they reported them and confirming whether or not the defect is in fact something they want rectified.

In my experience, most tenants will immediately make it clear which defects concern them, and which have been brought to their attention only by the visit of a claims management company employee or a surveyor.

There is often a significant difference between the defects mentioned in the LOC and those thought by the tenant to be worth mentioning. Almost by definition, if a tenant does not raise a particular defect, or says that it does not concern them, it is unlikely to be worth remedying, unless the surveyor concludes that it is causing loss of amenity which troubles the tenant.

Using the information gained from the survey/visit

Such information needs to be taken into account in deciding first whether there is any merit in the complaint, in respect of each defect, and second whether any works are necessary and compensation payable.

Often tenants will frankly tell their landlord that they are not worried about certain of the defects/works identified by their solicitors on the LOC. The landlord will never know that information unless it comes out in the complaints process. It is otherwise only reliably discoverable at trial – not ideal.

The complaint finding does not have to involve a complete legal analysis, although it is essential for the officer to be able to identify disrepair and unfitness. They must also know how much in compensation a court would award a tenant if it found that works had not been carried out within a reasonable time of notice being given.

Complaints processes can deal both with disrepair allegations and with service failures, whereas the court will only be tasked with deciding whether there has been a breach of the legal duty to repair. That distinction is fundamental.

Service Failures vs Disrepair / Unfitness

For instance, a tenant may be complaining about condensation dampness, which would be preventable if they were (a) given the right advice and (financial) assistance, or(b) if improvements or design changes are made to the property. Under section 11, there was no duty to carry out works. The fitness provisions may require a landlord to make improvements, if the dwelling is not reasonably fit for human habitation as a result of the defect in design.

The presence of condensation is now frequently said to mean a property is not reasonably fit for human habitation. Predictably, such claims have become a major issue. Tenant surveyors say either that defects should be rectified because there is a breach of section 9A/10. Rarely they say that the condensation is so bad that it renders the home 'unfit' under section 9A. In fact, defects should not be considered individually when determining fitness, the court must determine whether the property as a whole is other than reasonably fit– see Chapter Twelve.

Landlords may be required to complete design improvements to reduce condensation. It depends whether (1) the property is not reasonably fit for human habitation and (2) the landlord has a statutory defence under the 1985 Act, most commonly that the defect was caused wholly or mainly by the tenant. This has caused a significant increase in maintenance expenditure on damp and mould issues Landlords often take a cautious approach and carry out works even though it is obvious to them that the property would not be unfit but for the environment the tenant is creating. See Chapter Twelve for a discussion of fitness issues.

If a tenant is in fuel poverty and this results in significant condensation, the complaints officer might offer assistance. That might include referral to agencies to help with debts and financial management, the provision of physical assistance at home or of furniture or floor coverings.

A complaints process should look at service failures as well as breaches of duty and there may be cases in which although there has been no breach of duty under the 1985 Act, the officer concludes that the tenant should have received a different or better service.

Thus, recommendations for works and payment of compensation may be made within the complaints process when a tenant would not recover anything in a legal claim.

Compensation payments

If the Complaints Process is to provide a genuine alternative to litigation, a tenant ought to be able to recover within it a similar amount to that which they could expect at court. Compensation for service failures was historically very much lower than that obtainable within the legal process. There is an obvious reason for that where it concerns service failures, but if dealing with a breach of the legal duty to repair, complaints officers need to know the appropriate compensation levels.

For present purposes, it is enough to mention that damages for disrepair can be calculated in various ways and practitioners will need to be familiar with the principles in a number of cases[12]. For further details see D & R and Housing Conditions. In reaching a decision, the complaints officer must consider whether there was notice (if required – see Chapter Five), and if so, whether any delay in carrying out works was reasonable, if not whether works can be or have been carried out within a reasonable time, if not how much compensation should be offered.

Communication of complaints decisions

Complaints decisions must be provided in writing, in narrative form, complying with the Complaint Handling Code. A good complaints process will produce a decision letter which is often several pages long. Undue brevity may indicate a lack of proper analysis of the history of defects.

A complaint finding will give a clear outcome-either upholding or dismissing the complaint in respect of each individual defect. If there is a finding that works are necessary and have not been carried out, there will be a list of recommendations as to works, and if appropriate, an offer of compensation. A Stage 1 finding must also provide details of how Stage 2 can be initiated, along with other formal requirements.

Benefits of the complaints process

Properly operated, a complaints process should address the concerns raised by the tenant in their LOC. If it does not do so, it means either that the process is inadequate or that the tenant's solicitors are unduly optimistic.

---

[12] including *Calabar Properties Ltd v Stitcher* [1984] 1 WLR 287, *Wallace v Manchester City Council* (1998) 30 HLR 1111 and *English Churches Housing Group v Shine* [2004] EWCA Civ 434

If proceedings are then commenced, they can be defended on the grounds that the tenant's concerns as to fitness or repair have been addressed through the specification and/or carrying out of works, and if there was any delay, the tenant has already been offered or has accepted compensation.

The complaints process does not replace litigation, and decisions **must not be made** *"in full and final settlement"* of any legal claim. Quite the opposite, the finding should point out that the tenant retains the right to go to the Ombudsman and to pursue another form of ADR or a legal claim.

They should compensate for loss of amenity and therefore will be taken into account in any subsequent claim, but they must not supplant the legal process. Thus, tenants should not be asked to sign confirmation that the payment is made in full and final settlement of their claim, or any similar such wording.

Claims for costs following completion of the complaints process

If the claimant has been persuaded not to pursue their claim until they have tried the complaints process, only if it fails to satisfy the claimant should the steps in the Protocol be continued.

But if the tenant is satisfied with the works and compensation, claimant solicitors might still ask for their costs. If the claim has been resolved within the complaints process rather than with the assistance of lawyers, it should be argued that those costs are not payable.

In the context of Payment Protection Insurance ("PPI") claims, HHJ Jeremy Richardson QC decided[13] that summary judgment should be

---

[13]   In *Binns v Firstplus Financial Group Plc* [2013] EWHC 2436 (QB)

entered against the claimant and the claim struck out when the claimant had received the same amount that she was offered within the ADR/FSA scheme for the same amount which they could expect at court.

Paragraph 11 of the Protocol and *Birmingham City Council v Lee* following settlement under the Protocol

Paragraph 11 of the Protocol says that if it is settled "*on terms which justify bringing it, the landlord will pay the tenant's reasonable costs.*"

Of course, if interacting with claimant solicitors within the Protocol (rather than the ICP), landlords who carry out repairs and offer compensation through solicitors in response to a claim will normally have to pay the costs (on an FT or SCT basis) if they settle in certain circumstances.

But take the example where despite not having received notice of the defects previously, a landlord carries out any significant (e.g. perhaps even under £1,000 worth) works in response to a Letter of Claim and possibly offers a small amount of compensation. The claim Is settled on that basis.

On the authority of *Birmingham City Council v Avril Lee* [2008] EWCA Civ 891 ("*B v Lee*"). Hughes LJ said that when the involvement of lawyers in a claim is justifiable, a claimant can expect their reasonable costs to be met, although only *"according to whether the claim would fall within the FastTrack or the small claims track if it were to be made in court."* (Paragraph 16).

He further said (at paragraph 33) that the object of the Protocol *"is very clearly that, provided the claim was justified, it ought to be settled on terms which include the payment of the tenant's reasonable costs: and costs calculated according to the track which the claim would fall to if made by way of litigation."*

Does that mean the terms of settlement always "*justify bringing it*"? Invariably, tenant solicitors say that it does. In my view they are wrong. However, the judgment in *B v Lee* complicates matters.

Pre-allocation costs are not affected by allocation unless no order for costs is made upon allocation and any order for costs made before a claim is allocated is not affected by that allocation (CPR 46.13). The court's powers in respect of costs are unrestricted in relation to those costs. Therefore, an order for costs can be made in respect of them if it is necessary "*in order to ensure that the protocol does not operate to prevent recovery of costs reasonably incurred in achieving the repair.*" (paragraph 35).

Costs will be ordered on the FastTrack basis at the date on which repairs are carried out if the claimant subsequently wins at trial. Also, when a claim is settled, the parties are entitled to apply to the court asking it to determine who should pay the costs. It is wrong to assume that where costs are not included in a settlement, the normal order is "no order as to costs".

The Court of Appeal gave guidance on the determination of unresolved questions of costs in *BCT Software Solutions Ltd v Brewer & Sons Ltd* [2003] EWCA Civ 939. If it is clear which party has succeeded on a settlement, the court might be more willing to determine outstanding issues of costs, but it should be slow to embark on a determination of disputed facts just to do so. On the contrary, it should base its decision on the normal order as to costs unless it is in a clear position to do so on a proper basis of agreed or determined facts which allow the court to decide what order for costs should be made.

Obviously, if a defendant landlord agrees to carry out works and pay some compensation, within the ICP it looks as if successful party is the claimant. The argument that this was achieved within the complaints process and not by lawyers allows a claimant to say that it is inappropriate to conduct a mini trial and therefore it looks to the court as if the claimant was successful. The correct position in my view is that a landlord is entitled to argue that they are excused from further compliance with the Protocol if a tenant refuses unreasonably to engage within the ICP. This means that a legal claim ought not to have been started. But it presupposes that the court will find that paragraph 4 of the Protocol must of necessity be complied with before the remainder is instituted. As tenants can rely on *B v Lee*, this can potentially result in an unfair order for costs.

The facts of the decision itself seem to indicate that Ms Lee's claim involved only minor works and was not settled for anything significant, so it is a mystery to me that she ended up with FastTrack costs. It was presumably the eloquence of Jan Luba, KC which persuaded the Court to do something which has had serious financial consequences for landlords and has greatly enriched many firms of solicitors in the North of England.

Obviously, if a landlord did not know of the defects alleged (as is often the case in respect of most defects) then at trial the tenant will not win. Liability might not be established at all, or only be established in respect of, e.g., one defect, the repairing costs of which would be minimal. The court should find that the claim was not "justified", so the claimant would not be entitled to their costs.

Additionally, in my view, it is only when there was a well-founded claim for specific performance at the time solicitors had to follow the PAP that a defendant landlord should pay costs on the Fast Track basis. A claim for housing disrepair will be allocated to the Fast Track when the judge is of the view that there is a valid claim specific performance and either the claim for damages is worth more than £1,000 or the cost of the works necessary is over £1,000.

If the complaints process has run its course and works have been carried out, there should be no outstanding works. So, if the initial approach by the claimant's solicitors has been rebuffed with a direction that the complaints process should be exhausted and they have accepted that contention, by the time they are involved, there should be no reason that specific performance is necessary at all.

This should result in a decision by the court that the case was never one which would have been allocated to the Fast Track and that only Small Claims Track costs are recoverable.

However, they rarely agree to halt the Protocol while the ICP is exhausted, and there is then an argument about costs if the tenant accepts the works and compensation offered. Currently *Birmingham v Lee* provides some succour to claimant lawyers, as they can argue it applies to claims where the ICP offer has been accepted.

District Judges have made various costs orders on these claims, based on Hughes LJ's judgment, some in favour of the landlord and some against, or costs neutral. There is limited consistency and every decision is unpredictable.

In my view it is time for change, and I hope that a number of claims can be appealed to provide the forum for reconsideration of the authority. It is illogical, except in its wish to protect claimant lawyers, and unjust to landlords if applied strictly.

The level of costs in disrepair claims settled under the Protocol

If the landlord decides to settle on the basis, it is paying the claimant's costs, the level of those costs is almost always a significant issue between the parties. In *Birmingham v Lee* the court made observations by way of a postscript (at paragraph 37). They were not asked to deal with the amount of costs recoverable but said that *"in view of the information which we were given, some things ought to be made clear."* Even at the stage of the allocation questionnaire, the claimant was saying that her costs were about £7,100, back in 2008. The court observed:

"We do not know whether there is some special reason for such a level of costs, but Mr Luba did not attempt to suggest that they were justified. We say no more than that, unless there is some special factor, costs at that level look prima facie vastly disproportionate, and that if costs ever fall to be assessed they will need to be scrutinised with some little care."

This is a warning which is ignored by many claimant solicitors. If a landlord does settle using the Protocol, they can expect often exorbitant claims for costs, of between £5,000 and £10,000 when no work has been done other than the issue of a LOC and some negotiations, perhaps the obtaining of a surveyor's report. Such costs are clearly totally disproportionate to almost every disrepair claim encountered.

Claims of that nature can be contested by the instruction of good costs lawyers. Claimant solicitors' unreasonable demands for costs should be challenged.

At the conclusion of proceedings, if the ICP resulted in an outcome similar to that achieved, even if the claimant is awarded some damages, it is still reasonable to argue that they should not be awarded any costs or should even pay the landlord's costs – see Chapter Twenty-One.

Chapter summary / Key Takeaways

- An efficient complaints process should put an end to most disrepair claims, but if it does not do so then it should at least protect against a claim for specific performance of the repairing covenant and part, if not all of the damages. That is likely to have consequences in costs.

- If a landlord has instigated its formal Complaints Process and its officers have made a proper investigation and findings, the tenant should be satisfied with the state of repair of their home and with any offer of compensation.

- Despite the decision in *Birmingham City Council v Lee*, claims settled under the complaints process should not involve the payment of a tenant's costs. As the claim was resolved through the complaints process, rather than litigation, I argue that it was not "justified" and or that the claimant's breaches of the Protocol should disentitle them from relying on the authority and recovering any costs.

- If the complaints process fails to placate a claimant, or more likely, their solicitors, the claim will carry on. The costs arguments can be raised again at the conclusion of the final hearing.

In the next chapter we will look at the identity of the claimant, the nature of the property and the locality, all of which are relevant to assessment of the merits of the claim, whether under the complaints process, the Protocol or the legal claim.

CHAPTER ELEVEN

THE IDENTITY OF THE CLAIMANT

The identity and type of occupants – why is it important?

The Protocol requires that the claimant is identified. This requirement should be borne in mind when the claim is intimated. Occasionally the LOC provides the name of an occupant who is not even the tenant. They may mistakenly believe that they have a joint tenancy, but enquiries reveal that it is in somebody else's name. While this may not stop a claim being made, the nature of relief available changes.

Claimant solicitors are unwilling to pursue claims made by occupants rather than tenants, because ordinarily they have no contractual remedy under sections 9A, 10 and 11 of the 1985 Act.

The LOC rarely says who else is living at the property other than the tenant. That can give rise to a problem, because after settling one claim, a landlord may face further, additional claims from other occupants who are said to have suffered as a result of the disrepair.

Other occupants claiming under the 1985 Act

Other occupants can only succeed if they successfully argue that the Contracts (Rights of Third Parties) Act 1999 gives them the right to sue under the tenancy or in statute. For instance, they may be named on the original tenancy as occupants and will be presumed to benefit from the terms of the statute/contract.

More commonly, other occupants in the house are provided for under the claim of the tenant, on the basis that the tenant can claim for their benefit as well as for themselves. Damages will be limited, as they are just hangers-on to the claim, but as it is only the tenant who is paying rent, there is some justification for this principle. Additionally, it is the responsibility of the tenant to provide a comfortable home for the other occupiers, so if they recover damages for themselves, those occupiers might expect a share of those damages.

Other occupants can claim if injured or their property is damaged

A claim can be made under the Defective Premises Act 1972, or in respect of injuries incurred in the common parts, the Occupiers' Liability Act 1957. Such claims are relatively rare.

Other occupants claiming under the Renting Homes (Wales) Act

The new provisions expressly allow any permitted occupier to bring a claim personal injury or loss/damage to possessions under the Act.

Therefore, whenever dealing with a claim, if you are going to settle it, you will need to confirm who is resident and to ensure that you get confirmation from all occupants that the settlement reached is in full and final satisfaction of all claims which could possibly be made by any occupant. If you do not obtain such confirmation, you may be in for an unpleasant surprise.

Costs in cases where additional claims are brought

If a claimant solicitor does issue a subsequent claim, they may be at risk as to costs: see the case of *Chin v Hackney LBC* [1996] 1 AER 973, CA. If there is no adequate explanation as to why the subsequent claim was not brought at the same time as the original one, the claimant's solicitor might be liable for any costs wasted by the landlord because of the duplication of work in the second set of proceedings.

The individual characteristics of the claimant

It is necessary to think carefully about the individual characteristics of the tenant concerned. There may be reasons why they are experiencing particular problems with the property. This sort of information may be on your tenancy file and will form part of disclosure in the event the claim proceeds. Otherwise, it needs to be considered within the complaints process.

Is there a 'typical' claimant?

Knowledge of the particular abilities and limitations of tenants is important in terms of the landlord's maintenance expectations. Estate management should take into account what can be expected of the person who covenants with the landlord.

A landlord will need to consider what each individual claimant tenant is capable of doing in terms of property care. Tenants may be unable to comply with the requirements of the tenancy and care must be taken to signpost or provide help those with disabilities or limitations with work that others might be able to carry out.

The majority of claims in which I have been instructed have been brought by female tenants, either living alone or with children. Many of the claimants struggle with property maintenance, DIY and decoration for a variety of reasons, e.g.-lack of available free time, poverty, lack of skills or children who cause damage.

Unexpected claims

In the past there were few claims from some tenant groups e.g., couples with children, single men, tenants of advanced years. This may be of no relevance, but when there is an unexpected claim, you might consider whether there is anything unusual or special about the tenant or a member of their family which has an impact on the physical condition of the home.

For instance, I have come across cases where children with autism or schizophrenic adult children have caused significant damage in the home. Of course, such damage must be treated sensitively when reported by a tenant. But in my experience claimant solicitors and their surveyors often include it within the allegations of disrepair – they blame the disrepair on the landlord without troubling to ask the tenant how it occurred. It is frequently not reported, presumably because the tenant is worried that they will be made to pay for it.

In one claim by a middle-aged man with no apparent disabilities, my clients were surprised to receive a counterclaim for disrepair on a rent arrears case. After careful investigations, we discovered that he had been living and working in London, drug-dealing. He had sub-let the property illegally and his tenants had failed to report any of the defects which arose. Over time rent arrears had accrued.

He had lied to his solicitors, and they had not been able to discover the real reason for the arrears. They made the counterclaim in good faith, on legal aid. The landlord obtained evidence mostly from neighbours, but also from the police, given the fraud uncovered. The disrepair counterclaim was dismissed and a possession order made against him.

But in general, early consideration should be given to whether the tenant is vulnerable and in need of help. This may in addition raise the question whether the solicitors have taken advantage of the tenant in obtaining their signature on a CFA. Recently I attended a trial at which the claimants' barrister approached me and said that the male tenant was illiterate. The landlord agreed to honour the compensation offer of £300 and the claim was withdrawn with no order as to costs.

The Decent Homes Standard

An unintended result of compliance with the Decent Homes Standard has been a dramatic reduction in the fresh air circulation in social housing.[14] Landlords have invested in the sealing of fireplaces and the blocking of other sources of draughts. UPVC double-glazed windows, cavity wall and other insulation have been installed. Draughty Crittall windows have been replaced with perfectly sealed units which have trickle vents. Those vents can be closed manually, or blocked using Sellotape etc.

Taken together, although these requirements may have improved living conditions for some, they have caused substantial condensation problems for many others. We will look at this more carefully later. Increasing the provision of automatic ventilation and remote monitoring of properties have become of paramount importance in social housing maintenance.

The DHS requirements have had unintended consequences for the tenant who either has insufficient resources or skills to look after their property properly.

---

[14] See the report by the UK Centre For Moisture in Buildings https://ukcmb.org/ entitled "Health and Moisture in Buildings" page 5: "*It is highly likely that, through the current changes to building form, construction, occupation patterns and use, we will increase the risk and incidence of illness in the UK. These changes to our buildings may make their moisture condition much more hazardous over the next few years.*"

Poverty-related issues in social housing

Poverty continues to be more of an issue in social housing than in private stock. About 75% of private renters are employed, as against in the social housing sector 40% in employment according to the English Housing Survey 2022–2023. 47% of social renters were in the lowest income quintile, in stark contrast to the private sector. This has an obvious implication for fuel poverty and ability to maintain/decorate. Landlords should be advising on and helping with claims for any possible benefits.

Disability issues in disrepair claims

The proportion of households across England with one or more members suffering a long-term illness or a disability is 36%, in social housing it is 56%. In my experience disability discrimination is rarely an issue in claims. The landlord must check whether there are any health issues which will have an impact on the care of the property. Your repairs policy will consider the individual needs of tenants and should ensure that they are not left unable to care properly for their home.

Most tenancy conditions provide that the tenant will be responsible for decorations. Often part of the cause of problems is either a total lack of decoration, or infrequent/sub-standard attempts at decorative works. There is a continuum, from the tenant who moves in, does not ever even put down floor coverings and never decorates, to the tenant who is fastidious about their living conditions and decorations.

An increasing number of social housing tenants live alone, and there may be family difficulties, so that help is not as readily available as it was when the tenancy agreement was drafted, and they were given responsibility for internal repairs and decorations.

As the person dealing with their disrepair claim, you need to think about where they fall along that line and think carefully about whether your assessment has any implications for your future conduct and your approach to the case.

Damage caused by the tenant's acts or omissions

If they fall on hard times, many tenants struggle to pay their heating bills. As a result, they turn the heating thermostat down and try stop warm air leaving and cold air from entering. Many tenants remove the fuse from their ventilation fans, or otherwise disable them. They close trickle vents, block air bricks/Brook vents etc.

The tenant might supplement or replace their heating by using an unvented or condensing tumble dryer, with the exhaust hose venting into the property. Alternatively, they might dry clothes on the radiators, with the windows closed. They might cook without any ventilation, either by way of opening the window or using the extractor fan. They may use propane gas heaters.

Such issues can combine with physical or mental difficulties which prevent a tenant from maintaining their home as well as some others to provide the ideal environment for condensation, damp and mould.

In almost every case, one or more of these factors is a substantial cause of problems with living conditions in the home. Condensation and mould provide the backbone of most disrepair/unfitness claims.

The Housing Ombudsman has said that landlords should avoid a culture of blame, but that cannot mean landlords are obliged to refrain from defending proceedings on the basis that they do not want to attribute fault to the tenant. If the tenant is wholly or mainly the cause of any unfitness, it is not actionable. Frequently, but for the acts or inaction of a tenant, a property would be reasonably fit for habitation. The acid test is whether other tenants in the same block or same type of housing experience similar difficulties with condensation and mould.

These issues will need to be addressed in the report which has to be prepared in response to the claim. Whether a landlord is proceeding with a formal complaint, or responding through the Protocol, an immediate visit to the property is essential, with the aim of preparation of a full report into each of the defects and the history of notice and repairs to every one of them.

Chapter summary / Key Takeaways

- Think about who is living at the property. Make enquiries and confirm that the tenant is there full-time. Check who is living there with them.

- Make an investigation of their living circumstances and consider disabilities.

- Use the information as part of the report, to consider and determine whether the living circumstances are the cause, in whole or in part, of any or all of the defects.

- Fuel poverty and poverty in general are significant issues in the current climate, and landlords need to consider how to address the question even though legally they often cannot remedy the problems as they have a duty to other tenants to be fair in the expenditure of the rent they receive.

- If there are matters with which the tenant needs urgent help, for instance claiming benefits or having DIY carried out, efforts need to be made either to signpost the tenant or to provide that help if at all possible.

In the next chapter we will consider the standard of repair necessary according to the Act and how that affects liability.

CHAPTER TWELVE

THE STANDARD OF REPAIR – DOES LIABILITY ARISE?

The subject headings of the LOC in the Protocol address the question of notice before it requires the claimant's solicitor to list the defects. This sometimes shifts the emphasis of the claim away from a central issue. It is all very well that a landlord has been told about a problem in a home, but that problem must amount to actionable disrepair if the tenant is to succeed in their claim.

Often the LOC includes defects which are not actionable. There is a great deal of law on the definition of disrepair, to which must now be added consideration of 'unfitness'. This is a practical book, about how the landlord responds in terms of processes, rather than a book of analysis of the law behind the claims, so we will look at defences first, concentrating on the likely allegations made in the LOC.

The standard of repair upon receipt of notice

In general terms, whether a defect occurs in the premises or outside, a landlord is liable in damages for loss of amenity if the tenant has given notice of the defect and fails to repair the property to an acceptable standard within a reasonable period, or it is repairable without notice.

But that rule is not absolute, e.g. it is subject to the general restrictions on the standard of repairs, to the principle that patch repairs may suffice and to other restrictions.

Defences to claims of breach of duty

Before thinking about individual examples, it is necessary to consider the circumstances in which a landlord is not liable for the loss of amenity caused by defects in the home even though they might be within the repairing covenant.

Prior to the coming into force of the 2018 Act, a defect in a property caused by design issues could not give rise to liability, so that a house which was otherwise in good structural repair but did not perform its function well (e.g. because it generated copious condensation as a function of its design) could not be said to be in disrepair.

Now that unfitness is a criterion, the question whether a defect is repairable is more subtle. For instance, it is no longer true to say that defects in design do not usually give rise to a liability to repair. But provided the dwelling is *reasonably* fit for human habitation, defects which can only be remedied by improvements in design are unlikely to be actionable. Subject to that distinction, there are still some principles relevant to the question whether, taken as a whole, the property can be said to be in actionable disrepair.

Claims where the defects are too small or too large

There are two broad reasons why a claim might fail because the defect is not actionable: first because, despite the presence of defects, the home is in a reasonable condition overall and second, because the property is near the end of its prospective life and the ordinary standards do not apply.

Limits on the standard – section 11 (3) of the 1985 Act and section 92 (3) of the Welsh Act

Everyone dealing with disrepair claims should have at the forefront of their mind the wording of section 11 (3) of the 1985 Act: "*In determining* the standard of repair required by the lessor's repairing covenant, regard shall be had to the **age, character and prospective life of the dwelling-house and the locality in which it is situated**".

The Welsh equivalent says that the standard is that which is *"reasonable having regard to the age and character of the dwelling and the period during which the dwelling is likely to be available for occupation as a home"* – with no reference to the locality, although that would appear to me to part of the age and character of the building.

These subsections of the Act set the standard to which repairs must be carried out. Homes, whether rented or owned by their occupants will rarely be in a perfect state of repair. The purpose of section 11 of the 1985 Act was not to impose on landlords an impossible standard of perfection. The key concept is reasonableness. That remains true in the Welsh equivalent.

Defects which are too small

So, hairline cracks in plaster, a cracked pane of glass, minor defects in finishes, uneven but safe floors, nails in walls etc are not repairable, provided the dwelling is in a 'reasonable' state of repair as a whole. But for instance, if the floor is so uneven that furniture wobbles and floorboards rise and prevent other normal uses of the room, the landlord must repair the defect.

In Elmcroft, on the issue of the standard of repair, Lord Ackner said *"To my mind it is unarguable that the state of that flat in particular, bearing in mind the age, character and locality of the flat was such as to be quite unfit for the occupation of a reasonably minded tenant of a class who would be likely to take it — very probably unfit for any tenant….'*

It is a question of good estate management. Some deterioration will be acceptable, particularly if remedial works would be expensive compared to the gain in amenity experienced by the tenant. If the defect is first identified and then an analysis made of whether it is causing loss of amenity, a reasonable decision can be taken as to whether to repair.

If there are defects in the structure which do not cause any loss of amenity, it might be good estate management not to expend valuable resources repairing those defects until there is actual damage to the tenant's amenity. Many decisions of that nature are matters of opinion and the court should be asked to consider whether the landlord is being reasonable.

In summary, to satisfy the 1985 Act a rented home subject to a tenancy of less than seven years need only be in a *reasonably* good state of repair. That standard is to be judged by the standards of similar homes (1) of that construction type, (2) age and (3) in that area.

Although that word is not used, if landlords work at being *reasonable*, they are unlikely to be criticised by the court. Of course, the tenancy might impose a higher standard. This does not necessarily follow below. If the phrase is something like "good and tenantable repair" the court is unlikely to conclude it means anything more than "repair".[15]

There is no significant difference between the statutory and the common law standard. The simplest way of looking at the limit on the standard of repair in section 11 is to consider whether the damage is either too inconsequential to merit repair, or so serious as to mean property is effectively at the end of its useful life.

Both in case law and under section 11 (3), the court needs to decide whether any damage is unacceptable, primarily in the context of the age, character and locality of the home and the objective expectations of the average tenant likely to rent such a property.

---

[15] see for instance *Proudfoot v Hart* (1890) 25 QBD 42

It is necessary to consider this both as a whole and individually in respect of each of the defects alleged.

Providing evidence of the standard required

This fundamental question is often ignored in disrepair claims. Claimant surveyors' reports rarely consider the issue. The court must determine whether the damage is unacceptable in the context of the four considerations.

In order to do that, the court needs evidence in respect of each aspect, individually and then collectively. This evidence should be given by an expert, because a degree of opinion may be involved, but a knowledgeable housing officer may be able to help on some aspects, at least by giving the surveyor hearsay evidence of conditions in other homes in the area.

If, despite the presence of the defects relied upon, it can be said that it does not fall out of the range of similar properties, the claim should fail because section 11 (3) provides a defence.

A skilled and knowledgeable surveyor will be able to describe these issues and state how they affect the standard of repair to be expected.

The age of the property

The court needs to consider the age as at the date of letting. In an 1890 case which is still relevant today, Lord Esher said that "*nobody could reasonably expect that a house 200 years old should be in the same condition of repair as a house lately built*".[16] When he said that, he was considering the difference between a house built in 1690 and one built at the end of

---

[16] *Proudfoot v Hart* (1890) 25 QBD 42

the Victorian age. This is different to considering the prospective life of the property.

It is the age as at the date of the start of the tenancy which is important. So, you need to look at the effect of age on the building. If the property was built in 1890, it is likely to have undergone significant structural repair and improvement over the years.

For instance, such homes are unlikely to have cavity walls, and a tenant will not be able to demand that the walls are re-built to include them. Similarly, the walls are likely to have suffered settlement cracks over the years and there may be hairline cracks in the render and plaster. The floorboards may be uneven and may sag toward the middle of rooms.

These defects might be considered unacceptable in a modern home. But they can be seen as normal for a property of this age.

Character of the property

The court should consider the type of accommodation – put at its most extreme *"because the same class of repairs as would be necessary to a palace would be wholly unnecessary to a cottage"*, according to Lord Esher.[17]

While this is as indelicately put as his other well-known comments in the case, it is fundamental. Social landlords have an obligation to provide the best housing they can to the greatest number of people possible. Shelter says: *"the key idea of social housing is that it is more affordable than private renting and usually provides a more secure, long-term tenancy."* Social landlords are not concerned in the building of palaces, but in providing functional homes which are habitable yet still affordable.

---

[17] ibid, in *Proudfoot*

The court must consider the overall condition of the property as at the date the tenancy began. This can have a significant impact on the standard to be expected. There will often be a detailed condition survey report available, although the court does not need detailed evidence of its condition.

In commenting on this aspect, a surveyor should separate the effect of anything done or not done by the tenant and other occupants on the differences between the condition when let and the date of the claim. Deterioration caused by wear and tear is repairable subject to considerations of age.

But damage to the structure etc caused by deliberate acts or omissions of the occupants or other breaches of tenancy is rechargeable and a tenant should not recover compensation in respect of those defects, even if they are repairable.

The locality of the premises

Another brilliant quote from Lord Esher: *"the locality of the house must be taken into account, because the state of repair necessary for a house in Grosvenor Square would be wholly different from the state of repair necessary for a house in Spitalfields"*.

What is the general standard of construction, type of building method, materials used, maintenance standard of the area? Are there local conditions, such as weather or geography which contribute to challenges?

These are usually questions to be addressed by the surveyor but lay evidence can be used. There may be staff members living in the area or in this type of housing who can give relevant evidence on the peculiarities or special characteristics of such properties.

What is the tenure mix in the area? How many social housing units are there in the area? How does your performance in terms of providing housing measure up to other social landlords and private landlords? What sort of standards prevail in their properties?

Social landlords can use their performance markers/Key Performance Indicators for useful information as to their position in the quality ladder and other data. If this is not something that you wish to shout about, perhaps it is time to improve your position!

Either way, you will need to adduce evidence about it if you want to respond properly to the claim.

The population of the area and the likely tenant

Another quote from Lord Esher in *Proudfoot*: "*the condition of the premises must be such as would make (it) reasonably fit for occupation of a reasonably minded tenant of the class who would be likely to take it*".

If a surveyor is asked to comment on the question, they should be able to give evidence of the nature of the expectations of the average tenant. Are there particular problems for tenants generally found in the area or in your property – high levels of poverty or social problems which are prevalent and should be taken into account?

Are there any other claims in respect of that area? Who is bringing them and against whom? If there have been or are other cases, what has happened or is happening in them? If there are no claims against other landlords, why not?

Do any staff members live in the area or type of housing? Otherwise, are there any tenants who might be able to give you an unbiased overview of the repairs team's performance?

The prospective life of the dwelling - the damages too large

At the other end of the scale, if works necessary to remedy a problem are so extensive that they cannot be described as repairs, unless the tenancy provides for renewal the landlord may not be liable.

The 1985 Act includes an additional consideration-the "prospective life of the dwelling house", which had not been specifically considered in the case law. In practice it is rarely likely to add anything in terms of a defence, because its applicability was limited by a 1987 case. [18]

It will only be of application in rare circumstances, e.g. where the landlord intends to demolish or reconstruct the whole property with vacant possession. Then it might be a factor in determining whether it is reasonable to carry out running repairs rather than more serious structural works.[19]

The general rule is that if the tenant is to be handed back something which is wholly different to that which they were demised, the works will not be repairs.[20] Since the coming into force of the 2018 Act, it is unwise to speculate how this principle might operate, because the remedial works necessary to remedy unfitness might involve significant improvement to the structure of the property.

---

[18] *Maclean v Liverpool City Council* (1978) 20 HLR 25

[19] see the case of *Dame Margaret Hungerford Charity Trustees v Beazley* [1993] 2 EGLR 143

[20] see the judgement of Forbes J in *Raveseft Properties Ltd V Davstone (Holdings) Ltd [1980] QB 12*

Possession claims where a home is in serious disrepair

The landlord may be able to obtain possession against a tenant living in a property which is due to be demolished or reconstructed. For housing associations this can be done under the mandatory Ground 6 (intention to demolish or reconstruct, or to carry out substantial works) or the discretionary Ground 9 (suitable alternative accommodation). For local authorities, Ground 10 provides a discretionary ground of possession where demolition, reconstruction or rebuilding works are contemplated.

In practice, when using Ground 6 or 10, although there is no requirement to provide suitable alternative accommodation, I have never come across a case in which a landlord has not done so. Tenants sometimes deny that the accommodation is suitable, for various reasons. Those arguments are outside the scope of this book.

In most cases, the question whether works are so major that they fall outside the scope of the landlord's repairing covenant is unlikely to arise. It is more likely to be pertinent where a tenant in commercial premises has a full repairing covenant.

Relevance to fitness for human habitation

When dealing with some defects, e.g. rising damp, it is tempting to say that the installation of a DPC would amount to an improvement and therefore it is outside the repairing covenant. This might have been true, but these days the fitness provisions may require one. DPCs are not expensive to install, costs and it is an argument that might not be worth making.

Some surveyors say that there is no such thing as rising damp, everything is attributable to a specific cause such as the existence of a major moisture source outside the building etc. This is relevant, in that a DPC might not cure a damp patch on an external wall without other works to address the source of the moisture.

There is a clear interrelationship between this question and the issue of whether a property is "reasonably" fit for human habitation. Expectations may vary according to the geographic region and the specific area. What is acceptable and reasonable for a tenant in one area may not be so in another.

Care should be taken to adduce the evidence relevant to this question as a precursor to the discussion of individual defects. Having considered both, a conclusion must be drawn whether the standard of the accommodation falls below that which is "reasonably" to be expected. In some areas, it may be considered acceptable to live with certain defects which in other areas tenants would expect to have remedied.

But it is not merely the presence of one or more Category 1 defect which will render a property 'not reasonably fit for human habitation' and the test of unfitness is not the same as the test under section 11 (3). A property might have numerous defects which would be classed as 'disrepair' under section 11 and would fall below the standard expected by section 11 (3) yet still not be unfit for human habitation. Equally, there may be a number of 'hazards' but the dwelling is still not unfit as a whole.

A surveyor working for a landlord should be asked to provide sufficient evidence on this question to allow the court to make the judgement required by section 11 (3) and fitness. These days it will be necessary in some cases to address the issue of whether in that particular area there are any unique characteristics which affect the question of fitness for human habitation.

PRC homes

With modern building methods and the drive towards remediation and restoration, it is unlikely there will be much social housing stock which has reached the end of its prospective life. The main exception is non-traditional and easily erected Precast Reinforced Concrete stock ("PRC").

Many of those homes were built after the Second World War when labour and materials were short. They were built between 1950s and 1980s, but critical structural problems emerged, particularly in the concrete, which degraded as a result of environmental factors.

They were never intended to have a significant lifespan. The Housing Defects Act 1984 classes them as "defective housing". Unfortunately, a significant number were sold under the Right to Buy legislation and owners were left with long-term problems. They can be repaired and given a significant boost to their lives, but many social landlords have significantly reduced or eliminated them from their stock by redevelopment.

If the claim concerns a PRC home, there is a distinct possibility that the landlord will be engaged in a replacement scheme and will be reluctant to carry out large-scale expensive repairs. It should also apply if a building is evacuated due to structural issues, as by definition this is likely to arise from age.

Therefore, this will be one of those rare instances where a claim may be defended on the basis that the property has reached the end of its prospective life and is due to be demolished and/or reconstructed.

In such a case, the court is likely to sanction running repairs, rather than major works. This might mean that the tenant lives in less than satisfactory conditions for significant periods, but provided a landlord is reasonable about its approach, the court is likely to support it.

Cladding issues

Cladding is an issue in fitness claims rather than under section 11, see Chapter Thirteen

Running repairs in place of complete renewal

Any single defect might be capable of repair in several different ways. At one end of the extreme, when tiles are dislodged from a roof, a tarpaulin could be placed over the hole, stopping water ingress. But no landlord would suggest that should be more than a temporary, emergency repair. It is reasonable in the circumstances.

The question is then what works should be carried out to remedy the defect. A landlord then has a choice whether to carry out a patch repair of the roof, or completely to renew it. Additionally, in making those choices, the landlord might decide to use a less or more expensive type of roof tile, for reasons of economy or thermal efficiency.

The choice is a matter for the landlord to take, provided it is reasonable. There will come a time[21] when *"the only practicable way of performing (the) covenant is to replace the roof altogether…"*. In that case the roof was part of the demise[22] and Slade LJ said that there was:

> *"no evidence to suggest that a piecemeal repair of the roof in 1976 right up to 1982 was not a perfectly practicable proposition. I, for my part, am quite unable to accept the submission that, merely because there had been some half a dozen, no doubt troublesome,*

---

[21] as it did in *Murray v Birmingham City Council* [1987] 2 EGLR 53

[22] in a case where the roof is outside the demise the landlord will be liable to repair as soon as there is disrepair, though the court may be disinclined to award damages to a tenant who has failed to report the defect or to suffer any loss of amenity as a result of water penetration before the defect is remedied.

incidents of disrepair occurring during those six years, it necessarily followed from that the roof was incapable of repair by any way other than replacement."

That is a situation which frequently occurs. Less intrusive and expensive works are carried out, the defect recurs, and different remedies are tried. Eventually a decision is taken to undertake wholesale, fundamental and expensive renewal of a part of the structure. The court should not criticise the landlord for such decisions, unless they can be shown to be unreasonable. To do that, the claimant needs to prove on the balance of probabilities that the landlord's surveyors were effectively negligent. This is not to say that the tenant should expect to live in sub-standard conditions, e.g. with a leaking roof. Each time water penetration occurs, appropriate repairs must be carried out. The point is that they need not immediately involve wholesale replacement of the roof structure.

This is a crucial concept and again, often ignored by tenant solicitors. Their misconception arises from the PAP. That tells both sides that the claimant should have a say in the repairs schedule. This is wrong in law, most of the time.

Tenants' solicitors should not be involved in the choice of remedy

There are numerous provisions in the PAP which wrongly suggest that the tenant should be intimately involved in the choice of works, or even dictate them, for example:

- In paragraph 6.3 (d) *"a full schedule of intended works, including anticipated start and completion dates"* is to be included in the Letter of Response.

- In paragraph 7.1 (d) it says that *"the expert should be asked to provide a schedule of works, an estimate of the costs of those works, and to list any urgent works."*

- In the LOC provision for expert evidence says[23] *"If agreement is not reached about the carrying out of works within 20 days of this letter, we propose that the parties agree to jointly instruct a single joint expert…"*

So, it is not surprising that since the Protocol came into force, tenants' solicitors have gained the impression that they should be involved in the decision as to which works should be carried out. This is something which should be resisted, even though it is in the express wording of the Protocol.

Given that wording, it was understandable that before Awaab Ishak died, many social landlords had a policy of refraining from carrying out works until the tenant's solicitors gave consent. Since then, the Ombudsman has clarified that landlords should get on with works. It is notable that in discussions about the case reference has not been made to these provisions.

In conclusion, the surveyor inspecting within the ICP should specify and order works and have them carried out as soon as practicable.

The choice of remedy is for the landlord

Provided the landlord is reasonable, the tenant has no legal right to dictate what should be done. If the landlord gets it wrong and fails to remedy the defect, damages may continue to accrue. But that is a risk which the landlord takes.

---

[23] the current version of the protocol at: https://www.justice.gov.uk/courts/procedure-rules/civil/protocol/prot_hou#8.1 duplicates provision for expert evidence

There are examples where a tenant might suggest works which are far more expensive than the remedy chosen by the landlord and in which the court has supported the tenant.[24] In that case, there was extensive rising damp, but the landlord refused to inject a damp proof course ("DPC"), wanting instead to carry out patch repairs to the perished plaster. The block was a relatively modern construction and had an ineffective slate DPC, which had been bridged because it had been inserted below ground level and the internal walls were damp up to a height of 1–1.5m.

The court ordered the landlord to insert an effective DPC, saying that it did not give the tenant a different thing from that which was let to them. That defect would now be addressed within the fitness provisions, provided the dwelling could be described as not reasonably fit for human habitation.

In a claim[25] in which the Council had carried on patch repairs to the roof in the face of the tenant's contentions that it had reached the end of its life, and the Court of Appeal did not interfere with the judge's decision that the tenant could not insist on replacement despite repeated leaks and the necessity for numerous works over the years.

This aspect of the law is invariably ignored by claimant solicitors, who use the Protocol to their advantage. They argue that although the landlord has carried out some works, those which have been recommended by their surveyor has not been completed and therefore they are still entitled to claim specific performance of the repairing covenant. They have no right to do so, provided that the works completed house ameliorated any significant loss of amenity caused by the defect. I recommend you look at the issue in Dowding & Reynolds,

---

[24] see, e.g., *Elmcroft Developments Ltd v Tankersley-Sawyer* [1984] 1 EGLR 47, (1984) 270 EG 140

[25] Murray v Birmingham City Council [1987] 2 EGLR 53. See generally Dowding & Reynolds 10-07-10-08,

where it is discussed under the heading "Different Methods of Repair". In practical terms, this argument should result in the dismissal of the claim for an injunction is under section 17 of the 1985 Act, and the allocation of the claim to the Small Claims Track.

Bringing together the four factors

It follows from the above that just because a dwelling is not in a perfect state of repair, it does not mean that it is in 'disrepair' sufficient to give rise to liability. If the damage is modest and no worse than that put up with by other reasonably minded tenants, the court will not hold the landlord liable.

Again, the landlord can rely on Lord Esher in *Proudfoot v Hart:* the home *"need not be put into the same condition as when the tenant took it; it need not be put in perfect repair."*

Should decorations be included in the landlord's repair works?

This is a point which can give rise to argument in claims. In a 1984 case[26] the Court of Appeal said that the cost of redecoration after works is recoverable, despite the possibility that it would result in an element of betterment (giving back the tenant something better than they had). But in that case the court assumed that the house was properly decorated when the repair works were started. Equally there is no discussion in that case as to the standard of decorations expected of the landlord.

---

[26] *McGreal v Wake* (1984) 13 HLR 107, 269 EG 1254

The Court of Appeal based the decision on betterment on an old case not involving landlord and tenant law decided as long ago as 1970.[27] The court in that case held that if the claimant cannot make good their loss without betterment, the defendant is not entitled to make a deduction to take it into account.

A landlord cannot dictate the quality and nature of any decorations. A tenant may, for instance, choose to apply expensive wallpaper in place of a couple of coats of emulsion. I would suggest that a landlord then carrying out essential repairs for the benefit of the tenant should not be expected to redecorate using the same expensive wallpaper. Such eventualities should be catered for by household insurance.

Additionally, if there is an express term in the tenancy that the tenant is responsible for decorations, one could say that when the tenant took the tenancy, they knew that they would have to remedy any damage themselves because their contractual obligation was clear. If then decorations are damaged during repairs, contractually the tenant has agreed to be responsible for reinstating them.

If the existing decorations were in a poor condition, only minimal making good is necessary

The solution to the conundrum is found in another 1985 case[28] in which the court said: "*the tenant, who has very torn, damaged wallpaper which is further damaged, may well not be in a position to complain that the landlord has failed to make good consequential damage to the decorations if he is presented with an emulsion-painted wall. It may even be that the existing*

---

[27] *Harbutt's "Plasticine" Ltd v Wayne Tank and Pump Co Ltd* [1970] 1 QB 447 at pp 468, 473 and 476,

[28] *Bradley v Chorley Borough Council* [1985] EG 801

wallpaper is so damaged anyway that there was no consequential damage to the decorations, looking at the matter in the round."

The 'decorations allowance' in social housing

In social housing, after repairing defects many landlords do not redecorate themselves but provide a "decorations allowance" to the tenant. That policy is always subject to exceptions, particularly where tenants are elderly or disabled, or otherwise unable to carry out decorations themselves. This seems to work satisfactorily, except when claims come to court, and lawyers argue that the tenants should be entitled to the cost of getting decorators in to do the work. That meets with mixed results.

It is suggested that there is an issue of reasonableness to be considered. The rent charged by social landlords is very much lower than commercial rents. Where the landlord is carrying out repairs for the benefit of the tenant, if the tenancy requires the tenant to do their own decorations, offering a decorations allowance in place of contractual decorating services may be viewed as a reasonable custom and practice.

Such an allowance saves all tenants from the substantial increase in repair costs across the estate which would be caused if social landlords employed contractors to carry out all post-works decorations. It allows the landlord to direct its finances towards more important works. The decorations allowance point has not been considered at appellate level and there is no authority for my proposition, other than experience in front of district judges.

However, the court is unlikely to agree that it is acceptable in a case where a tenant suffers from physical disabilities preventing them from decorating and has no family or other support networks to assist them.

In a suitable case, the court can imply a term into a contract for commercial efficacy. It is suggested that the decorations allowance is a good example of the sort of situation in which the court should find that the commonly adopted practice is a reasonable compromise between landlord and tenant.

Chapter summary / Key Takeaways

- There are fundamental, general considerations which fix the standard of repair necessary in contract and under statute.

- The court is not interested in an objective, fixed "one size fits all" standard. It is about providing accommodation which is of reasonable quality for the area. This question should be at the forefront of your considerations and response to the claim.

- Surveyors acting for landlords should provide factual evidence of the four issues raised in section 11 (3) so that the judge can make an assessment whether, despite the defects relied upon, the property is still in a reasonable state of repair. The ultimate answer to the question whether the state of repair is reasonable is for the judge.

- All this information is relevant and determinative in fixing the standard required. It will also have a bearing when it comes to fitness for human habitation, because it is part of the question whether the accommodation is *reasonably* fit for habitation.

- By providing factual material and opinions to guide and inform the assessment, an expert can give them assistance which is likely to be appreciated. Without that evidence they are unlikely to be able to form an opinion themselves, unless they happen to live in the area, in accommodation of a similar nature.

- We have looked at the fundamental limits on the standard to be expected.

In the next chapter we will look at the defects, commonly relied upon and at the sort of issues which arise in formulating a response.

CHAPTER THIRTEEN

THE SPECIFIC DEFECTS ALLEGED

Because this is a book about responding to claims, we will look at what constitutes disrepair from the point of view of the example LOC, addressing the most common forms of allegations.

Before considering the list itself, I should point out one of the most fundamental issues with disrepair claim allegations: "damp", the 'defect' most frequently alleged, is not a defect at all. It is a symptom, or the effect of numerous possible causes. This gives rise to immense confusion in disrepair claims and often makes cases needlessly complicated.

Because dampness forms the basis of most claims and gives rise to the most serious consequences for occupiers, the relevant principles will be of application in almost every other allegation.

The defects alleged in the LOC

The allegations in the LOC are often something like:

- the property is damp throughout
- there is rising damp
- the kitchen/bathroom/living room/bedrooms is/are damp
- the cavity wall insulation is defective
- the UPVC windows are draughty and defective, and the seals need replacement

- the window opening mechanisms are broken

- the windowpanes are cracked

- the toilet leaks/pipes leak

- the kitchen/bathroom ventilation fan is not functioning

- the roof and gutters are defective

- the exterior brickwork is defective

- the property is unfit for human habitation

Investigating Liability

The claimant's solicitors should have to prove in respect of each defect individually that it is repairable by the landlord. In almost every case this is either because the landlord is contractually obliged, or because statute implies an obligation. Liability can arise in common law, but that will rarely add anything to the contractual/statutory claim. Equally, claims can be brought in nuisance, but there are limited circumstances in which it will be relevant.

The source of the rights in respect of each defect is critical. Tenant solicitors will invariably write their LOC (and later the Particulars of Claim) relying on every possible legal right, without specifying in respect of each defect which of them will be relied upon trial.

This makes it much more difficult to respond to the claim, because you do not know the extent of the obligation relied upon and the way it is put. Of course, you can ask for clarification, but there are few tenant solicitors who have the inclination or ability to provide it.

So rather than approaching this book by setting out all the different rights and leaving the reader to work out which might apply in any case, we will look at the allegations and consider which rights might be relevant. The most frequent and serious of all allegations is that which normally appears at the top of the LOC – "damp throughout".

A study of the principles behind liability in cases where the tenant is suffering from "damp" will be helpful in considering many of the other defects commonly alleged.

"Damp throughout"

Usually, the list of defects includes an all-encompassing allegation that the property is damp throughout. This is rarely true. Further, even if there is damp in every room, it is unlikely to have a single cause, unless it is condensation dampness. Since 2003 the percentage of homes with damp problems has fallen from 10.6% to about 4% as a whole. In the private rented sector, 9% of homes were reported to have a damp problem in 2022, compared to only 5% in social housing.[29] That figure is still significantly higher than the 2% of owner occupiers.

Many properties will have some limited amount of damp of some sort, but there in social housing there are few in which damp can truly be said to be affecting the entire home.

Prior to the 2018 Act, it was often said that condensation was not actionable in County Court proceedings. That was and still is true, unless it makes the home unfit for human habitation and is not caused by default on the part of the landlord.

---

[29] English Housing Survey 2022–2023

Just because a home is damp, it does not mean that the tenant has a good claim against their landlord. The causes of dampness must be understood. A claim in which the claimant surveyor fails to identify the likely cause of dampness should fail even if a landlord does not identify the true cause.[30]

But before discussing the causes of damp for the purposes of defending claims, it is important to address remote monitoring systems, because they have become an essential feature of estate management.

Property condition remote monitoring

In many Letters of Claim, the existence of condensation caused by the tenant is not separated from the list of defects relied upon. Instead, the claim will often include an allegation that there is black mould on the walls, without reference to the cause. The Ombudsman's views in *"Spotlight on: Damp & Mould-It Is Not Lifestyle"* must be addressed, but nothing can be done before the landlord reaches a properly independent and considered view about the cause of damp.

If there is evidence that the tenant is wholly or mainly responsible for the creation of the condensation, liability will not arise, although this may also lead to a resolution of the problem. The collection of evidence is therefore critical.

It is possible to obtain such evidence from the tenant themselves, but in my experience few surveyors attending on behalf of landlords manage to probe sufficiently into the use of the property to provide the evidential

---

[30] see for instance *Southwark LBC v McIntosh* [2002] 1 EGLR 25 and *Ball v Plymouth CC* [2004] EWHC 134

basis for the defence. I have rarely seen a tenant surveyor's report which reflects any proper enquiry into the causes.

Technology can come to the rescue and fortunately is being used by many landlords both to prevent damp and mould and to ascertain its causes when a claim is made. Therefore, landlords should fit such systems in any stock which is susceptible to condensation dampness.

Failing that, when a claim is received, a remote monitoring system should be installed in the property immediately.

This can be as basic as the installation of data logging ventilation fans in the kitchen and bathroom. But there are now monitoring systems such as Switchee, Aico, Airex, Awaretag, Fire Angel, GEM Smart, Healthy Homes, Invisible Systems, Vericon and IoT Solutions, available to landlords which both control heating systems and analyse the performance of the property and the true cause of problems.

The intention behind any remote monitoring system when used estate-wide, or in properties which are likely to be problematic is to provide an early warning signal, whether of technical issues or of worsening living conditions. Once such a unit is fitted, a landlord will be aware of issues without the need for any intervention from the tenant.

In 2024, only limited numbers of landlords have installed such units, but they have become more common since the Ishak case. The evidence they collect is crucial. In London, the local government innovation team, LOTI is available to help with (amongst numerous other service improvement initiatives) remote data logging. I would hope that in the future LOTI information on will be open to housing associations.

Suppliers of such equipment are aware of potential privacy issues and will invariably have processes which protect tenants from intrusive surveillance. Landlords should consult the LOTI guide, in their Resources tab on their website, which will save a lot of work.

Causes of dampness

Damp may be caused by water penetration from outside the home or may be caused or generated within it.

Penetrating damp caused by structural deterioration or construction

A roof or an external wall or other feature may deteriorate and allow water penetration.

If the tenant can establish that there is a missing roof tile, damage to the chimney stack or other structural defect which is allowing water penetration, the landlord will be clearly liable to repair it under the contract or the section 11 implied covenant. It is unnecessary to look any further than those sources of liability, at least in respect of damage suffered by the tenant themselves.

If damp makes the home unfit for human habitation, it is also actionable under section 9A, which we will look at separately.

Alternatively, damp may remain in the structure from construction and the landlord may be liable. In a newly built house, such dampness might be obvious upon inspection, e.g., if the walls have high levels of moisture remaining in the render when plastered.

Damp which causes damage to the decorative layer of plaster applied over the render has been held by the Court of Appeal[31] to be an actionable defect because that plaster is part of the structure and exterior. Since the fitness provisions came into force this isn't such an issue as surface damp

---

[31] *Grand v Gill* [2011] EWCA Civ 554, the landlord was represented at first instance but not on appeal.

and mould are actionable if they make the dwelling other than reasonably fit.

Damp where the landlord is not at fault or responsible

But a landlord is not liable for all penetrating damp. If for instance there is a flood from an upstairs flat, caused by a neighbour leaving a bath tap running, the landlord will have to repair damage to the structure and exterior, but will not be liable for any loss of amenity, or for damage to property or to decorations caused. If the flood is caused by faulty pipework; the landlord or owner of the neighbouring flat will be liable for damage caused to others.

Tenants should be insured against such problems, although in social housing they often are not covered. As a result, many social landlords both carry out repairs and rectify decorations out of sympathy for the tenant.

Damage arising from defects outside the landlord's possession or control

Equally, the guttering or roof of a building in which a flat is located may fail and the landlord of the flat affected by the damp may not have any right to access and repair the problem because they do not have any proprietary rights.

The landlord will generally have a claim under the terms of their lease from the freeholder or in nuisance against the neighbouring owner or it may be possible to enforce 'mutual' covenants in the lease to gain access.

Alternatively, maybe the freeholder cannot obtain access because another leaseholder is refusing entry. It may be necessary for the landlord to seek an injunction to force a freeholder or neighbouring owner to repair.

In such circumstances the statute protects the landlord provided he uses all reasonable endeavours to obtain but is unable to obtain such rights as would be adequate to enable him to carry out the works or repairs.[32]

Some leases allow the mesne (i.e. the intervening) landlord to carry out works themselves, and to invoice the freeholder. This has many pitfalls and is likely to result in more protracted legal proceedings. The alternative is to claim an injunction against the freeholder/head landlord. However, that position should be explained to the freeholder so that they do not subsequently allege that the social landlord failed to take advantage of an easy remedy.

Penetrating damp without a structural defect

As discussed earlier, under section 11 of the 1985 Act, a landlord is not usually liable for the presence of damp itself which is not caused by a structural defect. Such damp can affect the property without damaging the structure. It can originate outside the property and flow into it. Usually that occurs from or near ground level and is often called 'rising' damp.

The Collins dictionary defines rising damp as *"capillary movement of moisture from the ground into the walls of buildings. It results in structural damage up to a level of three feet."* Some surveyors question its existence, but it is probably more accurate to query the frequency of its occurrence, because some types of damp can be misidentified as 'rising'.

It is rare for a property to be sitting on ground which is so damp that the structure soaks it up like a sponge. There are circumstances in which this might happen, such as a property with hygroscopic walls and no damp proof course ("DPC") which is situated very close to the level of the water

---

[32] section 11 (3A) added by the Housing Act 1988 section 116

table, or on a slope down which water is moving under the surface of the soil.

But such damp may give rise to liability because it renders the home unfit for human habitation.

Design vs structural defects

If there is no DPC, it is unlikely that the damp has penetrated the external wall because of structural deterioration. It is in the nature of the construction of the building. It only becomes disrepair under section 11 where either the damp itself causes damage to the structure (and particularly to the render and decorative plaster), or where it can be said that the only reasonable way of repairing a defect is the installation of protection against rising damp.[33]

The question can be phrased in terms of whether the works would involve giving the tenant back something different from the property which was demised. That would amount to an improvement, although sometimes repairs might even involve works which improve the property.

There are cases in which rising damp can be shown to have been caused by defective external works. Where the external ground level is above the DPC moisture will be able to bypass it and flow into the property.

This may have happened because the landlord has changed the ground level, for instance by installing a footpath too high, or the tenant has built up a flowerbed or decking against the exterior wall. The surveyor will have to ascertain the root cause and thus apportion responsibility.

---

[33] cf *Uddin v Islington LBC* [2015] EWCA Civ 369, although in that case there was some evidence of an existing DPC, so it is not as helpful to tenants as might be thought

Equally, if somebody else is responsible for the penetrating damp, they can be joined into the claim as a "Part 20 Defendant". A landlord should not accept the blame for internal dampness caused by the acts or omissions of others.

Condensation

Alternatively, damp in a property can be caused by the condensation on surfaces of moisture vapour within a property. Readers of this book will be aware of the serious problems which can be caused by condensation.

First, it will give rise to mould growth, the decorations and then the plaster will become damp and deteriorate, insect infestation can occur, and clothing and furniture will be damaged. Further it can have serious effects on the health of occupants.

Broadly, condensation can have two distinct causes – design and the occupants' treatment of the property. They are often interlinked. Most social landlords strive to remedy condensation dampness, because the Decent Homes Standard required them to do so, and now various other pressures have been brought to bear on them by the RSH and the Ombudsman. However, as discussed earlier, in complying with the DHS and reducing draughts and better insulating properties, many caused further condensation to occur (see below).

Defects in the design

Over the centuries, building techniques have changed. Older buildings may suffer design defects which cause intractable problems:

- the building may be single skin construction;

- there may be inadequate insulation in the walls and roof;

- the cavity wall insulation may have failed;

- windows may have been fitted before trickle vents were common;

- windows may not open at all;

- older properties might not have extractor fans in the bathroom or kitchen.

Condensation may also be caused by or related to the tenant's occupation and use of the property. Often upon inspection, landlords find that the occupants are causing condensation in a dwelling by their behaviour. They may have:

- removed the fuse(s) from the ventilation or PIV fan(s);

- blocked air bricks or other vents;

- closed trickle vents in UPVC windows;

- failed to open the windows;

- disturbed the insulation in the loft;

- dried clothes in the property (which both adds to moisture and blocks heat from radiators)

- failed to heat the property adequately.

Such condensation dampness did not and does not give rise to liability under section 11 of the 1985 Act or in most contractual claims, provided it is not caused partly or wholly by a structural defect but may do so under section 9A and 10.

The effect of the Decent Homes Programme ("the DHP")

When the programme was introduced in 1997, setting the Decent Homes Standard ("DHS") there were 2.2 million homes falling below the standard required. There were four main aims: freedom from Category 1 HHSRS hazards, a reasonable state of repair, modern facilities and services and a reasonable degree of thermal comfort. By 2010 over 1 million homes had been improved, but there were still issues of affordability for some social landlords in implementing fully all the measures required.

Shelter says that *"On average, social homes are more likely to meet the standard for 'decent' housing. They are better insulated, more energy efficient, and more likely to have working smoke alarms than other types of housing."*

In social housing, despite the DHP, reports of condensation dampness have increased steadily over the last two decades. Although falling incomes (and therefore fuel poverty) may be partially responsible for this, there are other concerns.

This is because the DHP has resulted in the hermetic sealing of homes – double glazing has been installed, door and window seals improved, homes insulated, fireplaces sealed and therefore draughts eliminated.

The unintended side-effect is that the natural opportunity for changes of air within a property will fall dramatically. At the same time, over the past decades, the use of moisture producing devices has increased – particularly tumble dryers and showers in place of baths. The moisture produced by human beings is trapped and has nowhere to go. It condenses on the walls.

The Decent Homes Standard was targeted for a review, because of recommendations in the Social Housing White Paper published on 17 November 2020. The two-part review was designed to understand the case for change to the criteria in the Standard and then how 'decency' should be defined. A review was launched and subsequently relaunched in June 2023 to consider various updates. In October 2024 the government said it will consult on a proposed new DHS in early 2025. The HHSRS will be changed at the same time. Awaab's Law will also result in changes to the approach to dealing with damp and mould, and particularly timescales for responses.

For present purposes, when responding to a claim it is worth considering the interrelationship between the works done under the DHS and the subsequent rise in condensation levels. If the property concerned has begun to suffer from significant condensation issues, the DHS will not have achieved its purpose.

Remedial works to address those issues may be expensive, particularly the fitting of sophisticated whole-home ventilation systems. But the individual capital cost of such works will be minimal compared to the potential legal costs of numerous disrepair claims. It makes commercial sense to carry out works of improvement in such situations.

While such works should of course be done, it is important to separate any defects for which there is no contractual liability from improvements, because an injunction cannot be ordered and nor should damages be payable if a landlord is not obliged to carry out works by contract or statute (or even under case law).

As this is often the major issue where modest condensation is concerned, it will wholly or mostly defeat the claim. There is no reason that tenant should recover compensation for the carrying out of works which are not legally necessary. Sometimes they are only needed because the tenant is not heating or ventilating properly, but often landlords find it is easier to do the works than to argue about it.

Contractual liability for condensation

In some cases, landlords agree in the tenancy agreement that they should be liable for defects in the condition of the property. There might be a covenant "*to keep the property in good repair **and condition**"*, or to comply with "*relevant health and safety legislation*" which would mean that mould and condensation should be repaired under the contract[34] even though they are caused by design defects even without the 2018 Act.

Prior to the coming into force of the 2018 Act, it was usually sufficient to separate condensation damp from the other defects if there was evidence that it was either caused by a defect in design or the tenant had caused it themselves.

Liability for condensation under the 2018 Act-fitness for habitation

The 2018 Act has lessened the importance of such covenants, because when the property is not *reasonably* fit for human habitation, many types of work which involve an improvement in design must be carried out under the covenants implied by s 9A and 10 of the 1985 Act. This obviously includes remedies for condensation dampness.

So today a tenant can rely on condensation damp if they can prove that (1) the property is not reasonably fit for human habitation as a result of something done or not done by the landlord, and (2) that works can be done which will cure that condensation. Put another way, provided the test for unfitness is satisfied, to escape liability the landlord has to prove one of the statutory defences, e.g. that the condensation is caused wholly or mainly by the tenant, or that it cannot carry out works because of legal restrictions preventing them (e.g. planning).

---

[34] see for instance *Welsh v Greenwich LBC* (2001) 33 HLR 40

Part of the consideration whether it is unfit involves identifying whether there are present any of the 29 types of hazard named under the Housing Health and Safety Rating System, created by the Housing Act 2004, Part 1 ("HHSRS").

They include damp and mould growth and excess cold. Today there is very little, if any, social housing which does not have any form of heating at all. But there may be some heating installations which do give rise to liability. For instance, it can be argued that a tenant in fuel poverty cannot be expected to heat their home using expensive electrical storage heaters. That might itself mean that the home is excessively cold. That cold, along with a lack of ventilation might also cause condensation. In any individual case, this will be a matter of expert evidence for a Surveyor, or preferably an environmental health expert.

If sufficiently serious, that condensation might stop the home from being "reasonably" fit for human habitation. If it is unfit, the landlord will be liable. They might be expected to improve the insulation and/or ventilation, and/or to replace the heating with some more economically viable method.

The 2018 Act has greatly increased the potential for liability. Today there might be cases in which liability arises under both section 9A and section 11, such as where the storage heaters are defective as well as expensive.

Distinguishing between penetrating damp and condensation

In cases where there is dampness, but the home is still fit for human habitation, the surveyor will need to ascertain the cause of the damp found and, if there is both penetrating and condensation dampness, attempt to apportion the split between the two.

This can be a challenge. Often, condensation dampness can be so severe that it effectively masks the damage done by a modest area of penetrating damp. A landlord might miss such damp in their assessment of the defects in a property, particularly where there is serious condensation.

Tenant surveyors are alive to this issue and tend to inspect the exterior carefully, then often attribute internal dampness to any structural defect found, without identifying any particular area within the home or separating the effect of condensation caused by the tenant.

That may or may not be justified. If they are right, there is obviously potential for a repairable defect to be overlooked by the landlord.

Since the 2018 Act came into force, this may not be a question of such fundamental importance. If condensation dampness makes a property not reasonably fit for human habitation, the question will then only be whether it is caused *wholly or mainly* by the tenant.

The scope for argument is greatly increased. There is, however, significant technological help available to ascertain the cause of the dampness, as discussed above. In the coming years remote monitoring will become standard in cases where a claim has been made, and costs will be fitted in many properties.

Patch repairs vs renewal

We have already looked at this issue, but it is of such importance that it bears repetition when considering the issue of penetrating damp when remedying roof leaks. There is often a wide range of possible responses to a report of penetrating damp. Of course, in most cases it would not be necessary to replace the entire structure, and a patch repair would be sufficient. A tenant, or more often their solicitor, might believe that a report of water penetration through the roof should lead to the replacement of the roof covering.

A landlord need only show that they are responding reasonably to notice of a defect, *provided* the tenant does not continue to suffer any unacceptable loss of amenity – it is not a licence to leave a tenant living in unacceptable conditions. A staged approach to ascertaining the cause is acceptable, eliminating potential defects sequentially, but it must be explained by the landlord's surveyor, to show how the landlord's repairs staff are "following the trail".

Other defects

Damp is at the root of almost all claims, because very few other defects cause any significant loss of amenity. It is also the most complicated of all the defects which might exist, so it makes an ideal subject from which to extrapolate to other issues.

Below I address briefly claims in respect of cavity wall insulation, defective windows and ventilation installations.

Cavity wall insulation ("CWI") claims

This was a further booming area for claims farming solicitors. In the nine months between August 2017 and April 2018 Axa experienced a 1700% rise in CWI claims.

However, in 2024, the largest claimant firm, SSB Group went into administration owing six litigation funders £200 million.[35] This has led to a major problem for all involved. It was reported that they owed many hundreds of thousands of pounds to various sets of Barristers' Chambers and experts' agencies.

After the event insurance was repudiated by the insurers (little surprise there, as I have found in standard claims after getting costs orders), so

---

[35] According to *Legal Futures* on 17 May 2024

landlords had begun pursuing tenants for their costs. MPs have asked ministers.to intervene on various questions, including that of "*legal firms pushing people into no-win no fee cases…*".

The Insurance industry anticipates that there are potentially 3.5 million homes which might be affected by failing insulation, but the urgent problem is how to prevent claims farmers from continuing to treat the problem as a cash cow. It would seem that some members of the government are interested, and it is up to landlords to take this opportunity to undo some of the reputational damage which they have suffered in recent years.

How do CWI claims work?

The claimant surveyor attends the subject property with a thermal imaging camera and obtains a heat map. This may or may not show 'cold spots' caused by defective cavity wall insulation. But the claims are being made that insulation should be removed and replaced, often at a cost of many thousands of pounds. This is an area in which surveyors will need to become competent, or social landlords will need to call in external experts.

Because it is sometimes outside the demise (in flats) there might be arguments about notice on CWI claims, as discussed above.

Defective UPVC windows

Following the DHP, most social housing now has plastic, UPVC windows. As they age, they need either maintenance or replacement. Capital programmes will often provide for renewal far more frequently than homes in private ownership. This can be a problem in blocks of flats where long leaseholders have to be consulted, as they are likely to object to what they see as unnecessary expenditure.

But not every defective DGU needs replacement. For instance, although a 'blown' unit leading to condensation between the panes results in an impaired view through the window unit it leads to only a modest loss of thermal efficiency. It is possible to justify a delay in replacement of the unit on the grounds that the dwelling remains fit for habitation and the unit is not in *actionable* disrepair as it does not cause any *significant* loss of amenity (s 11(3)).

There are also contractors who can replace DGUs from the interior of a flat, and for modest cost. The alternative is to patch repair, by replacing individual parts, seals etc. ad hoc, waiting until it is uneconomic to continue. There are also companies which will remove misting from the double-glazing unit without the need to replace the glass panes. The diversion of resources towards replacement of cladding will have delayed many replacement programmes.

Provided that the decision whether to delay, patch or replace is taken reasonably, even if the claimant surveyor argues that they would specify replacement, the court should support the landlord's approach.

Broken/inefficient ventilation systems

In many claims, the claimant surveyor correctly states that the ventilation system is not functioning.

Often that is because a tenant will have removed the fuse to stop it operating. Some tenants, frequently those in fuel poverty, or people who do not realise the damage they are causing, prefer to keep the heat generated by cooking, bathing and even the use of an unvented tumble dryer within the property.

Sometimes ageing ventilation fans lose their efficiency. This may be because they are left to become so dirty that they do not function properly, or they are old and in need of a service. That may be the fault of the tenant, in failing to clean it, or the responsibility of the landlord.

Inefficiency in an installation resulting from poor design does not mean that the fan isn't in "proper working order", so a landlord will need to investigate the cause. If it leads to unfitness, it must be remedied.

As a minimum, landlords will be introducing humidistat fans as they encounter issues with inefficient old ventilation units. Those with sufficient funds will be well advised to invest in remote data logging ventilation systems, either on an individual, case-by-case basis or across their stock of any properties vulnerable to condensation. In an ideal world, every home would have fitted a data logging fan or ventilation system which will tell the landlord whether it is working, how efficient it is and, if it stops functioning, the reason for its failure to ventilate.

Allegations concerning the external faces and guttering/drainage

The same principles of law apply to other defects. Frequently the allegation that the roof, external brickwork and gutters are defective is not supported by the surveyor's evidence.

Additionally, occasionally there is a more fundamental issue with the allegations, for instance external render is criticised when the property is brick-faced. The LOC is prepared from the initial inspection by the claims management company employees, together with comments from the tenants and it is often clear that not much thought is given to the allegations.

Sometimes, when defects are alleged with the drainage system, it is simply a matter of a blocked gutter or downpipe, but there will always be a significant additional item of work in the Scott Schedule. A drone inspection often allows a landlord to diagnose issues correctly where the tenant's LOC has merely guessed at the cause.

Fitness for human habitation

Since the first edition of this book, which came out 18 months after the fitness provisions came into force, no cases have reached the Court of Appeal. A few county court decisions have been reported, one of which I talk about below. The two decisions discussed on *Nearly Legal* concern cases where the landlord did not turn up at trial so make very poor precedents (much like *Grand v Gill,* but that is another story).

Fitness for human habitation in Wales

In Wales the concept of fitness for human habitation has been incorporated into the 2016 Act and there is now a statutory obligation on landlords which provides a complete code on fitness law.

It is supported by The Renting Homes (Fitness for Human Habitation) (Wales) Regulations 2022, which imposes strict requirements as to the provision to the tenant of gas safety and electrical certificates and smoke[36] and carbon monoxide alarms (which must be powered by mains electricity).

If the requirements are not complied with by the landlord, the dwelling is automatically unfit. If the contract provides for it, the tenant is entitled to withhold rent until the court has decided whether the dwelling is fit for habitation.

The Regulations include a Schedule of Hazards which is effectively the same as the English list.

---

[36] In 2023, the Fire Service in England attended 246,529, being 42% of all incidents and the highest on record since 2011, 8% up on 2014, presumably the result of increasing numbers of smoke alarms fitted. Over half of them were caused by faulty equipment or mistaken activation.

Guidance on its application is provided by the Welsh government.[37] This includes lists of potential actions by landlords to ensure fitness. It is thorough and comprehensive.

Fitness for human habitation in England

Since the Homes (Fitness for Human Habitation) Act 2018 came into force on 20 March 2020, this allegation has become standard, often with little factual justification. The allegation is made in the LOC as one of the conclusions which can be drawn from the list of individual defects, without specifying what features render the home uninhabitable. But on inspection by the landlord, the reason for that lack of specificity in the allegation becomes clear. Although there may be defects and/or hazards, they do not make the home unfit for habitation as a whole.

The question is whether the property has defects which are so serious that no tenant can reasonably be expected to live in it.

Determining whether a house is fit

The court must have regard to the condition of the property in respect of a number of factors listed in section 10 (1) of the 1985 Act.

This repeats the list from the old section 8, being repair, stability, freedom from damp, internal arrangement, natural lighting, ventilation, water supply, drainage, sanitary conveniences, facilities for the preparation and cooking of food and facilities for the disposal of wastewater.

---

[37] https://www.gov.wales/fitness-homes-human-habitation-guidance-landlords-html

To that list, the new version of section 10 adds any prescribed hazard, as defined at section 10 (2) which is *"any matter or circumstance amounting to a hazard for the time being prescribed in regulations made by the Secretary of State under section 2 of the Housing Act 2004"*.

Those hazards are, in one paragraph(!): damp and mould growth, asbestos and manufactured mineral fibres, biocides, carbon monoxide and fuel combustion products, lead, radiation, uncombusted fuel gas, volatile organic compounds, electrical hazards, excess cold, excess heat, crowding and space, entry by intruders, lighting (including natural), noise, domestic hygiene, pests and refuse, food safety, personal hygiene, sanitation and drainage, water supply for domestic purposes, falls associated with baths etc, falls on the level, falls associated with stairs and steps, falls between levels, fire, hot surfaces and materials, collision and entrapment, explosions, position and operability of amenities, structural collapse and falling elements.

Those categories are to be reconsidered in 2025 and will be amended.

The operating guidance for the rating system is contained in a 185-page book. It is extremely complicated to assess fitness and highly unlikely that any claimant surveyor will have carried out the necessary test. However, that does not mean that, in a plain case, the court cannot form its own view, even unassisted by expert evidence.[38]

An assessment and finding either way in respect of the current occupiers of the property would be strong evidence for the judge.

But it is only unfit for human habitation if it is *so far defective in one or more of those matters that it is not reasonably suitable for occupation in that*

---

[38] See *Jillians v Red Kite Community Housing*, 24 September 2024 (unreported), discussed below, a County Court decision after a two-day trial at Oxford

condition. We will return to discussion of this issue when considering defences to allegations.

The list of 29 possible defects gives wide scope for potential criticism on the part of a claimant in the LOC. Often those assertions are not supported by their surveyor upon service of the claimant's report. Alternatively, a bare assertion is made that the property is unfit, but no reasons are specified as to why it is so seriously defective as to be not reasonably habitable.

Historic case law on unfitness

Because the old section 8 of the 1985 Act had not applied to any lettings for many years, there is no recent case law on the meaning of the implied covenant. But the old case law will still be relevant to some extent. The new law has an important extension – the whole building in which the dwelling is situated is now relevant for the purposes of section 9A.

One of the historic cases[39] is in my view a poor precedent as the facts were highly unusual. The tenant suffered serious injuries (she lost the use of her left hand, and her general health was severely affected) by an injury suffered when a single broken sash cord caused a window to fall on her hand and trap it, and the House of Lords found the small house was unfit. The only way she would be able to recover any damages for these injuries was to prove that the whole house was unfit, so it is perhaps unsurprising that the court made such a finding. Looked at objectively, this finding related to one defect, quite difficult to remedy, which many people live with for years in my experience.

In the same judgment, Lord Atkin referred to other cases and said that previously there had been reference to phrases such as "habitable repair"

---

[39] *Summers v Salford Corporation* [1942] AC 283 (HL)

and "tenantable repair" "*both import such state, as to repair, that the premises might be used and dwelt in not only with safety, but with reasonable comfort, by the class of persons by whom, and for the sort of purposes for which, they were to be occupied*". But he went on "*I am bound to say that I find it difficult to draw a distinction between an obligation to put premises into habitable repair… and to keep premises 'in all respects reasonably fit for human habitation.' Too much emphasis should not be laid on 'comfort', but, taking a reasonable view of the meaning of 'comfort', it affords useful test of liability.*"

There are other authorities cited in Dowding & Reynolds such as *Jones v Geen*,[40] in which Salter J said that "(T)*he standard of repair …is… a humble standard. It is only required that the place must be decently fit for human beings to live in*" or that the standard is that of "*the ordinary reasonable man*" (as had been said in *Hall v Manchester Corporation*.[41]

Dwellings which cannot be remedied at reasonable expenses

There was case law limiting the effect of the old section 8, by allowing a landlord to argue that the premises could not be made fit for human habitation at reasonable expense.[42] That is an uncertain precedent on which to rely, because the tenant conceded the point in arguing the case despite there being no statutory restriction on the expense necessary. It is likely to be challenged if relied upon, because there is no exception in section 9 (2) or (3) providing a defence of 'unreasonable expense' – see below.

---

[40] (1925) 1KB 659

[41] [1915] LJ Ch 732

[42] *cf Morgan v Liverpool Corporation* [1927] 2 kb 131, CA, later approved in another case

There are arguments for and against and it is an important question. Take a very old property which can only be made fit by installing new windows, heating, insulation, ventilation, and by relaying the floorboards, increasing room sizes etc. It would be unfortunate if it was removed from the available pool of rental properties because there exist hazards which people have lived with for hundreds of years.

In Wales the fitness provisions to include a restriction on their applicability where works cannot be carried out at reasonable expense.[43] It is open to social landlords to ensure that this provision is replicated in the coming changes in English law. Those involved in pushing through the original 2018 Act are vocal in their advocacy and will undoubtedly try to avoid its inclusion in England.

Recent case law on unfitness

There is no Court of Appeal authority yet on the 2018 Act and cases at first instance are at best of persuasive influence on a court. Often, they may not provide good guidance on the law as judges are busy and time limited for preparation and discussion. In a trial at Oxford,[44] Her Honour Judge Melissa Clarke considered how fitness should be determined but it is only a first instance decision and limited authorities are mentioned.[45]

The tenant moved into the three-bedroomed semi-detached house in 2001 with two daughters but by the time she signed an assured tenancy with Red Kite in 2013, she had 8 children, all living with her. Although

---

[43] In section 95(1)

[44] *Jillians v Red Kite Housing* (24 September 2024)

[45] It was unfortunate that she heard the trial, as any appeal only lies to a High Court Judge. Such claims are suitable for trial by District Judges and the route of appeal is then to the Circuit Judge – much better for all concerned.

she had applied for larger housing, the landlord could not provide one for her and at the date of trial there were 9 people living in the house. Perhaps unsurprisingly given the number of occupants, the house suffered from condensation and mould.

Looking at the extent of the damp and mould it does not appear to have been a marginal case in which there was any real argument as to whether it was reasonably fit, because the descriptions indicate there was a clear risk of harm to the tenant and her children. The debate was about who had caused that unfitness, and the Judge found the landlord's evidence wanting. Although the judge found the tenant a defensive witness, she found her honest and rejected all of the landlord's allegations about causation.

Various defects had occurred throughout the tenancy, and for a variety of reasons they had never been addressed satisfactorily. Red Kite said that she had failed to give access for repairs and had caused the condensation by failing to heat and ventilate properly and using an unvented tumble (condensing) drier etc.

Shortly after the arrival of the Letter of Claim the landlord inspected the property in August 2021, raised works orders but instead getting on with the works, sought agreement from the claimant's solicitor, so works were not started until five months after the LOC. This is what had happened in the previous year in Awaab Ishak's case.

There were further delays and, on a home visit year after the LOC the claimant told the landlord's surveyor that the solicitors had instructed her not to allow the contractors into the property unless it had been arranged through the lawyers. Eventually other works were ordered but carried out poorly. The judge found that the "intermittent" refusals of access "*really (did) not come into it.*" But it is a frequent problem, and landlords are often reluctant to ask for access injunctions. So, the combination of needing to go through lawyers and frequently causes delay which then ramps up any damages claim.

The works to remedy dampness were eventually completed in January 2024. The evidence provided by the landlord does not appear to have included much in the way of explanation for the different specifications of works and the progression of the various orders, possibly because of surveyors 'following the trail' and attempting to eliminate causes sequentially as they are entitled to do. However, reading about the standard of some of the works, the judge's finding is more understandable.

The landlord adduced evidence that on a visit, an employee found that the thermostat was set to 14 C and that the tenant said (in November) that she did not use the heating. But in evidence the tenant denied making that admission and the judge accepted her word. This is curious, when the employee presumably had no reason to lie, but the tenant had everything to gain, but of course the staff member was not in court to confirm that record.

Additionally, over the years 2021–2024, the claimant's gas consumption had fallen from 16,100 kWh to 11,500 kWh. This was a period over which the judge found that the mould growth "*had continued to increase in severity*" (para 119). While the landlord could not point to any statistics showing that such consumption was low for the property size, that is consistent with admission made by her that she could not afford the heating and did not use it. The Judge found that the heating bills were not low for a 3-bedroom house and that structural or insulation defects were responsible for the problem rather than tenant fault.

The expert evidence adduced by the landlord does not seem to have addressed moisture production by 9 people in a small house. In the absence of excellent ventilation and heating, I would think it a reasonable conclusion that the number of people living in the home would have caused significant condensation. The combination of factors would seem to me to provide a clear explanation for the mould growth seen, but the judge concluded differently.

The use of remote monitoring would have avoided any argument in this respect, and it is unfortunate that Red Kite were not able to rely on evidence of actual average temperatures in the property, rather than attempting to reconstruct the historical conditions from a single visit, her evidence and her gas bills.

It also appears that Red Kite may not have disclosed and relied on all their computerised records (para 42), which did not impress the Judge. She said that she had only seen the repairs records and logs and "associated documents" (para 110), which suggests that the Communications Logs and Tenancy file had not been included in the evidence. It was not clear whether the tenant had made any formal complaints but the Complaints file for the property was not adduced.

Finally, the landlord criticised the tenant's surveyor but had not asked Part 35 questions or required him to attend for cross-examination, so the Judge rejected those criticisms.

The Judge concluded that the house was unfit from 2018 to February 2024, when the works were signed off, although from the chronology in the judgment (at para 46) much of the remedial work to the mould appears to have been carried out by December 2022.

Given the judge's findings of fact, there is nothing remarkable about the Judge's conclusion that the house was unfit in the light of her perhaps questionable definition of the fitness test. There was widespread mould which was found not to have been wholly or mainly caused by the tenant, and which remained unremedied for years. However, there does not appear to have been any evidence of actual damage to the health of the occupants, which is perhaps surprising. One would think that, if the mould had been a risk to the health of the occupants, there would have been sent evidence of that risk becoming a reality.

The legal authorities most discussed[46] do not address any limitations on the application of the test. and there are other cases which would be relevant in any trial where the question of fitness is debatable – see earlier.

The Judge found that some of the defects remained unremedied at trial and granted an injunction for specific performance for those works. It is not clear whether they had been ordered or not, but it is surprising that she thought it was necessary. She said at one point that the landlord had refused to do them, perhaps this was because they were alleged to be necessary because of tenant damage.

The Counterclaim for acts of waste

Red Kite also counterclaimed for the damage which Ms Jillians or her children caused in respect of 23 defects, which she denied in her Defence to the Counterclaim. In evidence she accepted that many of those items of damage were her responsibility but said they had been fixed at her expense.

But despite this admission, the Judge also dismissed the counterclaim I query whether the amount expended by the landlord in remedying that damage (£3,216) might have been better described as a set-off, in that it appears unjust not to allow that amount to be deducted from any damages payable to Ms Jillians.

---

[46] *Bole v Huntsbuild Ltd* [2009] EWCA Civ 1146, a case about defective foundations which was not defended at trial by the main defendant, and *Rendlesham Estates v Barr* [2014] EWHC 3968 (TCC); 1 WLR 3663, which while it discussed damp and mould, it was accepted to have been caused by defects in the roof, a lack of insulation and leaks from a shower.

The tenant asked for specific performance and <£5,000 damages. She adjourned the issue of damages for the parties to attempt to come to an agreement.

Perhaps the decision will be appealed, but for the moment it provides some useful guidance on the preparation and presentation of evidence. Potential for unmeritorious/exaggerated claims

It is easy to appreciate the seriousness of the potential threat to social landlords from unscrupulous claimant solicitors and surveyors. If every design issue in a 200-year-old home is analysed against the list of 29 hazards, numerous problems will be identified, many of which are insoluble at reasonable expense.

For instance, single glazed windows do not provide good heat insulation and allow draughts, so create a hazard of excess cold. They might be small and limited in number, so giving rise to a lack of natural light. Stairs in such property might be steep, causing a risk of falls associated with stairs. The structure of the building may contain lead. There may be limited bathroom space, perhaps only providing a bathroom with WC on one floor.

But landlords are not obliged to carry out works to remedy all issues found as there are statutory defences.

Statutory defences to allegations

There are various defences to the duty to let and keep the home fit for human habitation, found in section 9A (2) and (3) which are worth setting out in full:

(2) The implied covenant is not to be taken as requiring the lessor—

(a) to carry out works or repairs for which the lessee is liable by virtue of—

(i) the duty of the lessee to use the premises in a tenant-like manner, or

(ii) an express covenant of the lessee of substantially the same effect as that duty;

(b) to rebuild or reinstate the dwelling in the case of destruction or damage by fire, storm, flood or other inevitable accident;

(c) to keep in repair or maintain anything which the lessee is entitled to remove from the dwelling;

(d) to carry out works or repairs which, if carried out, would put the lessor in breach of any obligation imposed by any enactment (whenever passed or made);

(e) to carry out works or repairs requiring the consent of a superior landlord or other third party in circumstances where consent has not been obtained following reasonable endeavours to obtain it.

(3) The implied covenant is also not to be taken as imposing on the lessor any liability in respect of the dwelling being unfit for human habitation if the unfitness is wholly or mainly[47] attributable to—

(a) the lessee's own breach of covenant, or

(b) disrepair which the lessor is not obliged to make good because of an exclusion or modification under section 12 (power of

---

[47] note this does not exclude defects which are only **partly** caused by the tenant from giving rise to liability

county court to authorise exclusions or modifications in leases in respect of repairing obligations under section 11).

Applying the defences – section 9 (2)

Looking at that list in section 9 (2), it is apparent that there may be a number of reasons why works would not be appropriate.

Using the premises in a tenant-like manner – section 9 (2) (a)

Following the Ombudsman's "Spotlight on: Damp and Mould" report, care must be taken to avoid stigmatising the tenant for damp and mould, as he has said that landlords should take a 'zero tolerance approach to damp and mould '. This means proactively identifying potential issues and taking steps to remedy condensation in at-risk property types. In my view this really means undoing the damage caused by the Decent Homes Programme.

So, it is no longer acceptable to blame the tenant, the emphasis must be on avoiding criticism and identifying any competing causes for condensation: *"Landlords should review, alongside residents, their initial response to reports of damp and mould to ensure they avoid automatically apportioning blame or using language that leaves residents feeling blamed."*

The Ombudsman has remarked that the Decent Homes review is an opportunity to consider the damp and mould issue afresh. Item 10 of the recommendations for senior management is *"Landlords should ensure their strategy for delivering net zero carbon homes considers and plans for how they can identify and respond to potential unintended consequences around damp and mould."*

The report mentions one landlord which had risk assessed 300 homes and come up with interventions as follows:

- Low risk: 1-to-1 energy advice and anti-mould paint applied to affected room(s).

- Medium risk: as low risk plus a *smart heating controller*.

- High risk: as medium risk plus a *centralised mechanical extract ventilation system*.

This strategy apparently led to a 100% improvement rate, which suggests that the lack of ventilation is of paramount importance.

I have already mentioned the problems caused by fuel poverty, and this has continued to be a serious problem for social landlords in particular. In the near future it is likely that the results of remote data monitoring will cause landlords to install positive input ventilation systems and possibly heat exchangers in effort to address this issue.

Most claimant surveyors will not look at competing causes of condensation tests and mould. If neighbouring properties do not suffer from condensation dampness, and there are differences in the way in which the properties are being used, as opposed to structural differences causing the condensation, It is reasonable to defend the claim on the grounds that the tenant is wholly or mainly causing the damage

The question for the court is whether the tenant is wholly or mainly causing the damage, so while not all condensation might be caused by the tenant and their family, once their acts or omissions are taken into account the home may not be unfit. Evidence on this point must be adduced by comparison with other, similar properties which are not unfit, and/or remote data logging.

If the problem can be reduced to an acceptable level by amendments to the environment created by the tenant, the landlord will not have to carry out the works suggested by the claimant's surveyor, but this must be established in expert evidence by the landlord.

Works necessary to rebuild or reinstate after damage by fire, storm, flood or inevitable accident – section 9 (2) (b)

This applies, e.g. to works necessary where there has been a flood from the property above.

Works to fix anything which is not part of the structure and exterior – section 9 (2) (c)

It is not likely that this section will be used often, because the tenant surveyors rarely point out issues with, e.g., the tenant's appliances.

Works which would be illegal – section 9 (2) (d)

A landlord is not obliged to carry out works which would put him in breach of any legislation. So, for instance, in a listed building in a Conservation Area, a landlord will not be obliged to install heat efficient UPVC windows in place of Georgian single glazed units. Nor will they have to tear out an old, steep wooden staircase and replace it with a modern set of shallow stairs with wide treads (which would in any event be impossible to fit in the footprint of the existing staircase).

Works needing the consent of a superior landlord or other third-party- section 9 (2) (e)

This defence is only available when the landlord has used reasonable endeavours to attempt to obtain consent but has not been able to obtain it. There is much room for argument in terms of timing here-for instance, should a landlord apply for an injunction against another party to be able to show that he has tried hard enough.

It is likely to be of application in cases where for instance there is a serious, persistent flooding problem arising in a flat above the subject property, particularly where it is in separate ownership, or where the roof is not in within the landlord's title and a superior landlord has to be persuaded or forced to carry out works. In those circumstances it can pay to join them to the claim as a 'Part 20 Defendant', thus ensuring that if they do not carry out the works, they will end up paying the damages to the tenant, the costs of the claim and of the repairs.

Consideration of section 9 (3) (a)

This extends the section 9 (2) defence requiring a lessee to use the property in a tenant-like manner, by making it clear that the Act does not impose on the landlord any liability if the unfitness is caused by a breach of covenant on behalf of the tenant.

So covenants beyond that requiring the tenant to be "tenant-like" may protect the landlord, e.g. where the tenant is obliged to provide floor coverings to the property but has allowed them to deteriorate so seriously that the property is unfit because of trip hazards, or where the tenant has failed to report defects outside their home (e.g. a flood from above) despite a covenant in the tenancy requiring them to report any damage in the demise.

Section 9 (3) (a) – modifications to leases under section 12

Although it is early days, it seems there is good reason to ask for exclusions or modifications in respect of the repairing obligations in some social housing leases, given the particular structural characteristics of many properties.

The justification for an application must arise from the benefit to tenants in general from creating exceptions to the enforcement of the new law. Landlords and tenants must apply for such exclusion or modification by agreement, so it may be that the section is of relevance where properties would otherwise be taken out of the landlord's housing stock, so that tenants can occupy attractive but less than perfect housing.

This might be particularly useful if the landlord is intending to demolish and reconstruct the whole or part of an estate, but certain individuals ask to be allowed to use the accommodation on a short-term basis pending demolition.

Chapter Summary / Key Takeaways

- A thorough understanding of what constitutes disrepair/unfitness and what falls short is crucial.

- I have attempted to provide a short guide to some of the most important issues raised in disrepair claims.

- It is not possible in a short introduction to housing conditions/disrepair law to provide sufficient material on which a claim can be defended. Instead, you will need to refer to the more complete works which I use and recommend.

In the next chapter we will look at how to deal with a claimant's solicitors' insistence on disclosure under the Protocol.

CHAPTER FOURTEEN

DISCLOSURE IN THE PRE-ACTION PROTOCOL

Disclosure is likely to be one of the first battlegrounds for landlords who upon receipt of an LOC assert that the tenant's instruction of lawyers is premature.

This is because paragraph 5.3 of the PAP requires a landlord who is responding to an LOC to provide disclosure of the documents set out in the Protocol and a landlord should refuse if such a request is made before ADR has been attempted.

That refusal is likely to provoke an application for Pre-Action Disclosure from the claimant's solicitors. Therefore, you need to know how to respond.

The expense of providing disclosure

It is important to avoid having to provide disclosure unless it is unavoidable. The process of searching out and obtaining all the documents listed in the Protocol will be lengthy and expensive if it involves lawyers.

The extent of disclosure required by the Protocol

The documents which the PAP says a landlord should disclose are likely to be extensive-they include some which are easy to obtain, but some which can be difficult to access. It follows that if disclosure is unnecessary, the landlord should not agree to provide it.

- A tenant should have a copy of the tenancy agreement, including the tenancy conditions (and Handbook), but tenant solicitors always ask for the document again, without thinking to check with their client whether they need a further copy.

- The tenancy file may contain documents which should not be disclosed for various reasons, and it may be necessary to redact certain documents to remove third-party names or details. However, a tenant is usually entitled to inspect the whole of their file.

- Documents relating to the giving of notice, including copies of "any notes of meetings and oral discussions" may have to be searched for in the repairs records and can be difficult to find.

- Inspection reports or documents relating to works required cannot be provided until they are created.

- The requirement to disclose "any computerised records" means in theory that a search has to be made for every document which mentions the state of repair of the subject property.

The complaints process as an alternative to disclosure

Disclosure is unnecessary if the landlord is operating their internal Complaints Process, because a tenant does not need to have access to all the documents for their complaint to be considered.

It is in the landlord's interests to operate the complaints process fairly and to ensure that a careful, objective investigation is undertaken. It follows that there need be no adversarial process, as the landlord should approach the complaint in an open and fair-minded manner.

Landlords operating the complaints process

If the landlord is responding to the LOC by saying that it has not had prior notice of the defects and/or that it is going to put into operation paragraph 4 of the Protocol, both stances mean that it is premature and unnecessary to engage in disclosure before ADR is exhausted.

Availability of a Data Subject Access Request

Further, the tenant has the right to obtain those documents using a Data Subject Access Request ("DSAR" or "SAR"), so the landlord does not have to instruct its lawyers to make the enquiries and obtain those documents. This can be done by the individuals in the organisation who are responsible for responding to such requests.

Those individuals are unlikely to be working at the same salary as lawyers who would be doing the same work. As a result, the exercise can be completed for a fraction of the cost. Additionally, social landlord lawyers will often be very pressed for time and any reduction in their workload is a significant benefit to the department.

Response to the tenant's solicitors' request for disclosure

For this reason, it is necessary to tell the claimant's solicitors that disclosure will not be provided, because the material is available for free by other means and because their involvement is unnecessary until ADR through the complaints process is exhausted. If they have not said that their LOC should be taken as a SAR, they should also be directed to the process for making a subject access request and informed that no further correspondence will be entered into on the subject because it is a waste of the landlord's resources.

Pre-Action Disclosure applications

These days, most Letters of Claim will state that they also constitute a Subject Access Request so the landlord must provide disclosure through that process. However, there are still some solicitors insisting on disclosure within the Protocol and the material below is therefore still relevant.

The tenant's solicitors may respond with a warning that an application for "Pre-Action Disclosure" ("PAD") will be made if the landlord does not comply with paragraph 5.3 of the Protocol. Usually, once the tenant's solicitors issue such an application, the landlord will instruct lawyers to represent it.

The test for the grant of a PAD

A PAD application is made under CPR 31.16, which is entitled "Disclosure before proceedings start". An applicant for such an order will need to adduce evidence and satisfy the court that it should make an order. The remedy is an exceptional one and the words of the rule make it plain that there are only limited circumstances in which an order for PAD should be made. The conditions which must be satisfied are set out in CPR 31.16 (3).

The threshold requirements under CPR 31.16

There are three threshold requirements, and the applicant must then prove that disclosure is desirable in order to achieve one of three aims.

The threshold requirements are that:

- the respondent is likely to be a party to subsequent proceedings;

- the applicant is also likely to be a party to those proceedings;

- if proceedings had started, the respondent's duty by way of standard disclosure would extend to the documents or classes of documents of which the applicant seeks disclosure.

The discretionary hurdle under CPR 31.16

The discretion can then only be exercised if the applicant can show that it is desirable to order disclosure to:

- dispose of the anticipated proceedings fairly

- assist the dispute to be resolved without proceedings or

- save costs

Responding to a PAD application

Such applications can be defended, both on the basis that (1) there is a cost-free and swift process to obtain the personal data held by the landlord, in the form of a DSAR, and (2) because the Protocol requires the parties to consider properly whether they should engage in ADR through the use of the repairs, complaints and/or arbitration procedures.

This means that the respondent can show that it is not desirable to order disclosure to dispose of the anticipated proceedings fairly, or to save costs. Additionally, pre-action disclosure will not assist the dispute to be resolved without proceedings, because that can be achieved more cost effectively and faster using the complaints procedure.

There is much law on the subject of when the court will exercise its discretion and the argument in these applications is invariably centred on those last three elements of CPR 31.16. The relevant cases are to be found in the commentary to the White Book and the respondent lawyer will need to provide a skeleton argument setting out the landlord's case.

Now that the decisions of three County Court judges and of a single judge sitting in the Court of Appeal assist landlords, there should be little chance of a successful application for pre-action disclosure.

First, His Honour Judge Ralton allowed an appeal by Bristol City Council against the decision of a Deputy District Judge in *Hockett v Bristol CC*[48] to grant Pre-Action Disclosure. Judge Ralton gave a reasoned decision, and the tenant's solicitors asked for permission to appeal to the Court of Appeal. The single judge, Bean, LJ, considered the matter on the papers and gave a brief judgment dismissing the application.

Driscoll Kingston had applied for pre-action disclosure against Bristol City Council, which was allowed by the judge at first instance. The County Court judge allowed Bristol's appeal, and gave a reasoned judgment, although not finding that the failure to engage in the ICP could be relied upon by the Council. On the application for permission to appeal to the Court of Appeal, Bean LJ said on 20 August 2021:

> *I agree with Judge Ralton that the critical question in this case is whether a tenant in local authority housing should make a subject access request under data protection legislation before applying to a court for pre-action disclosure. I also agree with Judge Ralton that the deputy district judge was right to refuse to make an order for pre-action disclosure. Pre-action disclosure is always a discretionary remedy. To make an order when the tenant has not used the Council's complaints procedure, has not made a subject access request, and has apparently refused to allow inspection of the*

---

[48] B2/2021/1025, (unreported and therefore not authority for the proposition)

premises goes against both the letter and the spirit of the relevant pre-action protocol and the policy of the courts to encourage parties to treat litigation as a last resort. I can see no plausible explanation for the course being adopted on behalf of the Claimant other than to increase the income of his solicitors.

I am wholly unimpressed by the elaborate argument to the effect that the answer to a subject access request may consist of information rather than copies of documents. If the Council's answer to the subject access request turns out to be evasive or to conceal the contents of relevant documents in its possession, then the case for a renewed application for pre-action disclosure might well be strengthened."

In *Sayed & Ashbir v Bristol City Council*, the same Deputy District Judge had allowed another PAD application. His Honour Judge Ambrose overturned the decision.

In *Heys v Swindon BC*, His Honour Judge Wood, KC gave a reasoned judgment on an appeal from a decision of Deputy District Judge Henley at Liverpool, who had allowed a PAD application. He agreed that the threshold requirements were not satisfied, nor should the discretion be exercised. He did not address the ICP point, instead saying that there were numerous reasons why the application should be dismissed and criticising the solicitors' conduct, noting that: "*clearly, the profitable activity lies in the PAD itself*".

Practicalities of the response to a PAD application

In the unlikely event that the tenant's solicitors refuse to make a SAR or tell you that you should treat the request under the PAP as a SAR, you may need to defend an application for PAD. The landlord will need to reply to any PAD application received with a witness statement, setting out the factual history of the correspondence from its point of view. Often the tenant's solicitor makes an application following a formula and fails to bring to the attention of the court the landlord's reasons for refusing to provide disclosure.

The landlord's witness statement should address that fact and make any justifiable criticism of the tenant solicitors in response.

Common additional issues in PAD applications

Such PAD applications are issued in large numbers by claimant solicitors. From the way in which they are prepared and pursued; they appear to be something of a 'cash cow', as Bean LJ remarked in *Hockett*.

Applications issued in a distant court centre

Usually, these applications are issued otherwise than in the County Court hearing centre which is local to the property. Although this is permitted by the CPR, it is inconvenient and can be expensive for landlords, who have to deal with a court with which they may not be familiar. Sometimes they have to send an advocate to a court centre hundreds of miles from them. Occasionally they are issued in a court centre which is not local either to the claimant's solicitors or the landlord. Make sure you ask for a remote hearing, with a reasonable time estimate if it is issued anywhere the judiciary may not be familiar with the above decisions, as you will need to argue the issue.

Applications asking for a PAD order without a hearing

Often the first that a landlord knows of a PAD application is when they receive an order from the court, which not only requires them to disclose numerous documents in a short space of time but also requires them to pay the costs of the application.

This is because the applications are sometimes drafted to request an order for PAD without a hearing. Frequently, for some reason, those applications are not even served on the respondent landlord. Applications made without notice and without a hearing should be extremely rare in any circumstances and are usually only appropriate in cases of urgency and where it is necessary not to alert a respondent to the forthcoming application.

Therefore, if landlords come across this tactic, they should object to the court in strong terms to the making of orders, without a hearing, but more important without notice.

The hearing

If you are unable to persuade the claimant's solicitors to give up on their application, you will need to instruct a solicitor or barrister to represent you. The advocate will have to prepare a skeleton argument, using the above principles to establish the law and the reason that the threshold test is not met and further that the discretion should not be exercised.

Orders for costs in PAD applications

Even if the tenant is somehow successful in their PAD, the usual order for costs in a PAD application is that the *applicant* themselves should pay those costs pursuant to CPR 46.1 (2), unless the applicant can show that the respondent's defence of the application was unreasonable.

The claimant can recover them later only if they succeed in a claim at trial, when they can include them in their claim for costs.

Those costs include both the cost of making the application and of complying with any order for PAD.

There is express provision for the court to make a different order, whether that is no order for costs, costs in the case or any variation on the theme. That provision, in CPR 46.1 (3) says that the court has to have regard to all the circumstances, including the extent to which it was reasonable for the respondent to oppose the application and whether the parties have complied with any PAP.

Where a respondent landlord is objecting on the basis that disclosure can be obtained free of charge and the tenant should have attempted to get satisfaction through the complaints process, even if the court makes an order in spite of the decisions referred to above, these arguments should both be found to be *reasonable*. The tenant's solicitors' failure to comply with paragraph 4 of the Protocol is relevant to the issue of costs and the tenant should pay those costs.

Chapter Summary / Key Takeaways

- A landlord can successfully defend a PAD application.

- If tenant solicitors become aware of the pointlessness of making such applications, they may in time simply advise their clients to make an SAR rather than pursuing an application which they are likely to lose, or on which they are likely not to recover the costs.

- Three County Court judges and a judge in the Court of Appeal have now addressed this issue in *Hockett v Bristol CC, Said & Abshir v BCC* and *Heys v Swindon BC*. While these are not binding authorities, the County Court decisions provide useful guidance and Bean LJ gave a useful single page summary of the reasons why an application for Pre-Action Disclosure is not justified and should be dismissed.

In the next section of the book, we will look at what happens when the tenant's solicitors issue a claim, either after attempting the complaints process and failing to gain satisfaction (which rarely happens) or when they continue to refuse to attempt ADR and instead, they issue a claim.

PART IV

AFTER PROCEEDINGS ARE ISSUED

In this section we will look at the preparation of evidence and applications in the course of proceedings where it has not been possible to settle the claim without litigation.

The first task for a landlord will have been undertaken by the landlord, at least in part, when investigating the LOC and responding to it, whether by instituting the Complaints Process or by trying to agree to settle the claim.

Despite your best efforts the claim is still alive, and you need to get ready to fight it in court. This involves collecting the evidence, making sure that the pleadings match the facts of the case as you now know them and ensuring that interim applications are made to deal with any pre-trial issues.

The landlord needs expert evidence to decide whether or to what extent to defend the claim. Often some of that evidence will have been collected within the formal complaints process, although the report of any surveyor involved will not be CPR 35 compliant.

CHAPTER FIFTEEN

EXPERT EVIDENCE

The opinion of a competent surveyor, whether employed by the landlord or instructed independently, is crucial to the decision whether to defend a claim, and in providing the evidence needed to do so[49]. The expert's report needs to be CPR 35 compliant and should provide evidence on a variety of essential issues. Usually, a suitable individual will have inspected the property within the complaints process.

A surveyor will need to understand the principles behind liability – both in terms of (1) notice and (2) the nature of defects which give rise to a claim as against those which (a) a landlord does not have to repair and/or (b) will not give rise to liability in damages.

There will be a certain amount of duplication in this chapter, in respect of the principles of disrepair law, because the surveyor needs to understand the practical application of the law content of the report.

Using an employee as an expert

A surveyor in the employment of the landlord will have the advantage of knowing the system and the stock and being able to work on cases within the landlord's standard budget rather than on an hourly rate as a disbursement. This should mean that they can devote the time necessary to each job, rather than rushing a report through without proper consideration of the issues. It is also likely to be less costly.

---

[49] see *Tui v Griffiths* [2023] UKSC 48

Potential for conflict between complaints surveyor and expert

Landlords operating a complaints procedure upon receipt of a claim need to recognise the potential for a conflict-of-interest for their surveying team. If the landlord does not use an external surveyor for the expert's report, they will be fulfilling a dual role. they If the same surveyor is to perform both functions, will need to think carefully about the implications of this situation.

Ensuring objectivity in both roles

On the one hand within the complaints process it is necessary to inspect the property to recognise defects and to recommend any reasonable remedial works, while being ready to recognise breach of duty and accept blame on behalf of the landlord. At the same time, the expert appointed to deal with the claim in court has to gather the material to provide a report which can be relied on in the legal proceedings.

In fact, provided the surveyor is professional and objective, these two roles will not produce a conflict of interest for the surveyor. The duty of a surveyor compiling a report for the complaints process is to the tenant as well as to their employer-they must be fair and objective. The duty of an expert witness is not to their employer, it is to the court. This is a fundamental rule which surveyors must recognise. It means that they cannot be a 'hired gun' in either situation.

Provided they comply with that duty, their duty to their employer should be accommodated within that role as an expert to the court. It would be disturbing if the surveyor viewed their professional responsibilities as anything less than the need to provide an objectively unbiased opinion.

It might be said that there is a potential for this conflict-of-interest to arise where a landlord has a limited budget. But in my experience, this does not happen. Budgets for social housing repairs tend to be significantly greater than those of many private landlords. Investment in the health of the building is seen as a priority and the economies of scale available to social landlords often result in work programmes which err on the side of generosity rather than cost-cutting.

In the report, the surveyor should address this issue head on and confirm that they recognise the possibility, so that they can honestly say that they are being objective.

Landlord surveyor's qualifications

Similar care should be taken to ensure that the expert put forward is properly qualified for the job. A landlord should ensure that the individual is objectively properly qualified.

If an internal surveyor is to be used, they may not have an equivalent qualification to that of the claimant's surveyor. In the absence of equality of formal qualifications, perhaps they are more experienced and have sufficient vocational training to be able to satisfy the court that their opinion is as valid as that of the better qualified claimant's surveyor.

Claimant's expert's qualifications

Disrepair lawyers may have come across instances where claimant surveyors have exaggerated their qualifications. A check should be made with the relevant qualifying body or university in respect of any surveyor not known to the landlord. There are a number of claimant surveyors who say they are Chartered Building Surveyors but are registered at RICS as Quantity Surveyors. If the conclusions in the report are disputed, Part 35 questions must be asked of the expert.

Provision for inspection of the property

As soon as the LOC is received it is necessary to arrange an inspection whether the complaints process is going to be operated, or the claim is being fought within the PAP and legal process. The PAP does provide for such visits and the tenant should have been advised not to prevent access.

The surveyor will be reporting for two reasons – to inquire whether the defects alleged exist and to diagnose their cause, and to discover from the tenant whether notice has been given for each defect and, if so, when exactly it was given. If necessary, they need to analyse the effect of any actionable defects on the tenant.

The surveyor needs to investigate the repairs records, check them against the tenant's assertions on notice and confirm or refute each.

The content of the report

A proper analysis of cause and effect is essential. A methodical approach to each defect, using the relevant scientific methods will eventually uncover the cause of each defect. In the case of dampness, that can be a challenge. Investigations can be prolonged and technically challenging, particularly where condensation is either masking penetrating damp, or greatly worsening its effects.

The surveyor will need to look separately at the history of the defects. That involves an examination of the initial allegations made in the LOC, as against what is present at the premises upon inspection.

There should then be an investigation of whether the landlord was on notice and an assessment of what has been done and whether it has been effective.

The general standard of repair of the property needs to be expressly considered, both in the context of the rent payable and of the general standard of repair of properties in the area. If a property has particular defects peculiar to its construction type, these should be explicitly discussed, in sufficient detail to allow the court to draw conclusions as to whether the standard of repair falls below that expected by section 11 (3) of the 1985 Act.

If there is any defect in respect of which there might be liability, the surveyor will need to investigate any loss of amenity and compare it with the general living conditions of the claimant tenant, as affected by their lifestyle and expectations.

The history of each defect

The repairs records will reflect the history of each defect chronologically, rather than by property area or defect type. Obviously, this is not how they appear in the LOC.

It is necessary to investigate the defects as they appear the LOC rather than as they appear in the records. This means considering multiple sources of information and amalgamating the evidence uncovered in respect of each defect to present tell the story of each. The landlord can then admit or deny liability.

It is necessary to check the housing/tenancy file, together with the complaints records, to ensure that notice has not been given to another part of the landlord's organisation. A landlord may operate a policy requiring tenants to report defects only to the repairs team.

Provided that policy is reasonable, the court will not take issue with it. For instance, a landlord may have a policy that caretakers in blocks of flats are not required to pass on reports of disrepair. If then the tenant reports a defect to the caretaker, who informed them that it is not within their role to pass it on, the court will not find that notice has been given.

The history of notice

Unless liability arises without notice because the defect is within an area retained by the landlord (see below), initially, the surveyor needs to look at the records to see whether notice has been given and, if so, when. If it is possible to check the incoming telephone records for instances where a tenant has called their landlord (i.e. using their mobile number), this should be done. These records are disclosable. If a tenant is alleging that the telephone records are inaccurate, evidence need to be given to support any contention that they record all instances on which the tenant has called.

Defects of which no notice has been given

A tenant's solicitors will frequently simply list the defects and alleged that notice has been given of all of them. There may be some allegations of which there is no prior notice in the records and no reason to say that the landlord ought to have known of them, e.g. because they are consequential upon a defect of which the landlord was aware.

These should be addressed together, setting them out in a list and saying that investigations are to be carried out and works ordered if necessary. Those works then have to be done within a reasonable time.

Defects of which there is evidence of prior notice

The records will usually contain one or more defects which have been reported at some time in the past. The report will need to address whether, at the date of receipt of the LOC, there was any outstanding issue known to the landlord.

It will be necessary (depending on the repairs software) to go through each individual entry and the screens behind the summary to compile a coherent narrative, showing the date of the first report (if any) and what was done in response. A defect may have been remedied but has reappeared or, for instance, the actual cause of damp may not have been diagnosed correctly and the symptoms of reappeared after replacement of render and plaster.

Constructive knowledge

Alternatively, the surveyor should consider whether the landlord ought to have known of any remaining problems or is considered in law to have had constructive knowledge of them because they are outside the demise and within the title retained by the landlord. Those issues have been addressed earlier in the book.

The job of the surveyor is to consider whether the tenant suffered any loss of amenity and, if so, whether the landlord could reasonably have known of any loss of amenity being suffered by the tenant, whether by the exercise of an independent obligation to inspect (e.g. contractually mandated periodic inspections) or inspections arising from a statutory duty.

This question is important because a tenant may succeed on liability even though the landlord has no idea a defect has started to affect a tenant. In those cases, it will be necessary to concede liability for that defect in respect of any period throughout which a landlord ought to have or is taken to have known of the defect. It may be that, even if the landlord was aware, the defect would cause little or no loss of amenity.

Contractual obligations to give notice

Most tenancies will contain a term obliging the tenant to give notice of a defect. If then a tenant fails to do so, they will be in breach of the terms of their tenancy. Depending on the wording of the clause, they may be said to have broken the chain of causation. They should not be able to claim any or any substantial damages for loss of amenity caused by defects of which they did not inform their landlord.

Failing to give notice as a failure to mitigate

Alternatively, damages will be reduced, possibly to nothing, over the period for which a tenant failed to give notice of the existence of a defect when the landlord was unaware of it, or if the landlord knew of the defect but did not know that it was causing loss of amenity to a tenant.

The surveyor will need to make a clear statement in their report in respect of any defect where the problem existed but there is evidence that the tenant did not inform the landlord of its existence.

Tenant fails to mitigate by failing to complain

Further, if a repair does not succeed, a tenant still needs to inform the landlord that the works have failed to cure the problem, and the loss of amenity continues or recommences.

Some repairs policies provide for a post-works inspection and/or survey, to ensure that tenants who continue to suffer loss of amenity are not ignored. It is important that the landlord either obtains confirmation directly from the tenant of their satisfaction, or records that the property was left in a satisfactory condition using objective evidence (e.g. photographs and/or a written note on the file, preferably with a signature by the tenant).

The effects of the defects if liability is established

But if it is clear that the landlord did know or ought to have known of a defect and they failed properly to repair it, an assessment needs to be made of the harm suffered by the tenant as a result, both in terms of duration and extent of interference with amenity.

If on investigation it is apparent that notice of a defect had been given, and works have not been carried out, or if they have been unsatisfactory, liability in damages might start to accrue.

This will involve consideration of the condition of the property apart from the defect. Often, the effects of a defect are quite obviously minor compared to the other issues with which a tenant is living voluntarily, because they have caused those conditions themselves.

For instance, in a case in which there is evidence of a problem with penetrating damp, if the majority of the damage arises from condensation which has been caused by the tenant's lifestyle, it is necessary to provide clear evidence to allow the court to draw this conclusion. Sometimes the effect of the defect will be so negligible as to make no difference to the tenant's overall enjoyment of the property.

There may be other issues-the tenant or another occupier or visitor may have caused a significant amount of physical damage themselves or maybe failing to clean and decorate the property to such an extent that their lack of care eclipses the effects of the disrepair.

This evidence needs to be collected, both in photographic and narrative form, and included as a separate section in the report, suitably highlighted. A video of the interior of the property can provide powerful evidence.

Confirmation whether works intended

Where a surveyor finds defects which need works, the approach should follow the landlord's normal repairs policy, making it plain when works are carried out to remedy a defect under section 11, or to improve the design defect under section 9A and 10 (see below), or to repair damage caused by the tenant.

The surveyor will need to prepare a 'Scott Schedule' listing the defects alleged, the claimant's suggested remedy and their response, including an estimate of the cost of any works if possible. That document will be used by the court, so it is helpful to be able to add an extra column for the judge's comments if necessary.

Separating works of repair from works of improvement

Before the coming into force of the 2018 Act, there was a tolerably clear distinction between works of repair and works of improvement. Now, under the fitness provisions, works necessary to a dwelling may well include improvements to the structure and design.

This arises where there are deficiencies in the design which lead to the existence of issues making the home unfit for human habitation. Even if the home is not currently 'unfit' within the meaning of the Act, it may be good estate management to carry out such works. In the future surveyors will need to exercise their judgement carefully, balancing the findings of a claimant surveyor against what is necessary to remedy unfitness.

In any case where there is an arguable assertion by the claimant surveyor that the defects in the home render it not reasonably fit for habitation, the surveyor will need to decide what in their discretion and professional opinion will be sufficient to render it fit enough, without going overboard and to justify that conclusion.

Method of remedy is a matter for the landlord

A landlord is not obliged to carry out the works suggested by the tenant's surveyor. The choice of remedy is for the landlord, absent any self-evident unreasonableness. I would suggest that this effectively boils down to a test of whether the landlord's surveyor's approach is negligent – i.e. something which no reasonably competent surveyor would suggest as a means of remedy.

If it is possible to go into some detail as to alternatives and to discuss why the landlord's approach is better than the claimant's suggestions, this will help the trial judge to decide whether any suggestion by the tenant that the landlord's approach should be rejected.

Cases where a tenant has caused part or all the damage

Rather than indulging a tenant who has failed to look after the property properly, if there is evidence that the tenant has caused part or all the damage themselves, this needs to be clearly stated.

Any works necessary because of tenant waste or damage should be listed separately and costed. Most landlords do not bother to recharge impecunious tenants but that should not stop a record being made in the report. If appropriate, a set-off can be claimed, or a counterclaim for the recovery of the cost of remedial works can be made. Given the judgment in *Jillians v Red Kite* (above in Chapter Thirteen), care needs to be taken not to fall foul of the court in making such a claim. The reality is that most social landlords wholly fail to implement a recharging policy fully, because they are compassionate. This was used against the landlord in that case. Therefore, it may be necessary to enforce the recharge policy, even though that might result in unkindness to some tenants. Claimant solicitors taking advantage of a humane approach and turning it on the landlord.

The same argument can be seen if the surveyor does not differentiate between repairs and improvements carried out in the course of the works, perhaps to placate the tenant, or out of sympathy for them. The tenant's lawyer may then argue that such works would not have been done unless they are within the landlord's duty. It is best to avoid the argument by clearly specifying the differentiation.

Addressing section 11 (3) of the 1985 Act and fitness

It is a crucial function of the landlord's surveyor fully to consider the overall standard of repair of the property in accordance with the standards required. I have never seen a tenant's solicitor's surveyor's report address these issues in any more than name. That is partially because few surveyors (who almost invariably practice from the North of England, like their instructing lawyers) are unfamiliar with the housing stock around the property, so they are unable to comment.

Section 11(3): The wording of the statute provides the structure for the assessment and bears constant repetition. The standard of repair is to be determined by reference to the "*age, character and prospective life of the dwelling-house and the locality in which it is situated*".

This has been addressed earlier in the book, in the context of discussion of the standard necessary. In the preparation of the report, a reasoned, logical approach to each word needs to be taken, and care exercised to be objective and reasonable in the analysis. The judge will be relying on the surveyor's professional ability and knowledge, because the claimant is unlikely to be able to provide any competing opinion.

In most social housing disrepair claims, the standard of the particular property will be higher than that of local privately owned housing stock, whether rented or owner occupied. Private owners are unlikely to have carried out the expensive works necessary to bring the condition of the property up to the DHS. This particularly applies where the property is in a low-income area and the local private landlords struggle to charge sufficient rent.

Fitness for human habitation: the surveyor must assess whether the property is reasonably fit for human habitation, despite any defects they find. If it is unfit, they must say whether that is because of something done or omitted to be done by the landlord, or whether instead one of the statutory defences applies - see Chapter Thirteen.

Using hearsay evidence in the assessment of section 11 (3)

An experienced landlord surveyor will have knowledge of other local housing, or will be able to investigate, either with members of their team or with the Environmental Health team.

Experts are allowed to include in their report the opinions of other experts if their opinion forms a subsidiary part of the necessary material.

If the evidence is hearsay, it is admissible without restriction, provided the requirements of the Civil Evidence Act 1995 are followed. So, the evidence needs to be identified as such, and the source of the knowledge named.

Such evidence can be obtained from other surveyors, either employed by the landlord, or practising locally. Websites can be used to obtain an idea of the average rent for privately owned housing of a similar type and size. Examples can be attached to the report using rental comparison websites.

Assessing the weight of hearsay evidence

The surveyor will need to provide material on the factors set out in section 4 (2) of the Act. It is worth setting those factors out here, so you can understand how easy it is to include hearsay:

> *"(1) In estimating the weight (if any) to be given to hearsay evidence in civil proceedings the court shall have regard to any circumstances from which any inference can reasonably be drawn as to the reliability or otherwise of the evidence.*

(2) Regard may be had, in particular, to the following—

> *(a) whether it would have been reasonable and practicable for the party by whom the evidence was adduced to have produced the maker of the original statement as a witness;*
>
> *(b) whether the original statement was made contemporaneously with the occurrence or existence of the matters stated;*
>
> *(c) whether the evidence involves multiple hearsay;*
>
> *(d) whether any person involved had any motive to conceal or misrepresent matters;*
>
> *(e) whether the original statement was an edited account, or was made in collaboration with another or for a particular purpose;*
>
> *(f) whether the circumstances in which the evidence is adduced as hearsay are such as to suggest an attempt to prevent proper evaluation of its weight."*

Using the evidence for section 11 (3)

The subsection is intended to protect landlords from the imposition of an unrealistic standard. Few properties will ever be continually in a perfect state of repair.

Landlords will inevitably make mistakes, miss appointments or otherwise fail in some way. They should not be held to account by the court for doing so when, overall, they are providing reasonable accommodation at a fair rent.

The surveyor's evidence on these issues can be determinative of the claim. If there are relatively minor defects, even though they have not been repaired within a reasonable time or to a reasonable standard, the court may be persuaded that the property is not in disrepair, because it is in a similar state of repair to others in the locality.

Of course, a landlord cannot use its own failure to maintain its stock to a decent level as an excuse and a way of saying that a property in an unacceptable state is nonetheless adequately cared for, so that liability does not arise.

Report conclusions / summary

The claimant surveyor will invariably have condemned the property, usually for both being out of repair under section 11 and being unfit for human habitation under section 9A/10. On close examination, those assertions may turn out to be untrue.

For instance, a dwelling can be significantly affected by condensation damp, which is caused wholly or mainly by the tenant's own acts or omissions. Yet the claimant surveyor fails to mention the true cause of the problems and blames it instead on matters which the landlord could do something about. So, the job of the landlord's surveyor is to be inquisitive and objective. They must 'follow the trail' in respect of defects which they see and provide clear reasoned conclusions as to whether they amount to actionable defects or issues for the tenant to resolve themselves.

Questions need to be asked of tenant and answers noted carefully, preferably following up with a request to confirm what has been said.

Often there is an element of both – for instance if a tenant fails to heat and ventilate a property properly, a landlord might put in a whole house ventilation system, at considerable expense, to take the decision out of the tenant's hands. However, tenants have been known to switch these systems off, because they regard them as noisy or wasteful of energy or heat, despite the existence of a heat exchanger. Then, when the claim comes to court, they deny ever having switched off the system. Remote data logging avoids this possibility.

The landlord's surveyor must not hold back in any opinions, they should provide a foil for the tenant's surveyor's failure to address the issues objectively.

Chapter Summary / Key Takeaways

- The quality of expert evidence is crucial to the defence of a disrepair claim.

- The Landlord's surveyor will need to produce a report which addresses the issues raised in the claimant surveyor's report, item by item, either admitting responsibility or explaining why liability does not arise.

- Landlord surveyors should be familiar not just with the subject property, but with housing conditions in the area.

- They need to familiarise themselves with common defects, tenant expectations, rent levels and any other factors relevant to the question whether the subject property falls below the standard of others in the locality.

- Following the coming into force of the 2018 Act, they will also need to know about fitness for human habitation.

In the next chapter we look at the drafting of applications for summary judgement/strike out/stay,

CHAPTER SIXTEEN

APPLICATIONS FOR SUMMARY JUDGEMENT / STRIKE OUT / STAY

Just because a claimant issues a claim for damages and an injunction it does not mean that there has to be a trial on the various allegations made, or at least on all of them.

Additionally, the elements of a claim which remain in dispute will have a determinative impact on the track to which the claim is allocated. Finally, a landlord should apply to stay what is left of the claim for ADR, if appropriate.

Time to instruct a lawyer

Once a County Court claim is issued, lawyers will almost inevitably be instructed by landlords. Those lawyers will need to receive at the earliest possible time all the evidence necessary to respond to the claim.

Firms of solicitors who have a specialist housing management team may be able to help with these applications. It is also possible to instruct a barrister directly, without solicitors, provided the landlord has sufficient administrative skills and resources to run the litigation.

Such instructions can be given to barristers under the "Public Access Scheme", a.k.a. "Direct Access". Barristers are obliged to undergo training in handling claims under the scheme and to provide a client Care Letter together with the "Guidance for Lay Clients".

Summary judgment

Through careful analysis of the merits of any disrepair claim, it may be possible to identify elements which patently obviously have no merit. On those elements the landlord can argue that the claimant ought not to be allowed to pursue the claim to a trial at which the parties would have to give live evidence.

During the early stages of the trial the attention of the court is specifically drawn to the availability of strike out and summary judgement, by PD 26, para 10. which says that *"part of the court's duty of active case management is the summary disposal of issues which do not need full investigation and trial (rule 1.4 (2) (c))"*.

That can include strike out or summary judgement and the court can use the powers either on an application or on its own initiative. I However, CPR PD 26.12 provides that the court will give 14 days' notice of its intention to strike out or enter summary judgment. If the case for striking out or entering summary judgement against a claimant on a claim for specific performance is sufficiently clear, it may be possible to persuade the court to strike it out at the allocation hearing, without an application, but this is unusual.

PD 26.11 says that a party intending to make an application for summary judgment should do so before or at the time of filing the directions questionnaire, the court will not allocate until it is determined.

No judgment in default pending hearing of summary judgment / strike out application

Judgement in default of service of a Defence cannot be entered against a defendant who has issued an application to strike out a claim or for summary judgement-CPR 12.3 (3) (a) and the application has not been disposed of. This is important-if the application for summary judgement/strike out is issued when the claim is received, much work can be saved. This can have a significant effect on the complexity of the pleadings, particularly if it is possible to strike out or enter summary judgement against the claimant on the claim for specific performance.

Mechanics of the application

There is plenty of law on summary judgement applications. CPR 24 deals with the mechanics of the application and the test which needs to be met by the N244 application notice and the witness statement in support. The applicant must state that they know of "no other compelling reason for a trial" of the claim or issue.

An application can be brought if the landlord can show that there is no "realistic" as opposed to a "fanciful" prospect of success[50]. It must be "more than merely arguable".[51]

The court must not conduct a "mini trial", but *"this does not mean that the court must take at face value and without analysis everything that a claimant says in his statements before the court. In some cases it may be clear that there is no real substance in factual assertions made, particularly if contradicted by contemporaneous documents."*

The law is set out in the White Book and in drafting the evidence in support careful attention needs to be paid to the exact reasons why the claim is hopeless.

---

[50] see the case of *Swain v Hillman* [2001] 1 All ER 91

[51] *ED & F Man Liquid Products v Patel* [2003] EW Civ 472 at [8]

In reaching its conclusion the court must take into account not just the evidence before it in the application but also any evidence which can reasonably be expected to be available if the claim goes to trial.[52]

However, the court should not "*indulge in Micawberism*", and make a decision not to grant summary judgment on the basis that something may turn up. In the claim by HRH The Duchess of Sussex against Associated Newspapers Ltd[53] 'Mr Justice Warby said: "*Easyair principles (vi) and (vii) contain echoes of the law's traditional disapproval of a "a desire to investigate alleged obscurities and a hope that something will turn up ..."* as a basis for defending a summary judgment application; a case that is "all surmise and Micawberism" will not do[54]. The focus is not just on whether something more might emerge, but also – and crucially – on whether, if so, it might "affect the outcome of the case"; and the court's task is to assess whether there are "reasonable grounds" for believing that both these things would occur.*[55]

So, it is important to anticipate what a claimant may say in response to the application (any evidence in reply has to be served more than 7 days before the hearing and to reply to any evidence they do serve (more than 3 days before the hearing).

---

[52]   see *Royal Brompton Hospital NHS Trust V Hammond (No. 5) EWCA Civ 550*

[53]   [2021] EWHC 273 (Ch)

[54]   see *The Lady Anne Tennant v Associated Newspapers Ltd* [1979] FSR 298, 303 (Sir Robert Megarry V-C)

[55]   see *Doncaster Pharmaceuticals Group Ltd v Bolton Pharmaceutical Co 100 Ltd [2006] EWCA Civ 661 [2007] FSR 63, [18] (Mummery LJ)*"

Applications in respect of unnecessary claims for specific performance

The most obvious target for an application for summary judgement is the claim for a mandatory injunction for specific performance. There is much case law on the subject, but essentially such relief is intended for serious cases where a defendant needs to be forced by the court to comply with its obligations.

Bearing in mind that such injunctions are enforceable by imprisonment, it is obvious that in the vast majority of social housing disrepair claims, injunctive relief is totally inappropriate.

The promise of a social landlord that it will carry out repairs within a certain period of time should be enough to dispose of that aspect of the claim. But it is far better to have carried out the works by the date of the summary judgement hearing.

Claimant solicitors defend such applications by serving a witness statement shortly before the hearing, alleging that defects remain, and an order is necessary to make the landlord do the necessary works. It is essential to ensure that this cannot happen by filing evidence shortly before the application confirming the tenant is happy with the works carried out, supporting the statement with photos and invoices if possible.

It is essential to issue such an application if you wish to be sure of allocation to the SCT, as otherwise the claimant lawyers are likely to say that works remain outstanding, and the tenant is entitled to expect an order for specific performance even if the landlord has promised to do works.

Expert evidence

The landlord will need to adduce expert surveying evidence as there is usually something on which an opinion is required. The use of an internal surveyor as an expert is standard practice, approved by the Court of Appeal[56]. Provided the landlord prepares the evidence properly, such evidence will be admitted by the court if: "*(i) it can be demonstrated whether that person has relevant expertise in an area in issue in the case; and (ii) that it can be demonstrated that he or she is aware of their primary duty to the court if they give expert evidence*". (per Lord Justice Waller)

An expert's report prepared for an early stage in the proceedings can be used at the final hearing/trial if the claim lasts that long.

Strike out under CPR 3.4

Sometimes claims are so poorly pleaded that an application to strike out the particulars of claim can be included in the application for summary judgement. The applicant will need to prove one of the three conditions in CPR 3.4 (2).

A particularly poorly pleaded set of particulars of claim might generate an application to strike out, or at least to strike out certain parts of the POC.

Equally, if a pleading relies on an expert's report that on examination contains no allegations of disrepair (for instance a report where the only defect is condensation, and the only works recommended involve telling the tenant to ventilate better and carrying out a mould wash) it may be possible to persuade the court to strike out the claim as well as entering summary judgement against the claimant. But generally, the remedy of summary judgement will suffice.

At one point district judges were striking out disrepair claims for the claimant's failure to comply with a rule/practice direction because they

---

[56] *Field v Leeds City Council* [1999] EWCA Civ 3013

had failed to agree to ADR. Since *Churchill v Merthyr Tydfil CBC* that is unlikely to happen on the first hearing, but if a stay is granted and the tenant refuses to engage, the rules provide for sanctions to be imposed, which can include strike out. It is still worth asking the court to do so where there has been a serious breach of the provisions on ADR, perhaps when the claimant totally ignores the invitations and does not even answer the request made in the response to the letter of claim.

The best time to make the application is before or at the same time as directions questionnaires are filed. But summary judgement application can even be made at trial.

Preparing an application for summary judgement/strike out

Lawyers working for landlords will already have at their disposal their surveyor's report, which will have appended to it the full Repairs History for the relevant period, together with the Scott Schedule.

There are two areas of attack open to a landlord: (1) the claim for an injunction and (2) the claim for damages.

Asking the court to dismiss the application for an injunction

The first and most important target is the application for a mandatory injunction for specific performance of the repairing covenant. An order for specific performance is supported by an injunction, which is backed up by the threat of imprisonment.

There are very few landlords who positively refuse to carry out repairs. It is inappropriate for social landlords' employees to face imprisonment for failing to ensure that repairs are carried out, except perhaps in exceptional circumstances.

Often the landlord's surveyor will agree to a greater or lesser extent with the findings of a tenant's surveyor in respect of the existence of defects. In respect of every defect which is agreed to exist and for which a remedy is proposed, the landlord can argue that there is no dispute between the parties on either issue. It follows from that position that the court is entitled to find that there is no dispute on the point which needs to be determined at a trial.

In respect of application for an injunction, this goes to the heart of the claim. If a claim for disrepair does not include a justifiable request for a mandatory injunction, it is likely to be allocated to the Small Claims Track. We will address those issues in the next chapter in the context of allocation to track.

Challenging the value of the claim during the application

Tenants will invariably frame the claim in the LOC and POC as having a starting date of the beginning of the tenancy. Often it is alleged that defects were already present when the tenant moved into the property.

Such claims are subject to challenge, because the pre-letting/void survey will often record, with photographic evidence, the condition and state of repair before the arrival of the tenant.

Responding to a claim for damages framed in the usual wide and all-encompassing way demands attention to detail and a careful investigation of each of the allegations, so that they can be shown to be wholly or partly misconceived.

Addressing allocation in the application for summary judgement

There will be instances where even though there might remain after summary judgement a valid claim for specific performance, but the outstanding defects are so minor that the works will cost less than £1,000, and the period of claim is so short or the historic loss of amenity is so minor that it should be obvious to the court that the claim for damages will not exceed £1,000.

It is the cost of the works according to the landlord's repairs team, which is relevant, not the cost as estimated by the claimant's surveyor. In this regard it is helpful if the landlord can justify their assessment of the cost of works, by reference to their schedule of rates or any other credible evidence.

In many cases, the court will agree that the hearing that after entering summary judgement on part of the claim, the remainder of the claim should be allocated to the Small Claims Track

Evidence-the tenancy file

Useful information and evidence can often be found in the tenancy file. Sometimes there are reports in the file which relates to repairs and provide facts which can be used in the explanation of the history of a defect or a repair.

Alternatively, the file might show occasional or frequent contact with no mention of repairs issues. Most social landlords will require their housing officers to pass on reports of disrepair or have a policy that they must tell the tenant to use the disrepair call centre or report online.

Individual recollection

Sometimes individual surveyors, housing officers or other employees will be familiar with the property and its repairs history, or they will know other helpful information about the tenant. The landlord's response policy for disrepair claims should provide for information gathering from any individual who may be able to help.

Collation of evidence and assessment of liability

The material obtained from the various sources can be presented to the court as a surveyor's report and possibly additionally, as a witness statement, for instance when a housing officer knows a substantial amount about the tenant. The conclusions reached will determine whether an application for summary judgement should be made and, if so, in respect of which parts of the claim. Lawyers involved in these claims will be familiar with the drafting of such applications. The aim is to dispose of the injunction claim as a minimum, on the basis that the landlord has never refused to do works and a claim for specific performance is inappropriate.

A decision then has to be made on whether there is any arguable claim and, if so, which defects over what period of time.

Landlords with broken repairs systems

Occasionally, a social landlord will face such technical and operational difficulties that the repairs system ceases to function properly and wholesale delays occur. The difficulties caused by the pandemic being such an example.

Social landlords will have long delays in the programming of routine repairs. This does not mean that the court should impose an injunction against employees requiring them to repair or face imprisonment. If works are ordered but cannot be done within a reasonable time and the tenant continues to suffer loss of amenity, the remedy should sound in damages at the most. Unless the landlord refuses to repair, the court should not impose an injunction.

Stay for ADR – *Churchill v Merthyr Tydfil CBC* [2023] EWCA (Civ) 1416

Additionally, after *Churchill*, if the landlord makes a request, the court is likely to stay a claim to allow or even require the parties to engage in alternative dispute resolution. While the landlord will suggest that should take place through its complaints process, the tenant's solicitors invariably criticise that proposed method and ask for a joint settlement meeting or other costs-bearing form of ADR.

CPR 26.5 provides that a party in filing the directions questionnaire can make a written request for is to be stayed for ADR, in which case the court will stay for a period of one month.

Alternatively, by CPR 26.5 (3A), "*if the court otherwise considers that such a stay would be appropriate, the court will direct that proceedings either in whole or in part, be stayed for one month or for such other period as it considers appropriate.* By sub-rule (4) "*the court may extend the stay until such date or for such specified period as it considers appropriate.*"

So, the CPR expressly provide for a compulsory stay of the proceedings, if the court considers that it would be appropriate. Unless a claimant can show that they have already tried the formal complaints process and have not gained satisfaction, it is difficult to see how a claimant tenant could be prejudiced by such a compulsory stay, provided that it does not delay the claim unduly.

The stay can be ordered for only a month, or for a longer period. Two or three months will provide sufficient time for the whole complaints process to be exhausted. Landlords should now be operating their internal complaints procedure on receipt of the LoC, but many landlords will not progress to Stage 2 unless the tenant requests to do so. In any event, there is no point in doing so if the reviewing officer does not know why the tenant is unhappy with the Stage 1 decision. So frequently, by the time the matter gets to a summary judgment application, Stage 1 has been completed but Stage 2 has yet to start.

The law behind the application to stay

There is much in the White Book on ADR – see Volume 2, section 14. It describes ADR as *"an integral part of the litigation process."* The Access to Justice Interim Report said that the range and availability of ADR procedures should be increased and that the use of ADR by parties had been encouraged by the court in various ways.

You can rely on the Ombudsman's Guidance on using the ICP, which is very helpful as he says that a landlord should continue to run the complaints process despite receiving a Letter of Claim. However, he does not say that the Protocol should be paused, so his guidance needs to be applied in an amended fashion.

Equally, the Civil Justice Council's Report of June 2021 concluded that compulsory ADR was lawful: at [58] that *"any form of ADR which is not disproportionately onerous and does not foreclose the parties' effective access to the court will be compatible with the parties' Article 6 rights"*, and [60] *"we think the balance of the argument favours the view that it is compatible with Article 6 for a court or a set of procedural rules to require ADR".*

The case law

Although the case of *Halsey v Milton Keynes General NHS Trust* [2004] EWCA Civ 576 held that parties could not be forced to mediate, the Master of the Rolls has laid that supposed rule to rest in *Churchill*.

It's worth setting out the law as the Court of Appeal found it, and then suggesting how it might be applied in housing conditions claims. Being as brief as I can, the following summary of my views on the issues raised in various paragraphs of the judgment might be helpful to you in understanding how to prepare:

Para 52: (Mr Churchill says that the) *ICP (i) does not allow the parties to be represented by lawyers, (ii) does not allow for the payment of the claimant's legal costs, and (iii) is not independent of the defendant's management.*

My observations on this:

- An ICP of its nature does not require lawyers on either side-it is a practical solution to a problem, which might at the same time resolve legal claims without necessitating the involvement of lawyers, with the attendant substantial costs;

- there is nothing to be lost by staying the claim for three months, and this should be balanced against the costs which will be incurred if it proceeds to a final hearing;

- If the Claimant is minded to accept any offer of compensation made by the Council at Stage 2, unless the Court has already made an order as to the costs to date, the question of the Claimant's solicitors' costs can be addressed at that stage, when the court will be in a better position to assess whether their involvement was *justified* (see also below on allocation). Further if a tenant accepts an offer of compensation within an ICP, it is not an award of damages and the 50% success fee would not be deducted from their award, so an ICP is much better from the tenant's point of view;

- the lack of independence from the public body is irrelevant when it is not a final method of alternative, appropriate dispute resolution. If a participant is unhappy, they simply proceed to the next stage, go to the ombudsman or continue their legal claim.

Para 61: (This will depend on) *(i) the form of ADR being considered, (ii) whether the parties were legally advised or represented, (iii) whether ADR was likely to be effective or appropriate without such advice or representation, (iv) whether it was made clear to the parties that, if they did not settle, they were free to pursue their claim or defence, (v) the urgency of the case and the reasonableness of the delay caused by ADR, (vi) whether that delay would vitiate the claim or give rise to or exacerbate any limitation issue, (vii) the costs of ADR, both in absolute terms, and relative to the parties' resources and the value of the claim, (viii) whether there was any realistic prospect of the claim being resolved through ADR, (ix) whether there was a significant imbalance in the parties' levels of resource, bargaining power, or sophistication, (x) the reasons given by a party for not wishing to mediate: for example, if there had already been a recent unsuccessful attempt at ADR, and (xi) the reasonableness and proportionality of the sanction, in the event that a party declined ADR in the face of an order of the Court.*

My arguments:

- ADR in the form of an ICP is intended to be simple, operated by an individual without assistance (unless they require some special form of help, e.g. people who cannot express themselves sufficiently clearly to inform a landlord of the nature of defects at their home);

- ADR in the form of the ICP is frequently effective, and in this case achieved a satisfactory result for the tenant, subject to any (unknown) objections she has to the works carried out by BCC;

- the involvement of lawyers from an early stage will have ensured that the tenant knew she could pursue her legal claim if she was dissatisfied with the ICP;

- there was no urgency in this case-no significant loss of amenity was being caused by any defects in the structure and exterior, and no interim injunction was sought requiring the landlord to carry out works urgently;

- the ICP did not cause the Claimant any prejudice at Stage 1 and will not do so at Stage 2. While the timescales involved have been longer than the Ombudsman anticipates, this has caused no harm to the tenant. Tenant solicitors frequently make these claims much more complicated than they are by including numerous defects in the Letter of Claim which, on careful examination by surveyors (on both sides) turn out not to exist;

- the claim has not been vitiated by the ICP and nor would it be if it goes to Stage 2, and there is no limitation issue in this claim;

- it is not possible to say whether Stage 2 will lead to a satisfactory outcome without trying it. At the moment the reasons for any dissatisfaction on the part of the tenant with the offer and carrying out of works at Stage 1 is not known. As far as the Council is aware she is happy with the current state of repair of his home;

- ADR in the form of the ICP in absolute terms is a very inexpensive process, involving only a few of the landlord's officers and, relative to the vast cost of litigation, it is difficult to see why it should not at least be attempted, even if it fails;

- there is a theoretical power imbalance between the parties within an ICP, but when addressing an internal complaint, it is only single, non-lawyer individuals who communicate with a tenant, ensuring the process is fair. But even if it is not independent and the tenant is not satisfied with the works or compensation offered, a tenant can progress to Stage 2 without restriction and can then carry on to the Ombudsman or with legal proceedings with no cost to themselves for having refused to accept Stage 1, even if they are eventually unsuccessful. They-are never required to pay the costs incurred by the landlord in operating the ICP;

- the reasons given by the tenant solicitors for their refusal to engage in the ICP never come from the tenant themselves, they are clearly legal arguments put forward by lawyers who will not get paid unless they succeed in obtaining a costs order in the proceedings. This is the same issue as is encountered in the dispute between the parties on Small Claims Track vs Fast Track. There is an obvious conflict-of-interest between the tenant and his lawyers in this respect;

- if a tenant refuses to engage in an ICP, the remedy can include a further stay, an order for costs or even strike out of the claim in a contumelious case, e.g. when they say they are not going to talk to the landlord solely because their solicitors had told them not to do so, or have threatened them with having to pay the costs if they accept a compensation offer.

Para 63:*Mr Churchill submitted that the internal complaints procedure in this case was, in any event, a disproportionate fetter on the right of access to court because (a) there was no neutral third party involved and the claim was dealt with by the manager of the Council's own knotweed department, (b) no legal advice was available to the claimant, (c) there was no settled written procedure by which it operated, (d) it had no statutory backing, (e) it was a process that had no fixed timescale and might take an open ended amount of time, (f) the limitation period was not suspended during the process, (g) there was no provision for the payment of a claimant's costs, and (h) there was no express provision allowing for the payment of compensation in addition to eradicating the knotweed.*

I would argue that:

1. this is not a disproportionate fetter on the tenant's rights of access to the court, for the reasons above and because he has had

plentiful legal advice. There is no need for any further settled written procedure over the ICP policy which exists. It is to be noted that the Council in this case has waived the exclusion of complaints over one year old, and equally does not object to addressing a complaint even though a claim has been issued. Both these exclusions are intended to protect the Council and there is nothing to stop it from deciding not to rely on them;

2. there is a statutory backing to this scheme-all social landlords have to be members of the Ombudsman's scheme, and they have to operate an ICP which complies with his Complaint Handling Code. In any event, this is not a final dispute resolution process if the tenant chooses not to accept the offers made.

Para 69: *The judge, as I have said, decided at [41], in addition to the Halsey point, that Mr Churchill and his lawyers had acted unreasonably and contrary to the spirit and the letter of the PD in refusing to use the internal complaints procedure. He said at [42] that he disagreed with Mr Churchill that true ADR had to be a wholly independent process. He rejected at [43]-[46] Mr Churchill's three other complaints at that stage, namely that (i) it was an inappropriate process, (ii) it did not deal with matters more than 12 months old, and (iii) it did not allow for the recovery of the claimant's costs.*

See the arguments above

Para 71: *Secondly, in fact, things have now moved on considerably. Mr Churchill has refused to allow the Council to treat the knotweed in his garden, standing on his right to seek compensation and costs from the court. Thirdly, whilst the stay was sought after the issue of legal proceedings, the Council's internal complaints procedure is plainly intended to operate before proceedings have been issued. ...*

The landlord's response:

- Tenants cannot refuse to have works done – their tenancy requires them to give access to inspect and carry them out.

- A tenant has no right to behave in a disproportionate manner and insist on a supposed unfettered right to litigate.

- While ICPs might say that the landlord can refuse to initiate them when there is litigation in existence this is an exclusion designed to protect the landlord, which can be waived. It is worth mentioning this in the witness statement and showing that a decision has been taken to do so generally.

Para 72: *In these circumstances, whilst it is obvious that the judge would have stayed the claim back in May 2022, had he been able to see this judgment, things have moved on. There is little point in doing so now, since nothing will be gained if a one-month stay were granted as the Council seeks. This court cannot properly grant a mandatory injunction against Mr Churchill requiring him to allow the Council to treat his knotweed. That has been neither formally sought nor argued.*

My reply:

- Much is to be gained from running an ICP in a housing conditions claim – it almost invariably saves a long wait for a decision on what works are necessary, and provides a speedy offer of compensation, which all goes to the tenant. (If the Master of the Rolls had not taken such a negative view of the benefits of running the Merthyr ICP it would probably have resolved the litigation).

- See above on getting works done– an access injunction can be granted and should be sought if a tenant refuses access.

Para 73. *It is better in my judgment to allow the appeal to the extent already stated and to allow the merits and demerits of this particular internal complaints procedure to be resolved on another occasion.*

I say in reply:

Mr Churchill's solicitors did not appeal the District Judge's finding that they had behaved unreasonably in refusing to hold off the issue of proceedings while the parties tried the ICP. Although the Court of Appeal did not stay *Churchill*, that was because things had moved on and it was about 21 months since the County Court had found the Claimant's solicitors behaviour was unreasonable and a stay was merited but it was unable to impose one because of *Halsey*.

Cases involving public authorities

In *R. (Cowl) v Plymouth City Council* [2001] EWCA Civ 1935 (mentioned in Churchill and probably the most useful decision of all) the Court of Appeal said that in disputes between public authorities and members of the public for whom they are responsible, 'insufficient attention was being paid to the paramount importance of saving costs and reducing delay by avoiding recourse to the application to the judicial review procedure'. The court was enjoined to use its powers to ensure that the parties tried to resolve their dispute with the minimum involvement of the court. That could involve telling the parties that they had to attend a hearing at which they would be asked to explain what steps they had taken to use ADR.

The decision of the single judge in *Hockett* on an application for permission to appeal following the dismissal of a pre-action disclosure application, to the effect that legal proceedings should not be instituted prior to an attempt ADR through the complaints process is still helpful as it's so succinct, but overtaken by the above.

Other helpful cases

In *Churchill* the Master of the Rolls referred[para 49] to a number of cases in which it had been held that the Court had power to stay a claim: "Arden J in *Guinle v. Kirreh* [2000] CP Rep 62 under the heading "ADR", Woolf LCJ, in *R. (Cowl) v. Plymouth CC* [2002] 1 WLR 803 at [14], Blackburne J in *Shirayama Shokusan Co Ltd v. Danovo Ltd (No 2)* [2004] 1 WLR 2985 at [12]- [20], Smith LJ in *Uren v. Corporate Leisure (UK) Lt*d [2011] EWCA Civ 66 at [73], Mostyn J in *Mann v. Mann* [2014] EWHC 537 (Fam) at [16]-[17] and [36]), Norris J in *Bradley v. Heslin* [2014] EWHC 3267 (Ch) at [24], and Moylan LJ in *Lomax v. Lomax* [2019] EWCA Civ 1467, [2019] 1 WLR 6527 at [24]-[32])."

Just before Churchill was decided, Senior Master Fontaine had dealt with the issue as it relates to ICPs, in the claim of *David Hamon & others v University College London* [2023] EWHC 1812 (KB)] (referred to in submissions but not mentioned by the Court in *Churchill*). The Master found that the court had power to order a stay for ADR even where a party opposes it [at paragraph 49 of her judgment] and that a stay should be imposed in that claim.

As in housing conditions claims, in *Hamon,* the claimants' lawyers had raised objections to UCL's cost-free ICP (for the same reason as they do in our claims, relating to costs recovery etc). However, the Judge said that UCL's ICP appeared to be the appropriate form of ADR, subject to clarification of the two objections raised by the claimants' lawyers, relating to the scope of the process and the ability of UCL's complaints team to cope with the thousands of complaints it would have to address.

As a result, Master Fontaine did not at that hearing stay the claim with an *express* requirement that the claimants engage in ADR through the UCL ICP. Instead, she stayed it saying that she expected the parties *"to engage constructively in some **appropriate** form of ADR"*. She listed the claims for further hearing after a period in which the parties were to try to agree how to proceed with ADR.

Other recent cases not mentioned in *Churchill v Merthyr Tydfil*

Other pertinent cases include *PDF II SA v OMF Co-1 Ltd* [2013] EWCA Civ 1288 *and Jet 2 Holidays Ltd v Hughes* [2019] EWCA Civ 1858 and many others listed in the White Book at section 14-2. Now that the court has a duty actively to case manage, there are various arguments which can be raised in support of the contention that a stay can be ordered despite one party objecting – see the commentary in the White Book at section 14-6.

See also *Uren v Corporate Leisure (UK) Ltd* [2011] EWCA Civ 66 and the other cases listed in the White Book at 14-7.

In the context of PAD applications, in *Wimpey Homes UK Ltd v Harron Homes [2020] EWHC 1120 (TCC)*, Fraser J dismissed a PAD application because the respondent sought ADR through the means of expert determination and the applicant had refused. He held that the fact that ADR had been rejected was material. In a case where a party has sought to refer the dispute to ADR, there is a question whether the disclosure stage will ever be reached, although whether such issues are questions of threshold or discretion is arguable.

He cited *Hutchison 3G v O2* [2008], in which the Court reminded itself that PAD is appropriate only where the circumstances are outside "the usual run" to allow the hurdle to be surmounted of showing that it is necessary because it would be useful in achieving a settlement or otherwise saving costs. He also referred to *Birse Construction Ltd v HLC Engenharia SA* [2006] EWHC 1258 (TCC) saying that disclosure before the proper time is not something which should be lightly ordered in cases where disclosure is a labour-intensive exercise and a major head of costs.

Most important, he said that ADR has "*a vast number of advantages to parties to commercial agreements*" and "It is almost always far quicker than litigation, and almost always far cheaper, to have disputes resolved in this way. The court in all cases will be astute to prevent pre-action disclosure being used either to frustrate, impede or interfere with contractually agreed ADR mechanisms."

The court should be reminded that litigation can cause significant damage to the relationship between a landlord and tenant by contested litigation, whichever party wins. It is therefore in the interests of justice to discourage litigation between parties who will have to continue to deal with each other whatever the result – see *Shirayama Shokusan v Danovo Ltd* [2003] EWHC 3006 (Ch), in which the Court also held that the Court could stay the proceedings for the parties to mediate – the case was decided before *Halsey*.

Rules made by the Solicitors Regulation Authority Board (6 June 2023).

The mainstay of the application is the law relating to paragraph 4.1 of the Protocol, the relevant provisions of the CPR and the Pre-Action Protocol, as discussed earlier in the book.

There is no specific obligation under the Rules that solicitors should advise ADR over litigation, but under Rule 1.2 "*You do not abuse your position by taking unfair advantage of clients or others*" is in my view relevant in these claims. That is what claimant solicitors do, exploiting often vulnerable tenants most of whom are only interested in getting works done rather than extracting large sums from their landlord.

Rule 2.4 is often relevant too: "*You only make assertions or put forward statements, representations or submissions to the court or others which are properly arguable.*" Most applications for orders for specific performance are hopeless from the outset, as the works have been completed before the signature of the Particulars of Claim.

Various provisions relating to service and competence might be in play too.

Although it is worth mentioning, it does not add much to the now substantial body of law giving the court the opportunity to stay for ADR.

Preparing an application to stay the claim for ADR

The legal basis for the application can be supported by factual details showing the disproportionality of proceedings compared to an ICP.

It is necessary to compile a witness statement which deals with the enormous cost in terms of officer time and public funds which disrepair claims generate. That can be supplemented by information about the number of claims made in the past and the number being received at the present time. It is also possible to get figures from other social landlords about how many claims they are experiencing. The overall message is that these claims are disproportionate and should not be allowed to go to court unless the parties have attempted ADR.

Obviously, the cost-free version, in the form of the complaints process, is preferable. If that does not work, the parties can try other types of ADR, but mediation and joint settlement meetings are likely to be very expensive because the tenant's lawyers will be involved.

Further, reliance on paragraph 4.1, which says that the parties are required to "*consider whether some form of ADR procedure would be more suitable than litigation and if so, try to agree which form of ADR to use*" can provide helpful evidence.

Either party might "*be required by the court to provide evidence that alternative means of resolving their dispute were considered.*" This paragraph is worth stressing-if the claimant's solicitors refuse to advise their client to exhaust the ICP, the landlord should be asking the court ideally to speak directly to the tenant and discover their objections. Solicitors will never let this happen, either drafting witness statements themselves saying the claimant is implacably opposed to talking to their landlord or prepare a statement containing hearsay evidence that the tenant holds this view.

Requests for further information to supplement applications

When investigating the merits of the claim it may be necessary to tie the claimant to their case and ensure that no further arguments will come out of the woodwork when making the application for summary judgement/strike out.

Requests for further information are made under CPR 18 and need to be made under the procedure in PD 18. First the party making the request must serve a written request for clarification or information, giving a date by which the response should be served, which must be a reasonable time hence.

Brief requests can be made by letter, more complex requests should be made in a separate document. The maker must state that they are making a Request under Part 18, and they should deal with the other matters set out in CPR PD 18.1.6.

Replies to requests

Responses must be in writing, dated and signed by the party providing the information with a Statement of Truth. This is important, as a claimant can be reminded in cross-examination that any answers given in their Part 18 Replies were provided in the knowledge that they could be sent to prison if they knowingly misstated a fact.

If replies are not provided

If objection is taken to answering the questions or to doing so within the time allowed, a response must be given, whereupon the party requesting will have to make an application to the court under Part 18, for which the procedure is set out in 18 PD.5. That will need to be served on the other side.

If the recipient does not reply, the maker of the request issues an application which need only contain a brief statement in box 10 of the N244 that a request has been made and not answered. They need not serve the application on the other party (CPR PD 18 5.5 (1)).

The court will then make an order without a hearing, provided at least 14 days have passed since the Request was served and the time allowed for a response has expired.

Requests for specific dates on which notice is said to have been given

It is particularly important to use this procedure to force the tenant to commit to dates of notice alleged to have been given, or to elicit a concession that they cannot provide any dates.

The tenant will have to answer the Request with a signed Statement of Truth. Once a tenant has said that they cannot be more specific, their witness statement should not contain any allegations that they gave notice on specific dates and in court they can be cross-examined if they then unexpectedly remember dates.

Request for information on alleged loss and damage

If the claim for loss and damage is broadly pleaded, or personal injury is alleged without a medical report being provided, a request can be made to particularise the alleged damage and application can be made for summary judgement on the personal injury claim if no medical report is served.

Content of the N244 application form

A decision must be made as to which parts of the claim are to be attacked and which allowed to continue to trial. Sometimes the entire claim can be attacked, if the documentary evidence is good enough. Often it will be the application for an injunction which is the best target. In some (unusual) cases, it may not be appropriate to make an application for summary judgement at all.

Occasionally an application can be combined with an application to strike out the claim as an abuse of process. This might be appropriate where a tenant has behaved in a way which is clearly and seriously in breach of the CPR, or of the Pre-Action Protocol.

There are specific requirements of an application for summary judgement, and it is important to get the procedural aspects right.

The application notice will contain the orders sought, the reasons for asking the court to make them (in box 3), and the bare bones of the evidence (in box 10). The surveyor's report and, if drafted, the additional witness evidence will be attached.

Requests for remote hearing

It is much more cost effective for most landlords to appear at these hearings remotely. The N244 should refer to CPR PD 23 paragraph 6.3: "*Hearings to deal with allocation or listing **or with a time estimate of two hours or less** may be conducted remotely, depending on the normal practice at a particular court.*" Claimant solicitors are likely to agree because their barristers will not have to travel long distances to court.

Conduct of the hearing

It is wise to prepare a skeleton argument, setting out the basis on which the application is pursued. Some district judges will be familiar with such claims, but most will need help when it comes to disrepair/unfitness law.

The idea of compulsory stay for ADR is also novel to some judges, at least at present.

Review of the application before the hearing

The decision whether to make the application should be reviewed when, or if the claimant files evidence in response. It is necessary to keep an open mind on the issue, encase the tenant adduces evidence which could cause the application to fail.

Chapter Summary / Key Takeaways

- The availability of the remedy of summary judgement/strike out/stay is a powerful weapon in the armoury of a social landlord, provided that they know when and how should be used.

- Such applications require careful planning and collection of evidence if they are to succeed. Most social landlords will have records which are sufficiently detailed to provide them with an opportunity to rebut much of what a tenant says.

- An application can be made simply to stay the claim for ADR, or to seek summary judgement or strike out on part or all of the claim, and a stay of the remainder. That hearing might also deal with allocation, which is addressed in Chapter Eighteen.

The next chapter considers the drafting of the Defence. If an application has been made for summary judgement/strike out, this should not be attempted before the landlord knows which parts of the claim are left in contention. This leads to reduced legal fees.

CHAPTER SEVENTEEN

DRAFTING THE DEFENCE

The Defence gives the landlord an opportunity to take issue with the various respects in which disrepair claims are usually defective or lacking.

Time for filing the Defence

The acknowledgement of service must be filed within 14 days after service of the claim form if the particulars of claim come it, or within 14 days of service of the POC if they are not served contemporaneously.

Provided that a defendant has filed an acknowledgement of service under CPR 10, the Defence has to be filed and served 28 days after service of the particulars of claim, which themselves must be either served with the claim form or within 14 days after service.

If the Defendant fails to file an acknowledgement of service, they only have 14 days in which to serve the Defence. It follows that it is important to serve that acknowledgement of service in every case.

That time limit does not give a landlord very long to gather the information necessary to plead the Defence properly. Fortunately, in most cases, the pre-litigation skirmish will have meant that most of the relevant information is to hand, and the pleading can be done relatively swiftly.

If it turns out not to be possible to file the Defence within the time limit, most claimant solicitors will allow extra time for the preparation of a

Defence if requested. The parties can agree an extension of up to 28 days between themselves.

If the claimant does refuse to give such an extension, the court will usually exercise its discretion in favour of extending time, provided good reason can be given for the delay.

No Defence need be filed in some circumstances

As I have already said, if you are making an application for summary judgement/strike out Defence-relying on CPR 12.3. After hearing the application, if any of the claim remains, the court will direct that a Defence is filed. If the court allocates to the SCT at the same time as dismissing the claim for specific performance, it may agree that the landlord's witness statements can serve as its Defence.

The mechanics of serving a Defence

CPR 15 contains the rules as to when a Defence must be filed and what it should contain. Disrepair claims will almost inevitably involve disputes as to the facts, so they will have been issued under Part 7 rather than Part 8. If a claimant uses the Part 8 procedure, the defendant should not follow the rules in CPR 15.

Counterclaims

It is sometimes necessary to include a counterclaim against a tenant, particularly if they have caused substantial damage to the property, bearing in mind the cautionary tale of *Jillians v Red Kite*.

Reply to the Defence

Most Defences are met with a Reply. It is up to the claimant to file their Reply with the Directions Questionnaire and to serve it on the defendant at the same time it is filed. The parties are not allowed to exchange any further pleadings without permission of the court.

This means that all the issues must be raised in those three preliminary documents.

The parties can amend their existing statements of case. The normal order for costs on any amendment is that the party making the changes pays the costs of and occasioned by those changes.

The content of a Defence

A defendant landlord will need to plead in the Defence all the facts on which they rely, but not the law.

The best way to approach the content of the Defence is to give an example of what might be included in such a document, so I have included one as an appendix. It is very long as I have tried to anticipate as many issues in the claim as possible.

Chapter Summary / Key Takeaways

- If no application for summary judgement or strike out has been made, the Defence has to be drafted.

- In a disrepair claim the Defence can be lengthy and reasonably complex, and you probably will need lawyers to prepare it.

In the next chapter we will look at transfer and allocation to track, and in particular the importance of the Small Claims Track in disrepair claims.

CHAPTER EIGHTEEN

TRANSFER AND ALLOCATION TO TRACK

Transfer to the defendant's home court

Often claimant solicitors issue disrepair claims in their home court, or even in other courts which have no apparent connection to either party.

Landlords should ensure that the court transfers the claim to their home court, either using CPR 30.3 or if it has been issued as a money claim, by telling the court as soon the claim is issued that it should be transferred pursuant to CPR 26.2A (2) and in the case of a claim for damages and an injunction, under sub-rule (4) or (5).

There is no automatic transfer to the defendant's home court if they are a company or a corporation, so landlords need to ensure that transfer happens. If it is only an interim matter with which the court is dealing (e.g. pre-action disclosure), it may be reluctant to transfer the claim before hearing.

Criteria for transfers

The relevant criteria in CPR 30.2 (2) are:

"(a) the financial value of the claim and the amount in dispute, if different;

(b) whether it would be more convenient or fair for hearings (including the trial) to be held in some other court;

245

(c) the availability of a judge specialising in the type of claim in question and in particular the availability of a specialist judge sitting in an appropriate regional specialist court;

(d) whether the facts, legal issues, remedies or procedures involved are simple or complex;

(e) the importance of the outcome of the claim to the public in general;

(f) the facilities available to the court at which the claim is being dealt with, particularly in relation to –

(i) any disabilities of a party or potential witness;

(ii) ... "

If a substantive claim has been issued, the court should transfer to the hearing centre in which the property is situated at the earliest possible moment. It is usually up to the landlord to ask the court to do so, as the tenant's solicitors will usually prefer it to remain in their home court.

Allocation to track

Claimant lawyers will be primarily interested in the potential for the recovery of costs. They work on conditional fee agreements and the track to which a claim is allocated by the court can have a fundamental effect on the pursuit of the claim, as claimant solicitors will not wish to pursue claims on the Small Claims Track ("SCT"), subject to *B v Lee*. They will carry on with the claim, because they are obliged by their CFA to do so, but will not run up costs in the same way as they do on the FT. There is much greater potential for them to recover costs on the Fast Track ("FT") but there are still significant restraints on the quantum of those costs.

The Intermediate Track

There will be few disrepair claims which could ever be valuable and complex enough for the parties to contemplate allocation to the Intermediate Track ("IT").

Benefits of allocation to the SCT

Therefore, this chapter concentrates on the choice between the SCT and the FT. My preference is that claims should be dealt with in the SCT, where the implications for both parties are far less serious in terms of costs and hearings will be listed much more swiftly, with a minimum of unnecessary preparation. This saves both landlords significant investment in legal fees and officer time and further, it is less stressful for all involved.

The court will be able to deal with the claim much more swiftly and will be able to allocate to it a more proportionate amount of time. The result is that neither party will expend as much effort and money on legal preparation and the saving in costs will be substantial. The normal rules of evidence do not apply in the SCT, but it is still important to prepare witness statements with exhibits properly.

In the SCT it is even possible that the court can be persuaded to deal with the claim on paper, without a hearing, if both parties agree. That might be an attractive option if a tenant's solicitors are worried that they will not recover their costs. But normally there is a conflict of evidence on the question of notice and the court will need to make a decision whether the tenant is telling the truth when they say they reported the disrepair many times.

In the SCT the costs regime is much less of a burden for the parties, so the loser will not be at any significant risk, subject to the rules about unreasonable behaviour and *B v Lee*, as discussed in Chapters Ten and Twenty-One.

In very few, rare cases, the claim for damages and an injunction is patently so modest that the case is obviously suitable for the SCT, and the claimant solicitors will issue in the SCT, but they will ask for *B v Lee* costs.

The landlord should be able to show in evidence, using a surveyor's report, invoices and preferably a certificate signed by the tenant, that no works remain outstanding, so SCT trial is appropriate provided that objectively the claim for damages is less than £10,000. Alternatively, after an application for summary judgement, it should be appropriate to allocate the SCT.

Upon the filing of a Defence, a court officer will provisionally decide the most suitable track for the claim and serve a notice of proposed allocation under CPR 26.4 (1). It is then up to the parties to decide whether the track decision suits them, or whether they should apply to have the claim allocated to a different track. The court may ask for further information on allocation, which must be provided within 14 days (ibid).

Alternatively, upon the filing of Allocation Questionnaires pursuant to CPR 26.5 (1) (a) the landlord can request allocation to the SCT, while the tenant's solicitor will ask for allocation to the FT.

The process of decision-making on allocation is set out in CPR 26 and its PD, at PD 26 4.1. The court will generally give brief reasons for an allocation decision, except when all parties agree on allocation.

Another opportunity to ask for a stay at the allocation stage

Upon allocation to the fast track, the CPR now provide, in CPR 28.7 (d) *whether to order or encourage the parties to engage in alternative dispute resolution*".

The small claims track has its own cost-free mediation service.

These provisions provide interesting possibilities for the future, although it is likely that the claimant lawyers would still insist that they should be involved so they can argue that they should recover their costs up to the date on which repairs are completed.

The importance of allocation to track

Cases which are listed in the SCT will not usually result in any significant award of costs against a party unless they can be shown to have behaved unreasonably or dishonestly. So, claimant solicitors will not be able to ask for the substantial sums which they claim in FT trials. But proceeding on the SCT also means that a landlord who wins at trial will not get its costs back, in normal circumstances (again, see Chapter Twenty-One on costs after the final hearing.

Even in cases allocated to the FT, issues of proportionality and fixed fees for the barrister's appearance limit the amount of costs recoverable by either side.

Financial limits for tracking of disrepair claims

A disrepair claim will normally be allocated to the Small Claims Track unless it includes a claim for a mandatory injunction and either the cost of works necessary is over £1,000, or the damages reasonably sought are likely to be more than £1,000. A claim made only for damages for disrepair will usually be allocated to the SCT unless it exceeds £10,000.

CPR 1.1(2) addresses the overriding objective, which is relevant to allocation as it requires the court to deal with claims at a proportionate cost, saving expense, in ways that are proportionate and take into account the amount of money involved, ensuring that it is dealt with expeditiously and fairly and allocating to a claim an appropriate share of the court's resources, and enforcing compliance with rules, practice directions and orders.

Amounts not in dispute

Usually, the first consideration on allocation is the value of the sum in dispute. In determining the value of a claim, interest, costs and *any amount not in dispute* are not included in the assessment – see CPR 26.13 (2) (a). *"Any amount not in dispute"* includes an admission made by the defendant prior to allocation which reduces the amount in dispute.[57]

Although there is nothing in the CPR which deals with admissions that works are accepted as needing to be carried out, paragraph 14.8 of PD 26 says, *"It follows from these provisions that if, in relation to a claim the value of which is above the small claims track limit of £10,000, the defendant makes, before allocation, an admission that reduces the amount in dispute to a figure below £10,000 (see CPR Part 14), the normal track for the claim will be the small claims track"*. Thus, even if works valued at over £1,000 were necessary, they would not be "in dispute" for the purposes of valuation even if they have not been carried out at the date of allocation.

General rule for allocation for matters remaining in dispute

This is set out in CPR 26: CPR 26.12 (1) says:

> *"In considering whether to allocate a claim to the normal track for that claim under rule 26.9, 2.1- or 26.11, the court will have regard to the matters mentioned in rule 26.13(1)."*

Rule 26.13(1) follows:

> *"Matters relevant to allocation to a track*

---

[57] Cf *Akhtar v Boland* [2014] EWCA Civ 872, at paragraphs 22 and 23

26.13 When deciding the track for a claim, the matters to which the court shall have regard include –

(a) the financial value, if any, of the claim;...

    (c) the likely complexity of the facts, law or evidence;...

    (i) the circumstances of the parties".

See also the allocation principles set out in PD 26.9 and 14 which supplements CPR 26. Essentially, it is for the court to assess the financial value of a claim, and PD26.14.6 says:

"(6) Where the court believes that the amount the claimant is seeking exceeds what they may reasonably be expected to recover it may make an order under rule 26.7(4) directing the claimant to justify the amount."

Also, under CPRPD26.14(7), in deciding whether an amount is in dispute, the court should exclude amounts for which summary judgment has been entered, any sum for which the defendant admits they are liable, and any sum offered by the claimant which has been accepted. So, offers made in the ICP should be excluded from amounts in dispute.

The proportionality of the claim has been a consideration since April 2013, when court was specifically enjoined to consider that issue in case management decisions. That has a clear and direct impact on the need to encourage claimant tenants to use a cost-free complaints process

CPR 26.1 addresses allocation. The rules provide that tracking must reflect the time and resources appropriate for the just disposal of a case at proportionate cost. It is important to understand the principles behind the crucial question of tracking.

Allocation in housing disrepair claims

Disrepair claims should not be allocated to the small claims track if they involve a claim for an injunction and either that claim **or** the claim for damages is valued at more than £1,000. The notes say:

> "*Housing disrepair—any claim which includes a claim by a tenant of residential premises against a landlord where the tenant seeks an order requiring the landlord to carry out repairs or other work and the costs of that are estimated to be no more than £1,000. This applies even if some other remedy is also sought in the same claim as long as it is also not more than £1,000 (CPR 26.9(1)(b)).*"

However, if the issue is marginal, there is leeway provided by the rules themselves: *"The court may allocate to the small claims track claim, the value of which is above the limits mentioned in rule 26.9 (1)."* (CPR PD 26, para 15 (5)).

Requesting allocation or reallocation to the SCT

CPR 26 on allocation specifies how the landlord should go about first asking for allocation to the SCT. When filling in the response to the claim and/or the DQ, the landlord will want to make it plain that they seek allocation to the SCT. If the court allocates the claim to track, it will serve a notice of allocation on the parties pursuant to CPR 26.17.

If the court allocates track of its own motion, a party may seek reallocation under CPR 26.18 if they believe the case has been wrongly tracked by the court officer. So, the question of which track is appropriate can be determined at a hearing upon the request of a party dissatisfied with the allocation.

Preparing to argue the question of allocation

The landlord's surveyor will need to address the question of what works have been carried out and what remains outstanding. Obviously, it is best to be able to prove that there are no works at all outstanding. Otherwise, the landlord will need to establish that both the claim for damages should be valued at less than £1,000 and there is less than £1,000 worth of work outstanding. If either of those heads of claim exceed that figure on valuation by the judge, the court will allocate to the FT.

In assessing the cost of any such works, in a social housing conditions/disrepair claim, it is the value put on the works by the landlord's surveyor/repairs team which is relevant for the purposes of valuation in allocation, which is likely to be at in-house rates.[58]

Where there is no genuine claim for specific performance

A disrepair claim will be allocated to the SCT if the claimant cannot show that there is a genuine claim for specific performance of the contract and the damages expected are less than £10,000.

The primary argument of tenants is that there is a genuine claim for specific performance. This is often untrue. An application for specific performance is ultimately enforced by injunctive relief, which carries a possible penalty of imprisonment. The question is whether as a matter of judgment (not on the balance of probabilities) the Court in valuing the claim accepts the tenant's allegation that *at the final hearing* an injunction will be necessary. The question whether the works remain outstanding at the date of allocation is not determinative.

---

[58] *Jalili v Bury Council* (17 June 2021) at paragraph 20, a decision of District Judge Haisley, although as it is only a first instance decision it should be viewed as non-binding

The claim amounts to an assertion that the landlord cannot be trusted carry out appropriate repairs and that the Court should reject its evidence (supported by a Statement of Truth), that it will carry out any necessary works to remedy the defects complained of by the tenant.

The law on specific performance against landlords

The restrictions on the grant of equitable relief do not apply to applications under section 17 of the 1985 Act (see Chapter Sixteen). Therefore, to guarantee that you will not face allocation to the FT, you will need to apply for summary judgment against the claimant on the claim for specific performance.

The authors of Dowding & Reynolds say that although there are no statutory restrictions on the enforcement of landlords' repairing covenants and the landlord has theoretically no statutory protection against frivolous or malicious claims by tenants requiring exact compliance with repairing obligations, *"it is thought, however that in practice the discretionary nature of specific performance will be protection enough: in general, the court will only make an order where there is a real practical reason why the work must be done, and in other cases, the tenant will be left to his remedy in damages."*

That must be right, because the court will not require works which would put the property in a better state of repair than that required by statute or under the contract. So, the restrictions of section 11 (3) of the 1985 Act and of the fitness for human habitation provisions do not require a landlord to provide a dwelling which is in a perfect state of repair and condition. It need only be reasonable and reasonably habitable.

Also, the relief is discretionary. The court will not grant a mandatory order, carrying with it the threat of imprisonment, unlimited fine or sequestration of assets against a party without good reason. It is difficult to conceive of circumstances in which any such reason might exist to make an order against a landlord which has adduced good evidence of its intention to carry out the very acts required of it in the claim for specific performance. In a claim in respect of the lifts in a Council block of flats the Court of Appeal contemplated making an injunction against the Council,[59] but it may be different where a landlord is doing its best to repair, cannot find the cause of a problem and damages would be an adequate remedy (i.e. the interference with amenity is not serious).

Finally, as discussed in Chapter Twelve, a tenant cannot ask for injunctive relief on the basis that their expert evidence suggests that works of a different nature should be carried out or different methods employed to rectify a defect, because the landlord as the covenanting party has the right to choose the way in which remedial works will be performed.

So, if the court is satisfied that there is no real prospect of the tenant establishing that contention at trial, it is entitled to find that the works are not "in dispute" pursuant to CPR 26.13 (2) (a) and therefore that there is no arguable claim for summary judgment. It makes no difference that the landlord has not applied for judgment on that element of the claim, as CPR 26 requires the same exercise of judgment, or an 'assessment' as described in the rule in valuing the claim.

But when told that the tenant is unhappy with the state of repair of the property, most social landlords will get on and inspect, then repair. Often works are carried out very shortly after the claim is intimated.

To recap, provided the result is that the tenant stops suffering any significant loss of amenity, the choice of works is that of the landlord and not the tenant. So, claimant lawyers should not succeed in an argument that their surveyors says that the roof should be replaced rather than

---

[59] *Parker v Camden LBC* [1986] Ch 162

patched, provided the patching provides satisfactory protection from the elements (see the facts of the *Trustees of Dame Hungerford* case.

Gaining access to do works-injunctions

It is worth repeating that tenants cannot refuse access for those works to be carried out. The Protocol requires tenants in paragraph 7.6 to allow landlords access to carry out works and there are no exceptions specified. Previously many tenant solicitors used to advise their clients not to allow a landlord in to do the works, particularly before they had sent a surveyor in to inspect.

It is incumbent on the tenant solicitors to get the survey done quickly, and they should not use that excuse to prevent access. Delay in the works can increase the number of damages payable, as the tenant will argue that although they had refused access, the landlord could have forced entry using their legal right if they chose to do so.

Therefore, any refusal of access by the tenant must be dealt with swiftly, by a written warning and either forced entry if the tenancy provides for it, or by application for an access injunction.

If there are any works necessary to remedy defects which may cause a nuisance or annoyance to anyone in the locality, or to employees etc of the landlord, an application can be made under the Antisocial Behaviour Crime and Policing Act 2014 – see Chapter Six.

Otherwise, the injunctive relief needs to be sought under the terms of the tenancy, using the Part 8 procedure.

Other arguments for allocation of disrepair claims to the SCT

In disrepair claims, apart from the expected value of the claim, there are likely to be two arguments raised on the part of claimants: the claim is too complex to be dealt with in the SCT and there is an inequality of arms if the claimant does not have the services of a lawyer. The proportionality of costs will also be relevant. Both of these can be defeated.

In two cases on the complex area of PPI law, judges have made observations which are helpful to landlords in disrepair claims: *Gillies v Blackhorse Limited* [2011] EW Misc 20 (19 December 2011) and *Loughlin v Blackhorse Limited* [2012] EW Misc 8 (CC) (13 January 2012). They were both appeals against the allocation of a claim to the SCT.

The claimants relied on the complexity of the facts and the law and on the parties' circumstances as they argued there should be equality of arms by providing for legal representation for both. Both appeals addressed the issues in the same way. The court held that it is actual complexity, rather than 'ostensible' complexity with which the court is concerned.

I will address each in turn.

Complexity

There is nothing in the principles listed in CPR PD 26.7 to provide guidance on how to judge complexity. The central allegation in both PPI claims was one of misrepresentation, although a variety of different legal claims were pleaded, in a similar way to disrepair claims, in which the central allegations is a failure to repair within a reasonable time, put under multiple heads of claim.

In *Gillies*, the judge said that:

> "Mr Gillies' claim is based on a number of familiar grounds; he alleges (amongst other things) misrepresentation, breach of the Insurance Conduct of Business Rules amounting to a breach of statutory duty under Section 150 of the Financial Services and

Markets Act 2000, an unfair relationship pursuant to the Consumer Credit Act, negligence and breach of contract. Those are all certainly pleaded allegations and they are issues raised in many of these cases".

In both cases, the court observed that the law had been carefully considered in the appeal courts. In *Loughlin*, the judge considered that, *"These matters are much more straightforward than they appear to be…Looking at the pleadings some of them have now been dealt with at a higher level ……… and the district judge is well able to take those matters into account in guiding the litigant through the small claim".*

Cases allocated to the SCT can involve complex issues and the court should not allocate to the FT on the assumption that any complex issues must be dealt with on that track. Again, in *Loughlin* the judge said, *"it is my experience of experienced district judges that, in dealing with these cases which are the subject of a significant number of claims, they become pretty experienced in the issues that arise and how to deal with them, and if something goes wrong then the litigant may appeal".*

In *Williams v Santander UK Plc* [2015] EW Misc B37 (CC) (21 August 2015) the court heard an application to re-allocate to the FT a case which had been allocated to the SCT. The claimant argued that it should be FT because of legal complexity and the inequality of arms.

As to inequality of arms, the district judge hearing the application for reallocation noted that *"…the court is and, as judges, we are, regularly faced with litigants in person and we try to ensure at all costs that the parties are helped through any difficulties that they may face in such a hearing".*

Equality of arms

Litigants in person in the SCT are protected by the overriding objective, which imposes an obligation on the court to ensure procedural fairness for all parties and to allow a degree of latitude to litigants in person.

In *Loughlin*, the judge accepted that if the case was allocated to the SCT, it was likely that the claimant would have to bring his case on his own (with Black Horse likely to be represented by lawyers) but said:

> "....given that the issues in this case are relatively straightforward and more or less the same issues as arise in Gillies, it does not seem to me that there is any real justification that this point is a good one. The real question here is whether this is a case which should be allocated to the small claim or the fast track in order to enable there to be a fuller argument by legal representation of the issues that arise".

Proportionality of costs

Costs must be proportionate to the matters in issue. In *Williams v Santander*, the District Judge responsible for the initial allocation to the small claims track noted in his order that *"the costs likely to be incurred by allocation to any other track would be wholly disproportionate to the sums in issue"*.

Evidencing the costs in a disrepair claim allocated to the FT

As part of the evidence in the allocation hearing, the landlord may need to show that costs of proceedings in the FT are disproportionate to the sums involved. N260s are frequently filed showing costs of £25,000 to £40,000. Even if the tenant recovers £2,000 in damages, those amounts are wholly disproportionate to the amount at stake.

Clearly there will be few cases in which such costs are proportionate. Admissible evidence needs to be produced to the court of those likely costs, i incurred to date and estimated to trial for both parties, in the form of a witness statement by the landlord or their solicitor. Alternatively, some courts ask for an estimate of costs to date and costs to trial, which will achieve the same purpose.

Chapter Summary / Key Takeaways

- Although claims are nearly always issued in a distant County Court hearing centre, they should be transferred immediately to the landlord's home court if possible.

- Careful consideration should be given to the issue of allocation and the claimant's assertion that the case should be listed in the Fast Track should not necessarily be accepted.

- Few landlords' representatives recognise the availability of this simple but necessary exercise in the assessment of a claim and the subsequent procedural steps or application necessary to address the serious issue caused by allocation to the Fast Track.

- A landlord needs to be confident of its stance on getting repairs done quickly-tenants should not be allowed to delay them. Landlords should ask for an injunction against the tenant for any persistent refusal of access.

- Landlords have a duty to carry out repairs as swiftly as possible following notice received through a Letter of Claim. They cannot be criticised for as soon as possible.

- The Court should not allocate a disrepair claim to the fast track if the circumstances do not justify such allocation.

- Where the claimant cannot honestly ask for an injunction for specific performance, and the damages claimed are less than £10,000, or both the cost of the works and the claim for damages are less than £1,000, the claim should not proceed on the FT and will be allocated to the SCT.

In the next chapter, we will look at disclosure and inspection, which is more relevant to FT trials, as the SCT does not require the parties to carry out the formal disclosure process.

CHAPTER NINETEEN

DISCLOSURE AND INSPECTION

This chapter considers disclosure regarding issues in disrepair claims and is unlikely to be relevant to other areas of law.

Almost all my claims are allocated to the SCT. I assume that there will be no claims that are so valuable they are allocated to the Intermediate Track. The rules differ substantially between the SCT and the Fast Track.

Directions and disclosure in the Small Claims Track

The court will send the parties a directions questionnaire to allow it to give directions for the final hearing, which will include an order that the parties file and serve copies of all documents on which they intend to rely at the hearing no later than 14 days before it is listed. If the claim is allocated at a hearing, the court will expect the parties to have filed draft directions.

There are some 'standard directions' available for certain types of disputes, and these can be adapted to suit housing conditions claims.

The court will also fix a date for the final hearing in the SCT when it sends out the Directions. That should be within weeks and not months (as is normal for the FT).

Using directions to address pleading of notice

In most claims there is a significant issue with the Particulars of Claim, in that they plead notice in very broad terms. You can address this in two ways:

First, when serving the Defence or at any time before allocation to the SCT (when the formal procedures should not be used), you can make a request for Further Information under Part 18 in respect of the pleading of notice. If the claimant fails to answer that you can ask for an order at the same time as making any application for summary judgment, a stay or allocation to the SCT. If the claimant is found to have refused unreasonably, the court should order them to pay the costs of the application.

Alternatively, or additionally you can include a draft direction to allow for the claimant to adduce their evidence first. So instead of simultaneous witness statement exchange, the claimant should file and serve their statements before the landlord. In that way the landlord can answer any allegations that there has been a failure to record instances of notice etc.

it is important to use one of these methods to avoid the claimant giving evidence at the final hearing that they called the landlord many times but cannot give any specific instances. Again, see the case of *Jillians v Red Kite* for an example of the court accepting the claimant's evidence that many instances of notice went unrecorded. The judge remarked that she had not seen the records which one might expect to have been disclosed if the landlord's contention that they had responded to notice every time was accurate.

Disclosure in the SCT

In the SCT there is no formal procedure for disclosure – CPR 27.2 (1) (b) expressly says so, but the parties must disclose documents on which they intend to rely and which may be helpful to their opponent.

It is worth asking for certain documents if they are relevant to issues in the claim, for instance copy emails, phone records, electricity and gas bills, medical records, evidence of loss or expenditure etc.

It is also important to remember that the duty of disclosure includes searching for documents which might be relevant in places to which the landlord has access. This means checking all the software systems. In practice this should include the repairs logs, communications logs, tenancy files (for both the current and historic systems if they have changed) and the complaints records.

In the past I have discovered that in its first disclosure exercise, one landlord did not check the complaints system, because of the separation of powers. It transpired that the tenant had made previous complaints, which proved that she had been mostly happy with the state of her home, as they related only to specific defects. See also my remarks below about disclosure by landlords in the FT.

When preparing claims in the SCT, the material below in respect of the FT may be relevant.

The Fast Track

In the Fast Track the process of Disclosure will take place in every case. It is governed by CPR 31, which you should read, along with the notes in the White Book.

Once a claim is underway, assuming that disclosure, or at least full disclosure has not been given at the Protocol stage (because you have successfully objected to pre-action disclosure) you will need to engage in disclosure within the trial process.

CPR 31 addresses disclosure and inspection and this is not intended to be a definitive guide to the process. Again, if you are litigating these claims, it is important to understand your general disclosure rights and duties. This means knowing what documents you are entitled to insist upon seeing and what documents you have to be certain that you have disclosed.

This is because the obligation to disclose is backed up by a binding confirmation that the party has complied with their obligations. CPR 21.23 says that *"proceedings for contempt of court may be brought against person if he makes, or causes to be made, a false disclosure statement, without an honest belief in its truth."*

Putting it bluntly, if you knowingly hide the existence of documents, you can go to prison, as can your opponent's solicitor, or the claimant themselves.

Meaning of 'Disclosure' in the FT

CPR 31.2 says that the meaning of the word is limited to a statement that a document exists or has existed. That means you do not necessarily have to produce the document for disclosure, in fact you may not even be able to do so-you have to say whether it is or has been in your control.

This can have relevance when a landlord's document retention policy results in the destruction of historical repairs records earlier than prudent. It is necessary to state in the disclosure process if you no longer hold records because they have been destroyed.

Equally, if as a defendant you ask the claimant to disclose certain documents, they must sign their disclosure statement confirming that they had the document in their possession, but it has been destroyed or lost etc.

'Possession or control'

The obligation to disclose the existence of documents does not relate only to those in your physical possession. It also covers documents which are in the 'control' of a party – see CPR 31.8.

This includes records held by others which can be obtained by application or request from them. The party only has to have a right to possession, or a right to inspect or take a copy of a document to make it disclosable.

Meaning of "document"

This word does not only mean paper documents. It also applies to anything in which information of any description is recorded. That includes computer files, email records, audio recordings and photographs/videos. It will also include mobile and landline call records where relevant. See CPR 31.4.

Therefore, landlords need to think carefully about what 'documents' tenants can be asked to disclose. For instance, it is important to ask claimant tenants for their phone records if they are alleging that they gave notice by telephone. Additionally, if they allege that the property is too cold because of disrepair, their heating bills are relevant. Further, if they say they have been caused any ill-health or injury, their medical records are disclosable for the whole period over which the injury is said to have occurred.

'Standard' disclosure

The extent of disclosure necessary is mandated by the track on which the claim is allocated.

In SCT claims there is no such thing as disclosure per se and the parties only have to comply with the limited obligation to provide copies of documents on which they rely and which might harm their case etc.

in FT claims, the parties are ordered by the court to give standard disclosure (under CPR 31.10) and the court may even dispense with or limit that process (by CPR 31.5 (1) (b)). Also, the parties may agree in writing between themselves to dispense with or limit standard disclosure.

In compiling the list, although documents have to be identified in a "convenient order and manner and as concisely as possible", it is possible to list classes of documents by date brackets-e.g. "Emails between claimant and defendant from [date] to [date]." Many people spend hours listing every single individual document, which is unnecessary.

In MT claims, the parties must follow the rather complicated timetable in CPR 31.5 (3) unless the court orders otherwise.

Disclosure relates to all 'relevant' documents

When giving standard disclosure you must disclose documents on which you rely, which adversely affect your own case or that of another party or which support any other party's case (CPR 31.6).

This is a very important principle – it is not permissible to hold back a document from disclosure because it might damage one's case. It is important to recognise that obligation and to check with the repairs team that there is nothing waiting to be discovered by people looking at other documents. Litigants, both claimant and defendant, have to remember that their credibility and reputation is at stake in each case. See the discussion above about disclosure in the SCT.

Disclosure by landlords in the FT

If disclosure has been provided within the Pre-Action Protocol the landlord should have little left to disclose, but a check still needs to be made that no documents have been missed out.

Sources of documentary records will include the various repairs team software databases, both reactive and long-term maintenance and improvement systems, the tenancy file and records of any complaints. There may well be email trails which are relevant to the carrying out of works and which explain decisions to proceed with or cancel various jobs.

It is likely to be necessary to update any of the computer records, because between the SAR and the final hearing there is likely to have been significant contact between the landlord and the tenant, and works will have been carried out. When it comes to the final hearing, it is good practice to avoid including in the bundle duplicates of any documents, including those records.

Disclosure by tenants in the FT

In theory a tenant ought also to have disclosed relevant documents in the operation of the Protocol. In practice they rarely do so and it is often necessary to ask for documents on which the landlord would wish to rely.

In the FT the court can order less than standard disclosure – see CPR 28, PD para 3.6(1) (c) and (4), but in disrepair cases this may not be a sensible course of action as the landlord needs to ensure that the tenant discloses all necessary documents.

There will be circumstances in which a tenant has possession or control of documents which are likely to assist the landlord in the defence of the claim. The most obvious of those (as mentioned above) are:

- telephone records when they say they have repeatedly called the landlord;

- medical records in cases where the tenant says they have suffered stress or ill-health. Reports are only privileged when prepared for the purpose of litigation;

- utility bills where they say that they have heated and ventilated a property adequately but it is still too cold;

- emails or texts which mention the state of repair of the property, whether to the landlord or to others.

Inspection

Once a document is disclosed, the other side has a right to inspect it unless:

- it is no longer in the control (not just possession) of the party disclosing it;

- the party has a right or duty to withhold inspection (most likely because it is privileged);

- the party considers that it would be disproportionate to the issues in the case to permit a category or class of documents, in which case inspection is not required and statement must be made to that effect;

- it is "closed material" under CPR 79-highly unlikely in a disrepair claim!

Duty of disclosure continues throughout the proceedings

Until judgement is given and an order made, the parties must remember their continuing duty to the court to disclose the existence of any document coming to that parties notice for the first time after disclosure has taken place.

This is particularly relevant where works are being carried out on a property as a case proceeds. It is crucial that those documents created during the works are disclosed to the other side. Another class of documents likely to be created during the proceedings is the data logging monitoring records. Landlords will need to obtain and analyse records created by remote or in situ property monitoring equipment.

Equally, it applies to a tenant who receives something as small as a card which informs them that the landlord called to carry out works but they were not available to give access. The same goes for updated medical records, continuing utility bills etc. useful evidence may be obtained from a tenant when works are carried out, for instance if they make no difference to the quantum of the utility bills.

Applications for specific disclosure

If a tenant's solicitor refuses to disclose the relevant documents, it will be necessary to make an application for specific disclosure pursuant to CPR 31.12. A party can ask for disclosure of documents or classes of documents (particularly anything named in or inferred to exist by the POC) and further documents which must exist as appears either from the face of a list or in the list itself.

The court has to consider the reasonableness of any search expected of the respondent. The applicant needs to give evidence why they are not satisfied with the disclosure afforded thus far by the respondent and why they anticipate that the specific disclosure sought would be proportionate and relevant to and probative of the issues.

Timing of applications for specific disclosure

Such applications should be dealt with at the same time as other case management decisions, if possible, to keep costs down, i.e. they should not be listed separately. This is particularly important because the court may consider that it is appropriate to reserve the question of costs to await determination of the question whether the documents disclosed have been probative and relevant.

Additionally, if an order for a further search is made but that search proves fruitless or the documents found in disclosed prove to be irrelevant, the applicant may be penalised in costs.

Disclosure can only be ordered in respect of matters which are expressly pleaded, so it is important to say in the Defence why particular facts are relevant if an application is contemplated.

An order for specific disclosure can include a requirement that the respondent carries out a search for any documents which are disclosable.

Documents mentioned in a statement of case

Such documents should be disclosed as a matter of course and are often attached as an appendix or schedule to the pleading.

If a party fails to disclose a document which has been mentioned in pleadings, a witness statement or summary, an affidavit or an expert's report, an application can be made under CPR 31.14 for disclosure and inspection of that document. Any documents which are privileged remain protected and cannot be inspected, unless it could be argued that privilege has been waived.

If a document is not specifically mentioned but its existence has to be inferred, an application needs to be made under CPR 31.12.

Some tenant surveyors do not include a copy of their instructions in their report and it is wise to request one, although only the substance of instructions need be disclosed.

Chapter Summary / Key Takeaways

- In the SCT disclosure is not a formal process.

- Frequently I find that it is necessary to ask for sequential exchange of witness statements, particularly useful if the claimant has failed in the POC to provide proper particulars of notice if not already conceded to be reflected by the landlord's records.

- You will need to ask for certain documents if you want to see them, as the claimant solicitors are unlikely to disclose material such as utility bills and medical records voluntarily if they do not assist the tenant's claim.

- When the tenant in an SCT claim serves witness statements and documents, it is important to consider what might be missing and ask for it immediately, because the final hearing is likely to be imminent.

- Social landlords often have sophisticated repairs software, which will need to be interrogated to provide proper disclosure on either track. It is sometimes a challenge to be confident that this has been done successfully by the repairs team, who are often overworked, so a careful check should be made.

- Disclosure in the FT should be used as an opportunity to reassess the strength of the claim against the landlord and to ensure that the witness statements can deal with all the issues of fact which are likely to arise.

In the next chapter we will look at drafting witness statements for disrepair trials.

CHAPTER TWENTY

WITNESS STATEMENTS

Some of the preparation necessary for trial will already have been undertaken in the earlier skirmishes concerning summary judgement, striking out, staying and/or allocation to track.

Those witness statements can be used in the trial but if they weren't sufficiently detailed or, more likely they are not up to date, updating fresh statements will need to be drafted.

Basic requirements of witness statements

It is surprising how many lawyers seem to be unaware of the need to follow the CPR. Anyone preparing a trial should read the requirements as to the format of witness statements, which can be found in CPR 32.8 and PD 32.17.

For instance, the statement must contain the heading as set out in CPR 32 PD17.1. It can be challenging to deal with witness statements from which this information is missing. At the final hearing the judge is likely to be irritated by a failure to comply, which is an own goal easily avoided by a litigant.

They must also be "*fully legible*" and "should normally be typed on one side of the paper only. Page numbers should be inserted and paragraphs should be numbered. All numbers, including dates should be expressed in figures rather than words. If any document is referred to, the reference to it should be included either in the margin, or in bold text in the body of the statement.

Exhibits must be clearly labelled with the exhibit number and paginated separately to the witness statement.

Witnesses who cannot speak English and/or read and write

A witness statement must comply with the requirements in PD 32 and, pursuant to CPR 22, be verified by a Statement of Truth.

Witnesses must prepare their statement in their own language if they do not speak English – see CPR 32 PD.18.1. They must then be translated by a certified translator. CPR PD 32.23.2 provides that the witness statement must be translated and certified. If this requirement has not been complied with it is self-evident that the witness cannot properly sign a Statement of Truth, because they do not know what is in the statement.

The same issue arises for a witness who cannot read and write. CPR 22.1 (9) specifies that the document must be certified by "an authorised person" and confirm that the document has been read to the witness, they appeared to understand it and approved it, the declaration of truth has been read and understood and that they have signed it or made a mark. See also CPR 22 PD .2 .4.

This issue is becoming increasingly important in housing conditions claims, as more tenants who do not speak English or cannot read and write are pursuing claims. I have been involved in a number of cases where it transpired only partway through the proceedings that the tenant could not possibly have read the earlier documents in the claim. The court will take a dim view if this only comes to light at all during the hearing. The claim is likely to be struck out if the claimant's solicitors cannot explain how being aware of the serious breach of the CPR.

Witness statements drafted for pre-trial applications

Occasionally there are issues which need to be addressed by the trial judge before the hearing. These can be last-minute disputes about the extent of disclosure, or the timing of service of witness statements. If the question concerns disclosure, it should have been dealt with long before, but the parties sometimes find themselves close to the hearing with outstanding arguments as to what should be disclosed.

Sometimes those arguments are so important that, for instance, they can lead to making a last-minute application for specific disclosure which ends up being listed before the trial judge. Such circumstances are thankfully rare and will cause significant wasted costs, which might be visited upon the party at fault. Occasionally, there are documents in the possession of one party or the other which can be obtained swiftly and produced, even on the day of trial.

Alternatively, one party or the other may serve their witness statements late. Arguments about service of statements are usually arid and pointless in most cases, despite what is said in *Mitchell* and the subsequent case law. If a party is not prejudiced the opponent by late service of witness statements, it is normally pointless to object to their admission. The attitude of most District Judges is that the parties should be encouraged to resolve the dispute on its merits, particularly if the trial is listed and would not take place if statements are not admitted.

However, there are some circumstances in which a judge might be inclined to refuse to admit witness statements and at this stage it need only be said that the question of trial preparation can throw up serious procedural issues which need to be addressed by the trial judge before the commencement of the evidence.

Any witness statement in support of arguments on legal issues will need to exhibit the chain of correspondence between the parties. If the facts relied on our clear from the correspondence, then the witness statement should not go into great depth about how and issue developed. The statement should just say that the correspondence is self-explanatory.

Witnesses as to the history of the tenancy

Although a good part of the dispute in a disrepair claim concerns the history of the condition of the property, in many cases the Housing Officer or other employees of the landlord will know facts on which the landlord will want to rely.

For instance, where a tenant has made no reports of defects yet the property is in a very poor state, it is necessary to investigate the reason for that situation. The tenant may have been living elsewhere, they may have been cultivating or selling drugs, or had other reasons why they did not want the landlord to attend at the property.

The evidence as to the history of the tenancy is unlikely to be found only on the repairs file. There may be material in the tenancy file which throw light on the situation. Often the tenancy application form will provide relevant material on the occupants.

The personal knowledge of the Housing Officer and others can expand upon those documents and notes. A detailed witness statement needs to be prepared, exhibiting the relevant diary entries and documents, explaining the landlord's point of view regarding the repairs history.

The witness statement should contain a reasoned chronological narrative, setting out the basic facts on which the landlord relies and referring to the documents for more detailed content. Brevity is desirable, because in a short trial (lasting only half a day or a day) the District Judge will not have time to read dozens of pages of history.

They will need to be told the basic facts and to be taken to the documentary exhibits which support the landlord's case.

The witness statement should refer to the exhibit by page number so any reference is easy to follow.

Chapter Summary / Key Takeaways

- The preparation of clear and informative witness statements is an essential skill. Because witnesses do not give evidence in chief, the judge needs to know the essential facts from the witness statement alone.

- You cannot rely on material beneficial to the landlord coming out in cross-examination. If there is a gap in the evidence, tenants will take advantage of it and the only weight to prevent that is to anticipate it.

- Getting the format and content of witness statements right will help the judge understand the facts and make it easier for the trial to be dealt with swiftly.

In the next chapter we will look briefly at the conduct of disrepair trials.

PART V

PREPARING FOR

FINAL HEARING / TRIAL

If the claim has continued despite your best efforts to refer it to alternative dispute resolution and to reduce the areas of dispute, you will need to prepare for trial. It is not possible in a book of this nature to give detailed instructions on how to prepare for a trial in general.

It is fair to say that you are likely to need lawyers, or at least a direct access barrister to help you from the outset. This is particularly true in getting ready to undertake a contested trial. I will therefore say a little about the particular features of preparing for disrepair claims which might be of help to those preparing for and attending trial.

CHAPTER TWENTY-ONE

THE FINAL HEARING / TRIAL

Housing conditions claims are usually listed before District Judges or, these days, Deputy District Judges. Occasionally they may be listed before County Court Judges or Recorders. This is not ideal, because any appeal from the latter will be more expensive and time-consuming.

It would not be possible in this book to address the conduct of a trial in any detail. Below I have included some features which may help in preparing the case to go to an advocate. That individual will know what to do in a trial, although I have made observations about peculiarities of disrepair trials.

Provision in the directions for a view of the property

In some cases, a landlord might want the Judge hearing the trial to see the property for themselves.

This is particularly so where a tenant is being difficult about the quality of works carried out but objectively, they are difficult to criticise. Alternatively, where the tenant's lifestyle is such that the landlord wants the court to make a judgement on the effect of any disrepair as against the loss of amenity caused by the tenant's own acts of waste.

If there is a hearing fixed before the trial to consider preparations, an application might be made for a view to take place. There is likely to be judicial reluctance unless good grounds can be proved. It helps if the property is very close to the court. These days, with the closure of so many county courts, that is often difficult to arrange. Further, judges are routinely given too much work and may not have time to fit in a view.

A view can be organised, if the court is willing, to start early in the morning on the day of trial, e.g. by 9:00 AM, and the judge can meet the parties at the building so that the trial can proceed as close to 10:00 AM as possible.

As an alternative to a view, the landlord might wish to attend and take multiple photographs or better still, produce a video showing the property, concentrating on issues which the landlord wishes to emphasise to the court. It will be necessary to file and serve copies and to ensure that viewing facilities are available at trial.

Ensuring that the judge can deal expeditiously with the hearing

Landlords need to be prepared to make up for failings on the part of claimant solicitors in trial preparation. Even if a reminder of the need for compliance is sent, it is common to receive a trial bundle which fails to comply with the Guidelines in one or more respects.

A Judge hearing a disrepair claim will sometimes have to get through 500–700 pages of trial bundle, a significant part of which will be relevant to the issues. They need every assistance they can be offered. They are unlikely to have been given any reading time by their listing staff and, if the trial is due to start at 10 AM and they arrive at court at 9 AM, they will have very limited time in which to consider the bundle. If that bundle is difficult to navigate, the judge is likely to begin the trial understandably annoyed.

As a result, it is sometimes necessary to prepare a trial bundle which complies with the Guidelines, so that the hearing can go ahead without the judge being inconvenienced from the outset.

Trial bundles

In the lead up to the trial it will be necessary to agree the content of a bundle with the other side, and for one or other party to create a PDF and possibly a paper version of that bundle.

Often, claimant solicitors do not appreciate the need to include certain documents in the trial bundle. This is particularly so if the evidence given in interim applications is still relevant to points in dispute at the trial. For instance, what a claimant tenant said in response to an application for further information or for specific disclosure may merit cross-examination at trial.

PDF bundles

It is essential that litigators are familiar with the "General Guidance on PDF Bundles" issued by the judiciary for the assistance of practitioners submitting them.[60]

Briefly, to comply with the guidance they must:

- be the subject of optical character recognition, so that the document becomes word-searchable and words can be highlighted;

- all documents should appear in portrait mode, but if the original is a landscape version then it should be inserted so it can be read with a 90° rotation clockwise.

---

[60] available at: https://www.judiciary.uk/wp-content/uploads/2020/05/GENERAL-GUIDANCE-ON-PDF-BUNDLES-f-1.pdf

- The default view should be 100%.

- if a core bundle is needed then it should be produced complying with the same requirements as a paper bundle.

- the number of PDF bundles should be limited so that the judge does not need to have a significant number of PDF files open during the hearing. If it is essential to separate documents, it should be done by document type rather than file size.

- bundles of particular types of document should generally be chronological if possible.

- all pages must be numbered, if possible using computer-generated numbering, or at least typing the numbers. Hand numbering is not permitted. If the bundle is split into sections then the page number should be preceded by the section identifying character, e.g. "B 17".

- pagination must not mask relevant details on the original document.

- scans should be of 300 dpi or less to avoid slow strolling or rendering all significant documents and all sections in bundles must be bookmarked for ease of navigation, with an appropriate description as the bookmark, together with the page number of the document.

- an index or table of contents should be prepared and if practicable each line should be hyperlinked to the individual document.

- all PDF files must contain a short version of the name of the case, the bundle number and the hearing date, e.g. "Claim No

………, Smith v Anytown Housing Association Ltd, bundle B, 1 July 2025".

- if adding supplementary bundle after the file has been transmitted to a judge, the party must check whether the additional material is to be added to the original or submitted as a separate file. But in any case, pages should be sequentially numbered. They should be added to the end of the bundle and the index should be updated.

- e-bundles must be less than 36 MB in aggregate if sent to the justice.gov eddress. The ejudiciary.net website will accept bundles of 150 MB in aggregate. Some courts will accept links to file uploads, e.g. Google Drive, OneDrive or similar.

- emails with a bundle attached for a remote hearing must contain in the subject line the case number, case name, hearing date, name of the judge and, in capitals "REMOTE HEARING".

Remote hearings

It is possible to undertake a disrepair trial remotely, though unlikely that the court will agree without good reason. Some claimants have a poor Internet connection and it is therefore difficult to see them clearly. This works to their advantage if there is any suggestion that they are not being truthful, as the judge will find it more difficult to see facial expressions and therefore to detect discomfort or nervousness.

Additionally, although views are rare in any event, is obviously not possible to organise one for a remote hearing.

Skeleton arguments

Many District Judges are not landlord and tenant lawyers and they are likely to need assistance with the background law relating to disrepair claims. This means providing a skeleton argument which addresses when liability will arise, how the court should approach the question of notice, whether there is an issue as to mitigation of any loss etc.

Further, in cases where the history of repairs to any particular defect is anything other than simple, it will be necessary to set out the page numbers of the relevant documents, so that the Judge can follow the history of each defect as evidenced by records, rather than as set out in the claimant's witness statement, which is unlikely to reflect the records.

It will also be necessary to deal with the expert evidence in the skeleton argument, which by the date of trial should be agreed. The claimant's surveyor is unlikely to have addressed the central issue of section 11 (3) or the history of repairs.

Scott schedules

The surveyors may have had some contact, although this should not be necessary if the landlord's surveyor has been efficient and has ordered the necessary works.

The court may expect the parties to prepare a Scott Schedule of the allegations, admissions and denials and costings and comments by each party.

It is very helpful to the advocate if a history of the defects is included, referring to page numbers of the bundle.

Attendance by surveyors

In the SCT the court will not normally allow experts to attend in any event.

If you end up on the FT, often the condition of the property on the day the surveyor inspected is not in dispute and it will be unnecessary to call the surveyors. This is a point which needs to be made both in the Defence and stressed in the skeleton argument. If there is no dispute between the parties as to the condition of the property and the works which need to be done, the value of the claim is commensurately lower and there is no arguable claim for specific performance.

The works as recommended by the tenant's surveyor will not ordinarily be of any relevance. This is because the nature and extent of remedial works is a matter for the landlord, provided that they act reasonably (discussed in Chapter Thirteen). If a tenant believes that the landlord's surveyor has not specified adequate works, unless the specification is clearly and obviously wrong or the tenant continues to suffer significant loss of amenity, the tenant's remedy lies in damages rather than an order that works should be carried out.

Therefore, even if there is some dispute as to method between the surveyors, it should be possible to avoid calling surveyors to give evidence at trial. This can be addressed in the Defence and repeated in the skeleton argument.

Procedure in the trial

Whether in the SCT or the FT, the trial follows the same format. The claimant tenant will give evidence first. They should not need to give any supplementary evidence once they are in the witness box but, for instance, works may have been carried out or further defects may be alleged to exist.

That might be because they have either occurred between the signing of the witness statement and the trial or are said to be original defects, not repaired by the landlord. Either way, the landlord needs to pre-empt any such allegation and to address it in evidence before the hearing.

It is important to anticipate that possibility and to obtain good, up-to-date evidence about the condition of the property, including confirmation that the tenant is happy with the current state of repair of the property.

Cross-examination

Cross-examination of a tenant will address issues such as how the tenant came to instruct solicitors, whether they did give notice as alleged in the claimant's pleadings and evidence or not, which defects they noticed themselves and which were pointed out by the claims prospector or the surveyor, the effect of defects, the reasons for tenant refusing access, the extent of any alleged loss and damage etc.

The landlord's surveyor (who will often be giving evidence of fact as well as opinion) and lay witness(es) will be cross-examined on methods of giving notice, repairs targets, specific delays in repairs, repair methods, policies etc.

Closing speeches and judgement

After the parties have called their evidence, the parties give their closing speeches, the claimant goes first and the defendant has the last word. The claimant has a right to reply to mistakes of law or errors of fact.

Judgement in disrepair claims is often reserved by the District Judge, because the issues can be factually complex and time is short in a trial listed for one day or even less.

THE FINAL HEARING / TRIAL

Costs to be paid by the claimant

Assuming that the defendant landlord is successful, the claim will be dismissed and the tenant will be ordered to pay the costs.

Costs to be paid by the defendant

These claims are a serious problem mostly because the costs incurred by tenant solicitors are so disproportionate to the amount of damages at stake that they are usually summarily assessed to a modest proportion of the original claim.

Tenant solicitors generate very substantial fees, often without much to show for them.

If the worst has happened, the claimant rarely ends up the true winner even in the Fast Track. There are numerous reasons why a claimant should not get their costs, or their full costs.

But in any event, many items of work will be obviously open to challenge and proportionality is likely to be of even greater importance. For this reason, when presented with an N260, it is worth getting a costs draughtsman to analyse it before the trial.

Fixed Recoverable Costs

The Ministry of Justice has implemented fixed costs in the fast track and in most money claims up to the value of £25,000, and costs are controlled on the Intermediate Track too, up to £100,000 claims. But housing conditions claims remain outside the regime for at least two years from October 2023. Unless the landlords lobby the Ministry of Justice before then to ensure that the exemption should end, I anticipate that claimant lawyers will benefit from a continued costs bonanza.

291

Bringing the fixed costs regime in for housing conditions claims would help to discourage the explosion of unmerited claims, which invariably result in disproportionate claims for costs. Fast track claims fall into four bands of complexity, Bands 1–4 from the simplest case to the most technical and complicated. Fixed sums will be awarded depending on the stage which the proceedings have reached: pre-issue, post-issue, post-allocation, pre-listing or post-listing, pre-trial. There are additional trial advocacy fees payable. Costs recovery will be limited minimum of nil and a maximum of what I calculate to be perhaps £15,000 when a complex claim goes all the way to trial.

Social landlords need to lobby the MoD and the government to ensure that the unfairness of this exclusion is ended and fixed costs are applied to these claims.

Costs in the SCT

In the meantime, in most claims, the SCT costs regime limits a successful claimant's total costs claim to less around £1,500 as the court will only order the costs appropriate to the SCT. However, if a *Birmingham City Council v Lee* order was made upon allocation, they may recover the costs on the FastTrack basis until repairs were finished.

A successful defendant can ask for their costs to be paid by the claimant if they can show that their conduct whether pre-action or during the claim was unreasonable, pursuant to CPR 27.14 (2) (g). It helps if the ICP team has made a reasonable offer which is still open to the tenant to accept, despite their solicitors' advice that they should not do so.

Dealing with *Birmingham City Council v Lee* at final hearing/trial

So even in the Small Claims Track, costs can be a problem because of the way *Birmingham CC v Lee* operates, as discussed in Chapter Ten in respect of claims settled under the Protocol. In my view the principle relies on a mistaken view as to the merits of these claims and also an arbitrary date for the termination of costs liability.

Lord Justice Hughes said (in paragraph 36) that the order should work as follows after a trial:

> *"if (a claimant) wins, (they) will have fast-track costs of making the claim up to that date. If she fails, she will have nothing. Any costs order, in favour of either side, relating to the period after (allocation) will remain governed by the allocation to the small claims track. The certain knowledge that that order will stand if she succeeds can inform any efforts to settle."*

He said that the court would expect that order to be made and it would *"inform any efforts to settle"*. Claimant solicitors thereby achieve uneven bargaining power, because it is phrased without qualification. If the case ends up on the SCT and the tenant recovers some modest amount in damages, but no order for specific performance, they are still arguably entitled to their costs on the FT basis to the date on which the works were completed. It is very unlikely these days that a tenant will succeed on their claim for specific performance, but the same applies.

B v Lee presupposes that a claimant has to succeed in their claim to benefit from the rule and that costs will only be awarded on the track to which the claim would have been allocated, but it can still be unfair.

For instance, in my view there is no logical justification for costs up until the works were completed when there was never any dispute that they would be carried out. Additionally, if the works were somewhat delayed for reasons which were partly found to be the fault of the landlord, the claimant may benefit from the rule

Alternatively, even if they were originally disputed, if those works were delayed by factors outside the landlord's control, e.g. because they were complex or because the tenant prevented their completion, the court might be tempted to make a costs order in favour of the claimant.

There is also no explicit prohibition on the claimant recovering costs where the claim was wrongly allocated to the FT (in hindsight because the amount in damages was less than the SCT limit and there was no order for specific performance), or because the ICP offered compensation in the same or similar amount to that awarded. In those circumstances the court must be dissuaded from any double counting, and should only enter judgment in the amount additional to that offered within the ICP. Then it may be that the tenant's success is so small as to be disregarded when it comes to costs. Further, in my view, the court should make an order for costs reflecting the fact that the claim was always only a SCT case in reality, and it was exaggerated by the claimant.

But hopefully, the landlord will have avoided the imposition of *Birmingham CC v Lee* order upon allocation. If the landlord has argued its corner properly at that stage, the court will have made an order that pre-allocation costs should be reserved to the judge at the final hearing.

At allocation a landlord should justify that order on the grounds it is for the judge who has heard the evidence to decide whether, even though claimant might recover some modest additional amount in damages over what they were awarded in the ICP, the claim was 'not worth the candle'.

If there is no *B v Lee* order, it gives the court scope for an order such as no order as to costs, or better still that the tenant's solicitors should because of unreasonable behaviour, either before and/or during the litigation.

Those limits can be overridden if either party can show that the behaved unreasonably – see CPR 27.14(1)(g). Given the way some claimant solicitors behave, this is a provision which is frequently relevant, although not necessarily easy to rely on successfully.

It is necessary to persuade the court that the claimant's conduct either before or during the proceedings was 'unreasonable' (CPR 27.14(2)(g)). This is defined according to a 1994 case, *Ridehalgh v Horsefield and*

Another & Ors [1994] 3 W.L.R. 462 at 232, per Sir Thomas Bingham MR:

> *"Unreasonable" also means what it has been understood to mean in this context for at least half a century. The expression aptly describes conduct which is vexatious, designed to harass the other side rather than advance the resolution of the case, and it makes no difference that the conduct is the product of excessive zeal and not improper motive. But conduct cannot be described as unreasonable simply because it leads in the event to an unsuccessful result or because other more cautious legal representatives would have acted differently. The acid test is whether the conduct permits of a reasonable explanation. If so, the course adopted may be regarded as optimistic and as reflecting on a practitioner's judgment, but it is not unreasonable.*

Wasted Costs

In some circumstances it may be possible to ask the court to make a "wasted costs" order against the claimant's solicitors as defined by section 51 (7) Senior Courts Act 1981, using the procedure in CPR 46.8. The court can also use CPR 44.11 to penalise misconduct on the part of a party or their legal representative. But case law has imposed strict limitations on the availability of the remedy.

The latest decision is *Williams-Henry v Associated British Ports Holdings Ltd & Anor (Re Wasted Costs)* [2024] EWHC 2415 (KB), in which the High Court judge denied a genuinely injured claimant her damages on the basis she had been dishonest about various aspects of her injury. The claim had generated huge sums in legal fees.

The court refused the defendant its wasted costs, on the basis that the claimant's solicitors conduct did not fall within the definition when considering 10 factors most pertinent to these claims.

Most important, the conduct must be improper. That includes behaving in a way which would ordinarily be sufficient to justify disbarment, striking off, suspension from practice or other serious penalty for the professional. You also have to get over the hurdle that the lawyers will almost certainly rely on professional privilege and say that their client has not waved privilege to allow them to tell the court what their instructions were. Further, just because a claim is doomed to fail does not mean the court will make an order. Finally, the applicant must show that the conduct caused the applicant to incur costs that they otherwise would not have incurred.

See the White Book for further helpful commentary.

Costs in the FT

if the claim has remained in the FT, either because the landlord has decided that they want to be able to recover their costs, or because they were unsuccessful in asking for allocation to the SCT, more substantial costs can be recovered by either party.

These days almost every tenant has legal expenses insurance, and in theory this should not be an issue. The court will ask for the defendant's N260 and costs will be summarily assessed. The court will usually order that those costs are payable within 14 or 21 days, as the money has to be obtained from the insurers.

It is not uncommon for a landlord to incur between £15,000 and £30,000 in costs defending a disrepair claim. These claims are more complex to defend than to pursue-usually a great deal of the response, both in terms of legal documents and evidence. After assessment, they are likely to recover a substantial part of that, providing they can show that the claimant put them to the trouble and expense of collecting the relevant evidence.

THE FINAL HEARING / TRIAL

Generally, the question of proportionality trumps all when it comes to costs in disrepair claims. It is the value at which the tenant's claim was put which is relevant to the question of proportionality in assessing costs which a claimant should pay, not the amount the landlord or the judge feels it would have been worth if it had succeeded. Additionally, if a claimant's conduct has unnecessarily increased the costs, whether by their being obstructive or failing to particularise their claim properly, the court will be more willing to reimburse the landlord's costs fully.

In the recent past numerous legal expenses insurers have repudiated liability when asked by the landlord to pay the costs ordered against the claimant by the court. They say that they are entitled to do so because the claimant told the court that they did not want to sue their landlord/had told the solicitors they wanted to stop the claim etc.

It may be possible to ask for a wasted costs order against the claimant's solicitors, but such orders are difficult to obtain these days. The courts protect their own, it seems (see above on costs in the SCT).

Damages in disrepair claims

In theory, landlords should not lose disrepair claims, because they will have spotted any cases in which there has been a genuine failure to repair and will have made offers to settle.

But some trials don't go so well; e.g. a claimant is believed despite the complete lack of corroboration of the alleged complaints, the landlord surveyor misses something in the records, or the claimant does not accept an offer (very rare).

Damages can be awarded on a variety of methods of calculation. I have already mentioned that the court can choose from the available cases, but most judges will rely on the method used in *Wallace v Manchester CC*, which gives a broad ranging tariff, which runs from a few hundred pounds a year to a few thousand.

If the court finds the landlord liable to some extent, it still needs to consider whether they should be reduced or wholly extinguished for a failure to mitigate on the part of the tenant. There are numerous ways in which this can be relevant, e.g.:

- failing to give notice of some or all of the defects

- refusals of access

- contributory behaviour e.g. failing to heat or ventilate

- whether the tenant continued to live in the property while the repairs were delayed

- delay in claiming or pursuit of the claim causing a worsening of the damage.

As I have said, the method of calculation is addressed in Dowding & Reynolds on Dilapidations and Luba et al on Housing Conditions. Hopefully it will be rare that you need to refer to it. In 30 years, I have only had to do so on a couple of occasions, so it is not worth spending significant time on the issue in this book, because we are concerned with defeating the claim rather than compromising or losing it.

Chapter Summary / Key Takeaways

- We have briefly looked at the conduct of disrepair trials, to the extent they differ from other County Court claims. There is plenty more that can be said about the conduct of the trial, probably another book's worth of work.

- Even if a claimant is successful at trial, they frequently do not recover significant costs from the landlord, because awards of damages are very much lower than those originally claimed and specific performance is rarely ordered.

- As this is primarily aimed at people who are involved in the preparation and pre-trial stages of the claim, and it is already quite long enough, I am going to refrain from going into further detail!

We have reached the end of the journey to trial, and I hope the book has been useful!

EPILOGUE / CONCLUSION

If you have got this far, you deserve a medal! I hope you will have taken on board the message. Unless you are working in an organisation which does not care about its tenants, most housing conditions claims are likely to be unjustified. With the material in this book, you should be able to begin to fight back against unjustified claims, or at least to know when to settle.

Please do tell me if you find any mistakes, of any sort.

APPENDIX ONE

EXAMPLE DEFENCE

This is single-spaced to compress it, but pleadings must be in 12-point font with 1.5 spacing. I have put in every possible point I could think of, so it is much longer than most Defences would be in practice.

IN THE COUNTY COURT SITTING AT
ANYTOWN CIVIL JUSTICE CENTRE

CLAIM NUMBER

MRS TENANT

MR TENANT

CLAIMANTS

AND

ANYTOWN CITY LANDLORD

DEFENDANT

DEFENCE

---

1. Paragraph 1 is admitted. The Claimants have been tenants of the Property since 5 June 2015 pursuant to a tenancy agreement signed by them on 1 June 2015. They have occupied it with their son, who is now aged 28.

2. Paragraph 2 is admitted. Further:

2.1. such obligations are subject to the condition that repairs should be done within a reasonable time of notification, and to a reasonable standard having regard to the age, character and prospective life of the dwelling house and the locality in which it is situated.

2.2. by Clause 10 of the tenancy agreement, it was an express term of the said tenancy that the Tenants would immediately report to the Landlord any blocked drains, defects in the structure and all other repairs required on the part of the Landlord and that the Tenants would refer to the leaflet "Getting Repairs Done" and follow the procedure set out therein in the event of the occurrence of disrepair.

2.3. the Tenants were under a duty to use the premises in a tenant-like manner.

2.4. By clause 13 of the tenancy agreement the Tenants were and remain under a duty to allow the Landlord access at all reasonable times to carry out inspections and any works considered necessary.

2.5. In determining the standard of repair required by the covenant implied by the Landlord and Tenant Act 1985 ("the 1985 Act") and under section 4 of the Defective Premises Act 1972 ("the 1972 Act"), the Court is entitled to have regard to the age, character and prospective life of the dwelling house and the locality in which it is situated, pursuant to Section 11 (3) of the Landlord and Tenant Act 1985.

2.6. As to section 9A and 10 of the 1985 Act, it is admitted that the Defendant is obliged to maintain the Property so that it is reasonably fit for human habitation, subject to the matters set out in section 9A (2) and (3).

2.7. It is admitted that section 4 the 1972 Act imposed a duty on the Landlord to take such care as was reasonable in all the circumstances to see that the Tenants were reasonably safe from damage to their property caused by a relevant defect and averred that such relevant defect means a defect in the state of the premises arising from or continuing because of an act or omission by the Defendant which constituted a failure by it to carry out its obligation to the Tenants for the maintenance or repair of the premises. It is denied that the Landlord was under any further duty to the Tenants. Further the standard of repair required is limited to that required by section 11 of the Landlord and Tenant Act 1985.

2.8. It is denied that the pleading in respect of section 4 of the 1972 Act is relevant so far as it relates to taking care to ensure that personal injury is not caused to the Tenants by a relevant defect, there being no subsequent allegation that the Tenants have suffered any personal injury because of such defects.

3. As to paragraph 3, it is admitted that the Defendant has not supplied a copy of the tenancy agreement to the Claimants. The Tenants should have in their possession a copy of the tenancy agreement as handed to them upon commencement of the tenancy.

3.1. Further, the Tenants have always been and are entitled to request a copy of that document outside the legal process and at no cost to themselves through a Subject Access Request.

3.2. It is denied that the Tenants are entitled to seek disclosure through the Pre-Action Protocol for Housing Conditions claims until they have complied with paragraph 4 of the Protocol and have attempted alternative dispute resolution or provided good reason as to why they should not at least attempt a cost free and speedy resolution to their concerns.

3.3. Pursuant to paragraph 4.2 of the Pre-Action Protocol, alternatives for social housing tenants include the repairs, complaints and/or arbitration procedure as the first step and, if that does not resolve matters, recourse to the Housing Ombudsman.

3.4. By a letter dated 30 August 2024 the Landlord informed the Claimants' Solicitors that they were obliged to consider alternative dispute resolution and referred them to the Landlord's formal complaints procedure, warning them of adverse consequences for failure to do so provided inter alia by paragraphs 13-16 of the Practice Direction Relating to Pre-Action Conduct and Protocols.

3.5. The Defendant then put into operation Stage 1 of its formal Complaints Process. It investigated the history of reports of defects and works done and concluded that certain works should be carried out, in accordance with the plans already made by its repairs team. It did not recommend the payment of any compensation because no breach of duty or service failure had been found in the investigation. It sent the Claimants a Stage 1 Finding on 21 September 2024.

3.6. By a further letter dated 23 September 2024, the Landlord informed the Tenants that if they were unhappy with the finding by the Landlord within Stage 1 of the complaints procedure, they should take their complaint further, using Stage 2 of the procedure.

3.7. The Claimants' Solicitors ignored the request to consider and attempt alternative dispute resolution and, instead, in a further letter dated 21 October 2024, disclosed a report by a Mr Anthony Smith, a Surveyor who had, according to the Claimants' Solicitors been instructed as a *"Single Joint Expert"*, despite no such instruction having been given by the Defendant. The report was unnecessary as works had already been specified and ordered within the ICP, which the Claimants' solicitors were told by a letter dated 23 September

2024 and so knew at the date of instruction. Further, it has been prepared without any reference to:

3.7.1. the records of the concerns of which the Defendant has been notified by the Claimants, which reflect:

3.7.1.1. the timing and extent of such notification and

3.7.1.2. the nature of their concerns as they were contemporaneously expressed by the Claimants themselves;

3.7.2. the repairs and improvements history as carried out by the Landlord;

3.7.3. the extent of any effect on the amenity of the Claimants of any alleged defect;

3.7.4. the effect of the occupation by the Claimants themselves on the state of repair and condition of the Property, for instance the manner in which the Tenants have used the Property, the condition and state of cleanliness in which they have kept it, the degree to which they have carried out or failed to carry out any minor repairs or improvements themselves and the standard to which they have decorated it;

3.7.5. section 11 (3) of the 1985 Act, so that no account has been taken of the age, character and locality of the dwelling house, or of its prospective life,

and it is therefore denied that the opinions expressed in the report should be given any weight by the court, save to record the physical condition in which Mr Smith found the Property during his visit on a date unknown prior to 15 October 2024.

3.8. By letter dated 7 November 2024, the Landlord reminded the Claimants' Solicitors of their obligation to advise their clients to consider alternative dispute resolution and queried the circumstances of their instruction.

3.9. Further, since the Defendant received the Letter of Claim, the Claimants have persistently refused to give access to its employees to inspect and to remedy any defects which might be found, telling the Defendant that their solicitors had advised them to refuse such access.

3.10. On 15 December 2024, the Claimants' Solicitors issued a premature, unnecessary and vexatious claim, despite the clear requests to consider ADR referred to above, and their knowledge that the Landlord was attempting to enter to inspect and carry out. In the circumstances the claim amounts to a serious breach of the Pre-Action Protocol and the Practice Direction and is an abuse of process.

3.11. The Claimants have served notice of funding by way of conditional fee agreement, which is not backed by any insurance policy, so that they remain personally liable for the costs incurred by their Solicitors.

3.12. The remainder of this Defence is pleaded without prejudice to the Landlord's contention that these proceedings should be struck as they are an abuse of process and, or otherwise likely to obstruct the just disposal of the proceedings and because there has been a failure to comply with the said Practice Direction and Pre-Action Protocol.

4. Paragraph 4 is admitted, save that it is denied that the obligation requires or imposes any further duty than that under the 1985 Act or within the tenancy. The implied covenant not to derogate from grant is not relevant to this claim.

5. Save as admitted herein below, paragraph 5 is denied.

APPENDIX ONE

PARTICULARS OF DEFECTS ADMITTED AND OF DENIALS

5.1. Throughout the duration of the tenancy the Claimants have reported defects and problems experienced in the Property, as set out in the repairs records, full particulars of which exceed three folios and will be served if this claim proceeds.

5.2. The Defendant has an extensive Estates department, which maintains approximately 15,000 properties in and around Anytown. It is specifically denied that repairs are not carried out because of impecuniosity, as pleaded by the Claimants. In administering its housing stock, a landlord is entitled to have regard to the likely cost/benefit ratio of any works of repair or improvement in its determination of the appropriate standard of repair.

5.3. On 4 March 2022 the Claimants complained to the Defendant that they were unhappy with the condition of their kitchen and of their bathroom and sought replacement of both. The Defendant responded by email dated 14 March 2022 and informed them that a full survey of the Property was to be ordered. Through administrative error the survey was not carried out until 12 June 2022.

5.4. By email dated 18 June 2022 the Defendant informed the Claimants that the survey had revealed the need to carry out damp proofing works and re-plastering works behind the kitchen units and to fill any gaps in the plaster behind the units.

5.5. In the same email the Defendant informed the Claimant that it was to carry out the following works:

5.5.1. on 26 September 2022, rewiring of the kitchen and works to the distribution board;

5.5.2. on 28 September 2022, refitting of the kitchen after those works;

the units were not to be replaced but repaired with new plinths, replacement drawers and easing of all doors, and with better support to the worktops;

5.5.3. damp contractors were engaged to replace the extractor fan in the kitchen and in the bathroom with an upgraded version of those fans (such fans not being in disrepair but being replaced by upgraded and more modern versions, such that they were works of improvement rather than repair within the meaning of the 1985 Act);

5.5.4. the bath was to be replaced after the kitchen work was completed and a mould wash to the bathroom ceiling was to be considered after the bath had been replaced (it being admitted that the bath was in need of replacement, but not that it caused any significant loss of amenity, and otherwise it being denied that such works were works which remedied any defect within the meaning of the 1985 Act;

5.5.5. loft insulation was to be investigated and improved (such works not being within the ambit of the 1985 Act, in that they were improvements to the design of the Property).

5.6. By reply email dated 18 October 2022 the Claimants repeated their request for the replacement of the kitchen units because of the dampness. They made a further complaint, which was further investigated in October 2022.

5.7. Following such investigation, the Landlord decided that the kitchen would not be replaced as it was still fit for purpose and there was no structural damp in the wall behind the units, nor was there any mould or water damage to the backs of the units. In January 2020 contractors employed by the Landlord, "ACME Damp Control", repaired some damp areas in the kitchen wall behind. That damp was caused by condensation generated by two unvented tumble dryers belonging to the Claimants, situated in front of the damaged wall. Such damage amounts to an 'act of waste', for which the Claimants have not yet been recharged.

5.8. A decision was made to replace the sink base unit and repair the existing, together with a section of worktop to the left-hand side of the sink where there was some water damage where the mastic seal had broken down.

5.9. The Claimant were informed that their kitchen would be replaced in 2022, pursuant to the "Keystone" planned works kitchen program, which the First Claimant accepted orally at the time.

5.10. Accordingly, it is denied that the damp in the kitchen was caused by a defect within the meaning of section 11 of the 1985 Act, the Defendant's case being that the cause of such damp (and that of a small area in the lounge) has not yet been definitively ascertained.

5.11. Further, when contractors attended the Property in October 2022, they discovered that they needed to rewire it completely because they found further faults on several circuits which they could not rectify. The rewiring was due to begin on 16 January 2023 but on 9 January 2023 the Claimants informed the Defendant that they would refuse access for the rewiring because they had obtained an independent damp survey which alleged that the whole house was damp and they had instructed solicitors.

5.12. Since that date, the Claimants have allowed the Defendant into the Property on two occasions but have refused further access, either for inspections or for the carrying out of works.

5.13. As a result of the refusal of access and consequential breach of tenancy on the part of the Claimants, the Defendant was and remains unable to carry out such works as are necessary, or even to inspect the Property to determine what is necessary.

5.14. Further details of defects found and admitted are contained either in the report of Mr Paul Surveyor, dated March 2024 and attached as Appendix 1.

5.15. Once the works specified by Mr Surveyor and those before him have been carried out, the Landlord will be able to make a judgement whether any further works are necessary to alleviate any disrepair at the Property. Such a decision is a matter for the Landlord, rather than for the Claimants or their Solicitors or Surveyor, save that the Landlord as landlord may take into account the views and opinions of others in deciding how best to remedy any disrepair found at the Property.

5.16. In repairing such defects, the landlord of a property is entitled to approach works according to good Estate management principles in a reasonable manner, carrying out such works as it considers necessary and proportionate and, for instance, not being obliged to replace in the first instance rather than repair when necessary and to replace only when repairs prove ineffective.

5.17. Accordingly, it is admitted that, between March and October 2023 the Defendant was aware of alleged defects with the kitchen and the bathroom of the Property as set out in the Claimants' complaint concerning the condition of those rooms but not otherwise. It is further admitted that upon inspection in October it was found necessary to carry out works to both those rooms, but not admitted that such works reflect the existence of "disrepair" within the meaning of the 1985 Act.

5.18. If, which is not admitted for the purposes of these proceedings, any liability in damages for loss of amenity arises as a result of the Defendant's failure to proceed with the inspection in March 2023, such failure can be investigated within Stage 2 of the complaints process and, if fault is found in the service level offered by the Defendant, if compensation can be offered to the Claimants within that cost-free process.

5.19. Further, if during the Stage 2 complaints process further allegations are made by the Claimants of any breach of duty or failure in service levels on the part of the Defendant, such complaints can be considered and adjudicated upon within that process, at no cost to either party and without involving lawyers. If the Claimants remained dissatisfied with the result of their complaint within Stage 2, they can complain to the Ombudsman or pursue legal proceedings, in which the Council will rely on the Stage 1 and 2 findings to limit the amounts in dispute.

5.20. If, which is denied, the Claimants are entitled to any damages for loss of amenity, it is averred that recovery by way of this claim is unnecessary and premature and that such claims should not be permitted to proceed until alternative dispute resolution has been attempted.

5.21. Further, the Defendant will rely on section 11(3) of the Landlord and Tenant Act 1985 in that the standard of repair was reasonable having regard to the age, character and prospective life of the dwelling house and the locality it which it is situated and taking into account particularly that the Claimants occupy the Property pursuant to a secure tenancy at a rent which is substantially less than the open market rent of privately owned housing in the area.

6. As to paragraph 6, it is admitted that the Claimants have reported defects as set out in the records of such reports contained in the computerised repairs files, full particulars of which exceed three folios and will be disclosed if this claim proceeds to a trial.

PARTICULARS OF DENIAL

6.1. As pleaded above, it is admitted that Mr Atkinson inspected the Property and found it in the physical condition set out in his report.

6.2. To the extent that there are differences between the opinion of Mr Paul Jones, Surveyor for the Defendant and Mr Atkinson, the Defendant relies on the evidence and opinion of Mr Surveyor, as it is entitled to do as landlord.

6.3. The instruction of Mr Atkinson was unnecessary and premature, the Claimants having failed to pursue the complaints procedure properly or at all.

6.4. If, following further investigation, the Claimants are found to have suffered unnecessary loss of amenity as a result of any breach of duty on the part of the Defendant, they should be compensated within the complaints procedure.

6.5. It is admitted that, if they remain dissatisfied with any offers made pursuant to Stage 2 of the complaints process, or by the Ombudsman, the Claimants are entitled to proceed with litigation and to rely upon the findings of Mr Atkinson.

6.6. The Defendant reserves its position in relation to the findings by Mr Atkinson so far as they differ from those of Mr Surveyor and will plead further only if necessary in the event that this matter is not struck out, and after any stay imposed by the Court has expired.

6.7. It is not admitted that the Claimants have suffered discomfort and inconvenience because the house has been damp and has smelt of damp for an inordinately long period of time as a result of any breach of duty on the part of the Defendant.

The activities of the Claimants have caused/created significant condensation dampness, as set out in the report by Paul Jones. Further, some condensation dampness has been caused/created by defects in design rather than defects in the structure of the Property and are not actionable under the 1985 Act.

6.8. If, which is not admitted, the Claimants have suffered any loss of amenity, damage to property or other damage, such damage was caused by the Claimants' own 'acts of waste' or other failures to heat/ventilate/use the Property properly so as to avoid the formation of condensation damp and resulting mould, and they have failed to mitigate their loss.

6.9. It is specifically denied that the Defendant has refused, persistently or at all, to carry out repair work to merely as alleged, or that it has treated the Claimants in a contemptuous manner or in any way other than as secure tenants entitled to seek the repair of their Property pursuant to statute and under the tenancy agreement. It is denied that the Claimants are entitled to any higher standard of repair or remedy than that provided by the Act or the tenancy agreement, so that it is denied for example that they are entitled to insist on the installation of a new kitchen or bathroom, as claimed by them.

6.10. Further, to the extent that the works carried out and/or ordered by the Defendant involve works of improvement, there is no obligation on the Defendant to carry out such works and no liability in damages arises from any failure to order or to carry them out.

6.11. The Defendant has investigated, identified and remedied, or attempted to remedy the causes of dampness and mould growth so far as they are caused by disrepair and has gone beyond its contractual and statutory duties in the remedy of design defects, as set out in the records of repairs and above.

6.12. As to the claim for special damages, it is denied that the Claimants have suffered any damage as a result of any breach of duty on the part of the Defendant. By reason of the matters set out above, it is denied that the Defendant has been in breach of its duty under the tenancy or otherwise.

6.13. If, which is denied, the Defendant has failed to repair the property in accordance with its duty it is denied that any such failure has caused any damage which is more than "de minimis", as pleaded above. Further, the Claimants have failed wholly to mitigate any damage being suffered by refusing the Defendant access to carry out inspections and repairs.

PARTICULARS OF ACTS OF WASTE/FAILURE TO MITIGATE

6.14. The Claimants have, inter alia:

6.14.1. failed to give notice of the existence of defects within the Defendant's repairing obligations properly or at all;

6.14.2. failed to follow-up when works have not been carried out to their satisfaction if, (which is denied), they did give notice of such defects;

6.14.3. used an unvented condensing tumble dryer in the Property and have dried clothes on the radiators, significantly increasing the moisture levels in the Property;

6.14.4. spilt water in the bathroom in excessive quantities;

6.14.5. failed to ensure that the bathroom window was open during or after bathing activities;

6.14.6. failed to clean off condensation and/or mould as it has formed on surfaces in the property;

6.14.7. failed otherwise to use the extractor fans fitted in the property properly and have removed the fuses from them;

6.14.8. failed otherwise to ventilate the property by opening windows as necessary;

6.15. if, which is denied, after notification by the Claimants, such repairs as were necessary were not done within a reasonable period of time, they have failed to give further notice to the Defendant properly or at all and to follow the repairs reporting and the formal complaints procedure, which will be referred to at trial.

6.16. If the Claimants had pursued the formal complaints procedure through Stage 2, even if there were "disrepair" in the Property within the meaning of the Act or tenancy, and the Defendant had failed to repair it, such disrepair would have been detected and remedied by that process and the Claimants would not have continued to suffer any loss.

6.17. The Claimants' claim to any special damages is denied and they are put to proof thereof by the production of receipts or the date and place of purchase of all items set out therein and the facts on which they rely to prove that the items were damaged by any breach of duty rather than condensation dampness.

6.18. The Claimants are not entitled to specific performance of the repairing covenants, as since January 2024 they have refused to allow the Defendant access to inspect and repair save on the occasions set out in the evidence to be provided.

7. Paragraph 7 is denied for the reasons set out above. The Claimants' surveyor did not find that the Property was unfit human habitation and section 9A the 1985 Act is irrelevant, as is section 4 of the DPA 1972, there being no allegations of damage to property or injury to persons.

8. As to paragraph 8, the contents of paragraph 3 to 6 above are repeated, and it is averred that litigation is entirely unnecessary and that the Claimants have themselves caused any continuing loss of amenity by refusing access to the Defendant to carry out inspections and repairs. These proceedings should be stayed pending the

outcome of that alternative dispute resolution.

9. As to paragraph 9, the Claimants' belief as to the merits of the internal complaints process is not relevant, as their solicitors have advised them not to cooperate either in the complaints process or regarding access. The factual history as set out above reflects the nature of the breach on the part of the Claimants' Solicitors failure to comply with the requirements of the Pre-Action Protocol and Practice Direction to undertake alternative dispute resolution if practicable.

10. As to paragraph 10, the issue of these proceedings was entirely unnecessary for the reasons given above and the Defendant has on numerous occasions made proposals that the Claimants should pursue Stage 2 of the complaints process. The Defendant repeats that request, relying on the law set out in the Claimants' own Particulars of Claim.

11. As to the Prayer:

11.1. it is denied that the Claimants are entitled to proceed with unnecessary litigation in circumstances where an alternative and cost-free remedy is available to them. The claim should be stayed for alternative dispute resolution.

11.2. In the circumstances, it is denied that the Claimants are entitled to any damages at this point. If that alternative dispute resolution is unsuccessful and the Claimants remain dissatisfied with the remedies offered by the Defendant, it is admitted that the Claimants may be entitled to modest compensation for the delay in arranging a survey between March and October 2024 (and/or for any further breaches of duty or failures of service detected during the complaints process), but averred that such compensation would and should have been sought within the cost-free complaints process, so that no costs would be payable if this claim proceeds without completion of that process;

11.3. it is denied that the Claimants are entitled to an order for specific performance, as the failure to carry out works at the Property arises because of the Claimants' own refusal of access, rather than any refusal by the Defendant to carry out works of repair and/or improvement as necessary and as already ordered by the Defendant in 2023/the works necessary to remedy the defects found were completed shortly after receipt of notice given for the first time in the Letter of Claim, and no significant defects remain;

11.4. The Claimants' entitlement to interest is denied, no sums being due in damages;

11.5. the claim should be allocated to the Small Claims Track, there being no arguable claim for injunctive relief or for damages in excess of £1,000.

12. Further and in any event, the Claimants' claim is statute barred in so far as any act or default occurred more than six years prior to the issue of the claim, or, to the extent that any allegation of physical injury is made, three years prior to the date of issue.

13. Save as herein admitted the Claimants' claim is denied as if set out and specifically traversed seriatim.

DEFENDANT COUNSEL'S NAME

STATEMENT OF TRUTH

The Defendant believe that the facts stated in this Defence are true. I understand that proceedings for contempt of court may be brought against anyone who makes, or causes to be made, a false statement in a document verified by a statement of truth without an honest belief in its truth.

I am duly authorised by the Defendant to sign this statement

Full name: ....

Name of Defendant's Solicitor's firm:
Anytown City Landlord Legal Services

Signed ....   position or office held: Solicitor

Dated this .... day of ....20..

By

....

To the Claimants

And to the District Judge

BIBLIOGRAPGHY

Dowding & Reynolds (7th edition, 2022), N Dowding and K Reynolds Sweet & Maxwell/Thomson Reuters

Housing Conditions, Tenants' Rights (6th edition, 2019) HHJ J Luba KC, C O'Donnell and G Peaker, Legal Action Group

INDEX

Access to Justice ... 22, 83

Alternative Dispute Resolution ... 29, 31, 35, 39-46, 69-84, 91, 92, 108, 109, 183, 185, 187, 193, 213, 219, 223-232, 233, 234, 235, 239, 308

Breach of duty ... 20, 39, 54, 59, 98, 124, 198, 306, 313, 314, 315

Cavity Wall Insulation ... 119, 128, 145, 155, 161-162

Cladding ... 135, 163

Claims Management Companies ... 4, 5, 23, 24, 58, 75, 96, 104, 164

Compensation ... 4, 22, 26, 27, 29, 34, 36, 42, 43, 58, 59, 77, 96, 97, 103, 104, 105, 106-107, 108, 109, 110, 112, 119, 157, 225, 227, 229, 230, 294

Complaints policy ... 16, 17, 19, 90, 93, 94-100

Complaint Handling Code ... 17, 42, 85, 87, 90, 92-93

Condensation ... 76, 105, 106, 119, 121, 124, 147, 148, 149, 154, 155, 156, 157, 158-159, 160, 163, 164, 171, 172, 177, 178, 200, 205, 211, 218, 310, 314, 315, 316, 317

Conduct of Authorised Persons Rules 2014, The ... 24

Costs ... 5-8, 22, 27, 32, 40, 41, 83-84, 108-109, 110, 111, 112-113, 116-117, 191-192, 246, 247-249, 259, 291-292, 295-297

Counterclaims ... 22, 43, 45, 52, 61, 63-67, 118, 174-175, 207, 242

Damages (See also Compensation) … 1, 34, 47, 48, 49, 50, 51, 52, 53, 55, 66-67, 106-107, 111, 113, 116, 123, 131, 137, 157, 168, 171, 180, 204, 205, 221, 245, 248, 249, 252, 253, 254, 255, 256, 289, 294, 297-299

Damp (see also Condensation) … 5, 13, 52, 55, 76, 92, 98, 105, 106, 121, 138, 139, 145, 147, 148, 149, 150, 151, 157, 158, 159-160, 167, 171, 177-178, 200

   … rising … 132, 138, 139, 145, 152-153

   … penetrating…52, 55, 150-151, 152-153, 159-160, 200, 205

Decent Homes Programme … 14, 119-120, 154, 156-157, 162, 177

Disability … 117, 120-121, 141

Disclosure … 33, 56, 117, 183-193, 233, 263-274, 277, 285

Expert evidence (see also, surveyors) … 34, 137, 159, 167, 172, 178, 195, 197-212, 217-218, 255, 288

Fast Track … 111, 112, 228, 246, 248, 259, 263, 265-266, 291-292

Fitness for human habitation … 9, 21-22, 25, 96, 105-108, 121, 123-124, 131-133, 158, 164, 165-174, 176, 180, 181, 208-209, 254

Flats … 49, 53, 55, 162, 201

Grenfell … 85, 100

Housing Health and Safety Rating System (HHSRS) … 14, 156, 157, 159

Housing Ombudsman … See Ombudsman

Injunctions ... 34, 56-57, 65, 80, 88, 90, 91, 92, 139, 151, 152, 157, 174, 179, 213, 217, 219-220, 222, 226, 227, 238, 245, 248, 249, 252, 253, 255, 256

... Access ... 56-57, 171, 230, 256

Intermediate Track ... 247, 263, 291

Ishak, Awaab ... 56-57, 86-90, 100, 137, 157, 171

Law Society, The ... 22

Leasehold ... 151, 162

Letter of Claim (LOC) ... 7, 20, 21, 23, 25, 26, 29, 31, 32, 33, 34, 35, 39, 41, 42, 56, 57, 59, 72, 75, 76, 82, 88, 89, 90, 96, 104, 113, 115, 123, 137, 145, 146, 164, 166, 171, 183, 185, 195, 200, 201, 220

Liability ... 13, 48, 50-51, 52, 55, 98, 111, 123-143, 146-147, 148, 150, 153, 155, 157, 158, 159, 169, 176, 180, 197, 201, 202, 203, 204-205, 211, 222, 288, 293, 297

Mandatory alternative dispute resolution ... See Alternative Dispute Resolution

Monitoring (see Remote Monitoring Systems)

Ombudsman (see also Complaint Handling Code) ... 9, 13, 14, 16, 19, 22, 24, 26, 30, 33, 42, 73, 74, 85, 86, 87, 90-94, 97, 98, 108, 121, 137, 148, 154, 177, 224, 225, 227, 229, 306, 313, 314

Particulars of Claim (POC) ... 220, 241, 273

Possession order ... 22, 43, 63, 64, 65, 66, 118, 132

Poverty ... 92, 98, 106, 117, 120, 130, 156, 159, 163, 178

325

Pre-Action Protocol … 1, 16, 25, 29, 30-31, 39-46, 71, 72-73, 79, 80, 81, 183-193, 238, 269

Precast Reinforced Concrete (PRC) … 133-134

Regulator of Social Housing … 17, 86, 154

Remote hearings … 190, 238, 287

Remote monitoring systems … 86, 119, 148-149, 160, 164, 173, 178, 212, 271

Repairing covenant … 49, 56, 124, 125, 132, 219, 317

Right to Repair … 74

Small Claims … 22, 109, 139, 220, 221, 228, 246, 248, 249, 250, 252, 263, 292, 293, 319

Social Housing White Paper (2020) … 85-87, 156

Standard of repair … 123-143, 169, 201, 208, 304, 305, 309, 313

Statement of Truth … 236, 254, 276, 319-320

Structural defects … 150, 152, 153-154

Summary judgment … 64, 108, 214-218, 251, 254, 255, 264

Surveyors … 25, 34, 89, 96, 104, 105, 127, 129, 130, 133, 148, 153, 159, 160, 161, 162, 163, 172, 175, 178, 197-209, 211, 218, 219, 253, 273, 289, 290

Trial Bundle … 269, 284, 285-287, 288

Ventilation … 92, 119, 121, 146, 149, 155, 157, 159, 161, 163-164, 165, 170, 172. 178, 211

Windows ... 119, 145, 146, 162-163, 175

Witness statements ... 189, 190, 215, 217, 222, 230, 235, 237, 242, 259, 264, 275–279, 288

MORE BOOKS BY
LAW BRIEF PUBLISHING

A selection of our other titles available now:-

'A Practical Guide to Probation Breaches and Other Applications' by Mark Thomas
'A Practical Guide to Remarriage and Divorce' by Cordelia Williams & Claire Howard
'A Practical Guide to Privacy, Transparency, Reporting Restrictions and Closed Proceedings in the Court of Protection' by Laura Mannering
'Beaumont on Barristers – A Guide to Defending Disciplinary Proceedings (Second Edition)' by Marc Beaumont
'A Practical Guide to Payments for Environmental Services' by Ben Sharples
'A Practical Guide to the Law of Pregnancy and Maternity at Work' by Rebecca Thomas
'A Practical Guide to Redundancy – Second Edition' by Philip Hyland & Collette Moore
'A Practical Guide to International Issues for Scottish Family Lawyers' by Susie Mountain, Donna McKay, Ken MacDonald
'A Practical Guide to the Law on Deprivation of Liberty' by Ben Troke
'A Practical Guide to Rights over Airspace and Subsoil – Second Edition' by Daniel Gatty
'A Practical Guide to the Law in Relation to Inquests' by Ramya Nagesh
'A Practical Guide to the Construction and Rectification of Wills and Trust Instruments (Second Edition)' by Edward Hewitt
'A Practical Guide to Data Protection in Social Housing' by Clare Paterson
'A Practical Guide to Spousal Maintenance – Second Edition' by Liz Cowell
'A Practical Guide to International Parental Child Abduction Law (England and Wales)' by Dr Onyója Momoh
'A Practical Guide to Deprivation of British Citizenship' by Sean Ell
'A Practical Guide to Commercial Property Service Charges' by Rachel Garton
'A Practical Guide to Clinical Negligence – Third Edition' by Geoffrey Simpson-Scott (Geoff)
'A Practical Guide to the Rights of Grandparents in Children Proceedings – Second Edition' by Stuart Barlow

'The Electronic Communications Code: A Practical Guide – Second Edition' by Kerry Bretherton KC, James Castle, Mark Loveday

'A Practical Guide to the Independent School Standards – September 2023 Edition' by Sarah McKimm

'A Practical Guide to Estate Administration and Crypto Assets' by Richard Marshall

'A Practical Guide to Parental Alienation in Private and Public Law Children Cases' by Sam King QC & Frankie Shama

'Contested Heritage – Removing Art from Land and Historic Buildings' by Richard Harwood QC, Catherine Dobson, David Sawtell

'The Limits of Separate Legal Personality: When Those Running a Company Can Be Held Personally Liable for Losses Caused to Third Parties Outside of the Company' by Dr Mike Wilkinson

'A Practical Guide to Transgender Law' by Robin Moira White & Nicola Newbegin

'A Practical Guide to 'Stranded Spouses' in Family Law' by Mani Singh Basi

'A Practical Guide to Residential Freehold Conveyancing' by Lorraine Richardson

'A Practical Guide to Pensions on Divorce for Lawyers' by Bryan Scant

'A Practical Guide to Challenging Sham Marriage Allegations in Immigration Law' by Priya Solanki

'A Practical Guide to Digital Communications Evidence in Criminal Law' by Sam Willis

'A Practical Guide to Legal Rights in Scotland' by Sarah-Jane Macdonald

'A Practical Guide to New Build Conveyancing' by Paul Sams & Rebecca East

'A Practical Guide to Inherited Wealth on Divorce' by Hayley Trim

'A Practical Guide to Practice Direction 12J and Domestic Abuse in Private Law Children Proceedings' by Rebecca Cross & Malvika Jaganmohan

'A Practical Guide to Confiscation and Restraint' by Narita Bahra QC, John Carl Townsend, David Winch

'A Practical Guide to the Law of Forests in Scotland' by Philip Buchan

'A Practical Guide to Health and Medical Cases in Immigration Law' by Rebecca Chapman & Miranda Butler

'A Practical Guide to Bad Character Evidence for Criminal Practitioners by Aparna Rao

'A Practical Guide to Extradition Law post-Brexit' by Myles Grandison et al

'A Practical Guide to Hoarding and Mental Health for Housing Lawyers' by Rachel Coyle

'Stephens on Contractual Indemnities' by Richard Stephens
'A Practical Guide to the EU Succession Regulation' by Richard Frimston
'A Practical Guide to Solicitor and Client Costs – Second Edition' by Robin Dunne
'Constructive Dismissal – Practice Pointers and Principles' by Benjimin Burgher
'A Practical Guide to Religion and Belief Discrimination Claims in the Workplace' by Kashif Ali
'A Practical Guide to the Law of Medical Treatment Decisions' by Ben Troke
'Fundamental Dishonesty and QOCS in Personal Injury Proceedings: Law and Practice' by Jake Rowley
'A Practical Guide to the Law in Relation to School Exclusions' by Charlotte Hadfield & Alice de Coverley
'A Practical Guide to Divorce for the Silver Separators' by Karin Walker
'The Right to be Forgotten – The Law and Practical Issues' by Melissa Stock
'A Practical Guide to Planning Law and Rights of Way in National Parks, the Broads and AONBs' by James Maurici QC, James Neill et al
'A Practical Guide to Election Law' by Tom Tabori
'A Practical Guide to the Law in Relation to Surrogacy' by Andrew Powell
'A Practical Guide to Claims Arising from Fatal Accidents – Second Edition' by James Patience
'A Practical Guide to Asbestos Claims' by Jonathan Owen & Gareth McAloon
'A Practical Guide to Stamp Duty Land Tax in England and Northern Ireland' by Suzanne O'Hara
'A Practical Guide to the Law of Farming Partnerships' by Philip Whitcomb
'A Practical Guide to the Law of Unlawful Eviction and Harassment – Second Edition' by Stephanie Lovegrove
'A Practical Guide to Costs in Personal Injury Claims – Second Edition' by Matthew Hoe
'A Practical Guide to the General Data Protection Regulation (GDPR) – Second Edition' by Keith Markham
'A Practical Guide to Working with Litigants in Person and McKenzie Friends in Family Cases' by Stuart Barlow
'Protecting Unregistered Brands: A Practical Guide to the Law of Passing Off' by Lorna Brazell
'A Practical Guide to Secondary Liability and Joint Enterprise Post-Jogee' by Joanne Cecil & James Mehigan

- 'A Practical Guide to the Pre-Action RTA Claims Protocol for Personal Injury Lawyers' by Antonia Ford
- 'A Practical Guide to Neighbour Disputes and the Law' by Alexander Walsh
- 'A Practical Guide to Coercive Control for Legal Practitioners and Victims' by Rachel Horman
- 'A Practical Guide to the Law of Driverless Cars – Second Edition' by Alex Glassbrook, Emma Northey & Scarlett Milligan
- 'A Practical Guide to TOLATA Claims' by Greg Williams
- 'A Practical Guide to Elderly Law – Second Edition' by Justin Patten
- 'A Practical Guide to Responding to Housing Disrepair and Unfitness Claims' by Iain Wightwick
- 'A Practical Guide to the Law of Bullying and Harassment in the Workplace' by Philip Hyland
- 'How to Be a Freelance Solicitor: A Practical Guide to the SRA-Regulated Freelance Solicitor Model' by Paul Bennett
- 'A Practical Guide to Prison Injury Claims' by Malcolm Johnson
- 'A Practical Guide to Advising Clients at the Police Station' by Colin Stephen McKeown-Beaumont
- 'A Practical Guide to Antisocial Behaviour Injunctions – Second Edition' by Iain Wightwick
- 'Practical Mediation: A Guide for Mediators, Advocates, Advisers, Lawyers, and Students in Civil, Commercial, Business, Property, Workplace, and Employment Cases' by Jonathan Dingle with John Sephton
- 'The Mini-Pupillage Workbook' by David Boyle
- 'A Practical Guide to Crofting Law' by Brian Inkster
- 'A Practical Guide to the Law of Domain Names and Cybersquatting' by Andrew Clemson
- 'A Practical Guide to the Law of Gender Pay Gap Reporting' by Harini Iyengar
- 'NHS Whistleblowing and the Law' by Joseph England
- 'Employment Law and the Gig Economy' by Nigel Mackay & Annie Powell
- 'A Practical Guide to Noise Induced Hearing Loss (NIHL) Claims' by Andrew Mckie, Ian Skeate, Gareth McAloon
- 'An Introduction to Beauty Negligence Claims – A Practical Guide for the Personal Injury Practitioner' by Greg Almond
- 'Intercompany Agreements for Transfer Pricing Compliance' by Paul Sutton
- 'Zen and the Art of Mediation' by Martin Plowman
- 'A Practical Guide to Adoption for Family Lawyers' by Graham Pegg

'A Practical Guide to Industrial Disease Claims' by Andrew Mckie & Ian Skeate
'A Practical Guide to Conducting a Sheriff Court Proof' by Andrew Stevenson
'A Practical Guide to Vicarious Liability' by Mariel Irvine
'A Practical Guide to Applications for Landlord's Consent and Variation of Leases' by Mark Shelton
'A Practical Guide to Relief from Sanctions Post-Mitchell and Denton' by Peter Causton
'A Practical Guide to Equity Release for Advisors' by Paul Sams
'A Practical Guide to Financial Services Claims' by Chris Hegarty
'A Practical Guide to Financial Ombudsman Service Claims' by Adam Temple & Robert Scrivenor
'A Practical Guide to Running Housing Disrepair and Cavity Wall Claims – Second Edition' by Andrew Mckie & Ian Skeate
'A Practical Guide to Holiday Sickness Claims – Second Edition' by Andrew Mckie & Ian Skeate
'Arguments and Tactics for Personal Injury and Clinical Negligence Claims' by Dorian Williams
'A Practical Guide to Drone Law' by Rufus Ballaster, Andrew Firman, Eleanor Clot
'On Experts: CPR35 for Lawyers and Experts' by David Boyle
'An Introduction to Personal Injury Law' by David Boyle

These books and more are available to order online direct from the publisher at www.lawbriefpublishing.com, where you can also read free sample chapters. For any queries, call us on 0844 587 2383 or email us at mail@lawbriefpublishing.com.

Our books are all generally in stock at www.amazon.co.uk with free next day delivery for Prime members, and at good legal bookshops such as Wildy & Sons.

We are regularly launching new books in our series of practical day-to-day practitioners' guides. Visit our website and join our free newsletter to be kept informed and to receive special offers, free chapters, etc.

You can also follow us on Twitter at www.twitter.com/lawbriefpub.